Youth Sport, Migration and Culture

How do migrant youth negotiate their role in society through sport and leisure practices? How can political theory and qualitative critical research work together to make sense of these processes? These are among the questions that led to a long-term investigation of young males' sport practices in Ireland, possibly the most fertile contemporary setting for the analysis of questions of sport and identity.

Youth Sport, Migration and Culture emphasises the epistemological and ethical urgency of doing research *with* rather than *on* young people. Engaging with the social changes in Irish society through the eyes of children of immigrants growing up in Ireland, the book looks closely at young people's leisure practices in multi-ethnic contexts, and at issues of inclusion in relation to public discourses around 'national identity' and immigration.

Offering compelling analysis of how ideas of race and racism are elaborated through sport, this book is fascinating reading for anybody with an interest in the sociology of sport, sport development or youth culture.

Max Mauro is Lecturer in Sport Studies at Solent University, UK and Visiting Lecturer in Media, Sport and Communication at St. Mary's University, Twickenham, UK.

Routledge Critical Perspectives on Equality and Social Justice in Sport and Leisure

Series editors:
Kevin Hylton
Leeds Beckett University, UK
Jonathan Long
Leeds Beckett University, UK

This series presents important new critical studies that explore and explain issues relating to social justice and equality in sport and leisure. Addressing current debates and examining key concepts such as inclusion and exclusion, (anti)oppression, neo-liberalism, resistance, merit(ocracy), and sport for all, the series aims to be a key location for scholars, students and policy makers interested in these topics.

Innovative and interrogative, the series will explore central themes and issues in critical sport and leisure studies, including: theory development, methodologies and intersectionality; policy and politics; 'race', ethnicity, gender, class, sexuality, disability; communities and migration; ethics and morals; and media and new technologies. Inclusive and transdisciplinary, it aims to showcase high quality work from leading and emerging scholars working in sport and leisure studies, sport development, sport coaching and PE, policy, events and health studies, and areas of sport science that consider the same concerns.

Available in this series:

Sport, Leisure and Social Justice
Edited by Jonathan Long, Thomas Fletcher and Beccy Watson

Youth Sport, Migration and Culture
Two Football Teams and the Changing Face of Ireland
Max Mauro

Youth Sport, Migration and Culture

Two Football Teams and the
Changing Face of Ireland

Max Mauro

Routledge
Taylor & Francis Group

LONDON AND NEW YORK

First published 2019
by Routledge
2 Park Square, Milton Park, Abingdon, Oxon OX14 4RN

and by Routledge
52 Vanderbilt Avenue, New York, NY 10017

Routledge is an imprint of the Taylor & Francis Group, an informa business

© 2019 Max Mauro

British Library Cataloguing-in-Publication Data
A catalogue record for this book is available from the British
Library

Library of Congress Cataloging-in-Publication Data
A catalog record has been requested for this book

ISBN: 978-0-8153-8391-8 (hbk)
ISBN: 978-1-351-20523-8 (ebk)

Typeset in Goudy
by Wearset Ltd, Boldon, Tyne and Wear

This book is dedicated to all the young people, then teenagers and now young adults, I met during this research. The future is yours, make this world a better place!

Contents

Figures

Acknowledgements

I wish to thank several people who have been instrumental in helping me to complete this book. The original ethnographic study would not have been possible without the collaboration of the young and adult members of Mountview Boys and Girls FC and Insaka AFC. I am grateful for the openness and trust they showed to me throughout my fieldwork, and I wish to particularly thank my adult gatekeepers: Mick Harrop, Willie Maguire, Ken McCue, James Igwilo and Zuby Ufoh. Ken McCue provided me with an initial insight into Irish sport cultures and accompanied this long journey of mine over the years with updates and feedback. The ethnographic fieldwork was carried out during my PhD at the Centre for Transcultural Research and Media Practice, Dublin Institute of Technology. My thanks go to my main supervisor, Dr Alan Grossman, who offered helpful advice for the preparation of this book, and to Dr Harry Browne and Dr Aine O'Brien.

The writing of the book has benefited of the generous feedback to my thesis of the external examiner, Professor Michael Giardina, from Florida State University, USA. I am also indebted to my fellow PhD candidates in the Centre: Sally Daly, Veronica Vierin, Agnes Kakasi, Darcy Alexandra, Deirdre Lynch, Giovanna Rampazzo and Roisin Boyd for offering insightful feedback during the research process. The follow up to my ethnography has been made possible by the unexpected invitation of Simon Whitmore, of Routledge, and I wish to thank him for this. Professor Jonathan Long and Professor Kevin Hylton, from Leeds Beckett University, have provided precious feedback to my first chapter and encouraged me to complete the book. My colleague at Solent University, Dr Jaron Murphy has provided encouragement during the writing process. Finally, I wish to thank my wife, Bibi Agosto, who has always supported my efforts and expressed trust in my work throughout these years.

Introduction

A title of a book can be simultaneously simple and complex. We could even say that the simpler the title, the more difficult it gets to scratch its surface and discover what the content of the book is truly about. If we take 'youth sport, migration and culture' as three separate elements, for example, we would struggle to find a coherent definition of their meanings to which everyone agrees. 'Youth sport' may be easier to define than the other two, as youth is generally understood to be that phase in our lives before adulthood. At the same time, it is perceived to be slightly different from childhood. Thus, youth sport is sport played by people who find themselves in between these two central phases of human life. Still, despite the help of institutional definitions, such as the one provided by the United Nations Convention on the Rights of the Child, many in the Western world would find it hard to clearly identify the age when someone is no more 'young'. Does youth end at 18? In organised football, one arguably makes the transition to adulthood when they start to play at senior level. Quite often these days, players aged 16 or 15 are made to play with the first team, because they are considered mature enough for the challenge. According to the English FA regulations, at the age of 17 players are allowed to sign their first professional contract, and according to FIFA rules if they reside within the European Economic Area (EEA) they can be enrolled in a full-time elite football academy abroad at the age of 16. In every sense, they are professionals. In football terms, despite their young age, 'youth sport' is no longer their environment.

Things get even more complicated when we look at 'migration'. This is a topic that more than any other has influenced national and transnational politics in Europe over the last two decades. Debates about 'immigration' traverse many different fields, from policy, to labour, education, human rights, and obviously sport. In all these cases, views are divergent, sometimes extremely different and polarised, particularly due to the rise of far-right movements and parties who, in the name of their imagined version of the 'nation', oppose any form of 'multiculturalism' or whatever definition is used for a normal, naturally diverse society. According to certain, increasingly popular ideologies, almost anyone can be perceived as an 'immigrant'. In January 2018, Eric Descheenie, a member of the House of Representatives of Arizona (USA), was asked by supporters of the USA president Donald Trump during an anti-immigration rally if he was in the country illegally. Some shouted at dark skinned counter-protesters like him to 'get out of the country'. Descheenie is a Navajo, 'an indigenous to these lands', as he explained to a local newspaper. Given its highly mediatised dimension, sport is the field that probably more than any other brings to the fore the contradictory interpretations of 'immigration'. In May 2018, Mesut Özil, a German international football player of 'third-generation' Turkish descent, was heavily criticised for posing for a photograph with Turkey's president Recep Erdoğan. Despite having represented Germany 119 times, at youth and senior level, he decided to retire from international football, claiming that he was made to feel 'German when we win, but I am an immigrant when we lose'.

The third element of the title, culture, is the most difficult to define. It is a pervasive and ambiguous concept, which can be interpreted and used in contradictory ways. In an early attempt to put things straight, Raymond Williams (1961) identified three possible categories in the definition of culture: ideal (the description of universal values of human condition); documentary (the body of intellectual and imaginative work), and social (a way of life, expressed not only in art and learning but also in institutions and ordinary behaviour). He concluded that all three are useful, as 'it seems necessary to look for meanings and values, the record of creative human activity, not only in art and intellectual work, but also in institutions and forms of behaviour' (Williams 1961: 58). However, later in his life, he admitted: 'I don't know how many times I've wished that I'd never heard the damned word' (Williams, 1979: 154, cited by Bennet 2013: 110). In contemporary societies, culture is often associated with the nationality of a person or group of persons. It is assumed that because someone shares their country of origin (or simply the passport) with someone else, they automatically share a 'culture'. Multiculturalism and Interculturalism, as public policies rather than social processes, both originate from this assumption. Given the popularity of these terms, it is difficult to escape the strictures of dominant public discourses on 'culture'.

Ireland makes a compelling case study in this debate, as the history of the island, particularly since becoming a British colony in the early seventeenth century and emerging in the twentieth century split in two states, has been marked by tensions between 'cultures': religious cultures (Catholics and Protestants), political cultures (nationalists and unionists), and national cultures (Irishness and Britishness). The idea of 'Irishness' as a cohesive and distinctive form of identity found a fertile terrain in mass emigration, which took millions of Irish to seek a better future across the oceans, in the Americas or in Australia, or in Britain. Since the second half of the nineteenth century, sport has played no marginal role in affirming the boundaries of 'culture'. The creation of the Gaelic Athletic Association (GAA) and the definition of 'non-Gaelic Games', meaning essentially those originating from Britain, such as soccer, rugby, cricket and hockey, was a firm step in that direction.

In such a scenario, the cultures brought about by in-migration appear to be a novel actor; a narrative often reinforced by national media and political powers, bound to an understanding of Ireland, and specifically of the Republic of Ireland, originally as a mono-cultural society. No one can deny that the Republic of Ireland, as a central hub of economic globalisation, over the last 20 years has gone through deep social and demographic changes. In 1991, only 1.1 per cent of the population was born abroad; in 2016, more than 200 nationalities were registered in the national census. At the same time, ethnic, national and racial diversity cannot be considered a 'new' phenomenon in Irish history. Through their participation in British colonial history, in different roles and capacities, Irish people encountered different cultures and, to some extent, brought them back to the island. Moreover, in-migration and cultural exchange has been a trait in the history of the island for a long time before the economic boom of the 1990s.

One of the aims of this book is that of providing an original exploration of the intersections of sport, culture and immigration in Ireland. The focus is on youth, and particularly on adolescents, of different ethnic and national backgrounds who come together to play 'football', the most global of modern sports, and also the most widely played by young people in Ireland. MacDougall (2006) believes that children are the best 'students of culture'. Sport is the main field of socialisation outside school for adolescent males. Different from school, and family, however, it is a field they can decide to join or to leave. Their agency is tangible, and this makes it a particularly intriguing and challenging site of investigation. The contribution made by sport, namely football, to 'intercultural' dialogue between young people is read on the backdrop of the contrasting experiences of the two teams at the centre of the research that underpins this book. Issues of race and racialisation characterise sport participation of young people of migrant background, but they are also part of their everyday lives. Through the prism of sport, critical facets of public discourses about cultural and national identity and immigration come to fore. This notwithstanding, a central theme of the book is that teenagers living in-between cultures (Bhabha 1996) are at the same time appropriating and challenging cultural codes. They often function as transcultural agents of diversity, whose embodied forms of belonging slip easy categorisations.

Chapter 1 engages with theoretical and methodological frames of reference underpinning the ethnographic study. Drawing from different disciplinary fields, including cultural studies, migration, sport, and visual studies, the discussion foregrounds debates surrounding the inclusive potential of sport practices and questions of belonging among youth of immigrant background. After unfolding key elements of the research project, the chapter introduces to the reader the sites of the fieldwork. The chapter also includes a discussion of ethical issues in adopting visual methodologies in working with young people and the critical use of reflexivity.

Chapter 2 introduces Mountview FC, a local youth club, and its Under-13 team, composed of Irish (white) boys and boys of different African backgrounds. Questions of access and the creation of rapport with adult and adolescent participants are addressed. 'Community' emerges as a recurring facet of discourse of belonging among adult members of the football club and the local suburban area. The chapter further examines how boys of immigrant background construct notions of belonging. The final part of the chapter examines the production of a video clip about a day in the life of the team, which – following an expressed request from the boys – was eventually uploaded onto YouTube.

Chapter 3 addresses questions of ethnicity and class in relation to sport participation of teenagers of immigrant background. Hussein, a young boy of Sudanese background, emerges as a compelling protagonist of the ethnography. His social and economic capital – he is the son of a doctor, living in a more affluent neighbourhood than the rest of his teammates – appears to make him better equipped to establish dialogue with adults. The chapter analyses two episodes of alleged racial abuse against black players focusing on the understanding of the problem by the adults in charge of the team and the game. The concluding part of the chapter includes the discussion of ethnographic events which testify to the modalities of 'transcultural' dialogue among boys of different ethnic backgrounds.

Chapter 4 presents an unforeseen turn in the ethnography: the tragic death of a boy of Nigerian background, friend and schoolmate of several of the protagonists in the study, killed by two white Irish men. This nationally reported event established the possibility for further fieldwork with Insaka AFC – a football team exclusively comprising immigrant youth (of African and Eastern European backgrounds) and one in which the boy had played. Access to this club was made possible by the collaboration with Sport Against Racism Ireland (SARI), an NGO active in promoting 'positive integration and social inclusion through sport'. This chapter further engages with performative instantiations of belonging by teenage boys on the football pitch and via the production and sharing of hip hop music and home-made videos. The ethnography takes a collaborative form when two young players of Romanian origin agree to contribute with one of their songs to the production of video documentation of the SARI Soccer Fest, the most important sport festival in Ireland. This ethnographic event elicits a critical reflection on the possibilities of collaboration when working with young people, particularly with the help of visual media.

Chapter 5 starts with the discussion of the racialised position of the members of Insaka FC, and their strategies to counter episodes of racism and discrimination. In this context, the coaches' discourse on 'discipline' and its implementation is foregrounded. Drawing on the definition of 'informal anti-racism' and 'resistance through sport' by Hylton (2009), the chapter endeavours to analyse some significant events that enable a deeper understanding of manifestation of racism in youth and grassroots football. The final part of the chapter reconnects to questions of cultural and national belonging, drawing attention to the question of national football teams, their composition and how they discursively redefine the very meaning of national affiliation, thereby emphasising 'transcultural' forms of identification.

Chapter 6 looks first at the material changes in the setting of the study after a few years. It then returns to the questions introduced in Chapter 1, and which are explored throughout the book, with the aim of placing some of the themes into a longitudinal perspective. This chapter critically situates the discussion of sport, belonging, and migration in Ireland in a constantly evolving social and institutional reality. It further foregrounds a reflection from some young research participants on the contribution that sport, namely football, has played in the development of their subjective and collective identities.

References

Bennet, T. (2013). 'Culture'. In T. Bennett, L. Grossberg and M. Morris, *New keywords: A revised vocabulary of culture and society*. London: John Wiley & Sons.

Bhabha, H. (1996). 'Culture's in-between'. In S. Hall and P. du Gay (eds), *Questions of cultural identity*. London: Sage, 53–60.

Hylton, K. (2009). *'Race' and sport. Critical race theory*. London: Routledge.

MacDougall, D. (2006). *The corporeal image. Film, ethnography and the senses*. Princeton: Princeton University Press.

Williams, R. (1961). *The long revolution*. London: Chatto and Windus.

Chapter 1

Sport, youth and migration in the post-nation age

Play can be a contest for something or a representation of something.

(Johannes Huizinga 1980 [1938])

The year was 2000. While working as a journalist in my hometown of Udine, in the North-Eastern corner of Italy, I was presented with a story that elicited my interest. A member of the Moroccan immigrant community had invited me to meet a young football player. The 16-year-old son of a Moroccan couple, who was himself born in Morocco and brought to Italy at the age of three, was playing in the youth team of an Italian professional club. When I entered the family's house I found the father sitting on the sofa in the living room under a gigantic picture of his son, taken during a football game. It was the only image hanging on an otherwise empty wall. My informant had told me that the boy was making everybody in the Moroccan immigrant community proud of him. I waited half-way through my conversation with the boy and his father to ask what I thought could be the most sensitive of questions: given the opportunity to choose, I asked, would you prefer to play for Italy or Morocco? The boy remained silent, and before daring to answer he searched for his father's approval. The father seemed worried about what his son would say, while the boy seemed worried about what his father would think of his answer. In the end the boy uttered his answer in a feeble voice: 'Morocco', he said. But he immediately stressed that he also supports the Italian national team and that he would like to play for Italy as well, given the opportunity.

This apparent contradiction in the boy's answer caught my attention; it appeared to me as a vivid example of how sport offers a contested site in which young people negotiate subjective and collective identities and sense of belonging away from the arguably more restrained environments of school and family (Biesta et al. 2001). But how does this happen? What epistemological and theoretical challenges does the researcher face in approaching this particular field of inquiry? These were some of the questions that lingered in my mind as I considered making the transition from journalism to academia. Over time, I had developed towards my profession the kind of sentiment expressed by Siegfried

Kracauer in his insightful explorations of Berlin and other cities in the 1920s. I found myself in the position of the reporter who, in Kracauer's words, 'draws from life with a leaking bucket' (Kracauer 2009 [1964]: 72; translation mine). A few years later, I moved to Ireland, a country whose history has been defined by migration more than any other in Western Europe. For a long time, Ireland 'exported' migrants in large numbers and, from the 1990s, following a rapid and unprecedented economic boom, it started to receive steady flows of immigration. But Ireland is also a place where sports have historically been deeply imbued with social and cultural meanings, particularly in relation to national and cultural identities. Where could I find a better setting for the study I had in mind?

In this chapter, I introduce some of the key theoretical and methodological concepts underpinning the research on which the book is based. I do so by addressing a few questions that are central to the motive for this endeavour. What can youth sport tell us about the identity patterns of young people in multi-ethnic and multi-national societies? Which are the main epistemological and theoretical challenges in the study of youth leisure practices? What makes Ireland a particularly fertile setting for the study of sport, migration and belonging? I further explore the methodological decisions I took during the two years spent doing fieldwork, in particular the decision to adopt the video-camera as one of my means of inquiry and the choices I made in order to be able to 'construct the field' (Amit 2000), which eventually led me to question the possibility of the anthropological field per se. I will also address my transition from journalism to ethnography and how I conceptualised the need for a transdisciplinary approach to research, in particular in the study of migration and youth. This chapter will 'set the scene', in theoretical and conceptual terms, for the following chapters, which explicitly follow a more narrative and discursive approach. The rest of the book will, among other things, explore the possibilities of the text to meaningfully tell life stories (Berger and Mohr 2010 [1975]), and to create the conditions where 'the messy text becomes the place where ethnographers write for and not about the other' (Denzin 1997: 268). Before moving any further, however, I will briefly introduce the protagonists of the book.

Two football teams

The ethnographic fieldwork was conducted over two years, between 2009 and 2011, with the players of two youth football teams operating in North Dublin, and the adult members, namely coaches and officials, of the two clubs. After a few years, during which I kept in touch with some of the participants, I returned to the setting of my initial study and explored changes and possible continuities. Prior to commencing my research project I had made two visits to Dublin and made contact with Ken McCue, one of the founders of Sport Against Racism Ireland (SARI), a unique organisation in the Irish context, whose motto is to work for 'social inclusion and cultural integration' through sport.[1] Ken helped my initial orientation into Ireland's sport cultures and put me in touch with people who he thought would be relevant to my inquiry. From the outset, my goal was that of finding a youth football team with a diverse composition in terms of ethnic and national backgrounds, and to follow them over a season. This was by no means an easy task. At the time, Ken could not facilitate my access to any team, but he would later become the main gatekeeper in my field-work with Insaka AFC.[2] It took me approximately four months to finally estab-lish access to the Under-13 team of Mountview Boys and Girls Football Club,[3] a youth club based in Blanchardstown – a large suburban area located in North Dublin. Before starting fieldwork, I conducted interviews with immigrant youth, school teachers, social activists and sport officials to obtain a better under-standing of the youth football movement in Ireland and in particular of the sport participation of young males of immigrant background.

In the end, I spent two seasons with Mountview. Towards the end of the second season I was presented with the opportunity to conduct another period of fieldwork with a recently created team, Insaka. It was an unexpected event that led me to the encounter with Insaka – the death of a young teenager of Nigerian background, Toyosi Shitta-bey, a former player of this team, stabbed to death in Blanchardstown in early April 2010. This tragic event shocked the local community, but it also made headlines on national media. It not only marked an emotional turn in my ethnographic journey but also raised new crit-ical questions worth exploring. The encounter with the members of the team and their coaches showed participation in sport under a different light, from a different perspective.

The two clubs of my study could not be more different in terms of history and structure. Mountview is one of the oldest youth football clubs in the area; it operates in a mainly working class neighbourhood and, at that time, catered for several teams, including also a girls' team. Insaka was founded in the summer of 2009 by a former professional footballer from Nigeria with the help of Ken McCue of SARI, with the aim of nurturing 'African talent'. The club only catered for an Under-18 team. During my fieldwork, the Mountview Under-13 team fielded white Irish boys, together with boys born in Africa, mainly in Nigeria and DR Congo. Insaka fielded adolescent players originally from different African countries and from Eastern Europe. Understandably, in a country only recently touched by immigration, none of the boys of immigrant background, whether in Mountview or Insaka, were born in Ireland. They represented the first flow of migrant children in Irish grassroots sports. There was another vital element that characterised this fluid constituency: most of the boys of African background and one from Eastern Europe were living in Ireland under refugee status. All these elements of diversity are increasingly common in the 'new Ireland' (Ulin et al. 2013), but the history of the island was hardly devoid of cultural complexities and exchanges before the 'Celtic Tiger'.

The diverse history of Ireland

In his autobiography, *Back from the brink*, Paul McGrath – 'Ireland's best loved sportsman' (McGrath 2007: 1), as he was often referred to in his heyday – recalls his teenage years spent in a South Dublin orphanage in the early 1970s. In particular, he recounts how their inner city peers perceived him and his friends: 'We were seen as posh kids, you see. We came to school from Monkstown on bicycle. We spoke differently. We were Church of Ireland and that made us different' (McGrath 2007: 70). Here, his memory touches upon issues of social and cultural background in Irish society. Interestingly enough, it appears that McGrath's racial background – he was the son of a Nigerian father and an Irish mother – might not have been as important as his perceived social and cultural background (coming from South Dublin, being Church of Ireland) in defining his 'identity' in the eyes of other teenagers who he met at school and happened to play football with. However, he later points to football as the place where he could finally emancipate himself from one visible element of diversity – his 'blackness':

> I could play soccer. I could stand my ground against anyone in that yard and not feel remotely vulnerable. Within a few days, the change was unbelievable. I was no longer 'Nigger', I was Paul. It was the old cliché about football being the international language. Suddenly I was accepted. An ability to play amounted to a badge of respect.
>
> (Fanon 1987 [1952]: 72)

McGrath's lived experience of 'diversity' is a helpful starting point in the discussion of the role of race, class and locality as tropes of belonging among young footballers of immigrant background in contemporary Dublin. At the time when McGrath was growing up in Dublin, Irish society was not as ethnically diverse as it would become from the mid-1990s. However, as argued by Lentin and McVeigh (2006: 5), to some extent 'Ireland has always been multi-ethnic'. They write:

> Contrary to attempts to portray in-migration into Ireland as an entirely 'new' phenomenon, Ireland has long been a country of both emigration and immigration. Colonial plantation in the seventeenth century fashioned many of the cultural and political dynamics that continue today – especially in the north. Alongside Scots and English migrants came substantial other in-migrations including Huguenots, Italians, Chinese, Germans and Jews.
>
> (Lentin and McVeigh 2006: 120)

This 'history in the plural' (Olsen 2012) tends to be overlooked by casual observers of contemporary multicultural and multinational Ireland. When, in 2008, I moved to Dublin, I found accommodation in a part of the city that bore the traces – albeit weak – of the Irish-Jewish community that once used to live there

(Harris 2002; Rivlin 2011). The same area, located at the crossing of Clanbrassil Street and South Circular Road, is today home to new immigrant communities. Goldstone highlights how,

> The South Circular Road in Dublin, which once boasted the greatest con-centration of Jews and was the heart of a vibrant Jewish life, now has more Muslims, drawn from Bangladesh, Somalia, Pakistan and Malaysia living in the side streets off its long and sinuous bends.
>
> (2009: 106)

My flat was around the corner from one of the four mosques operating in the city centre at that time. The mosque was visited by my neighbours, a young couple of academics from Pakistan. Over time, the Irish-Jewish community had slowly dispersed, a combination of a geographical relocation to the suburbs and outward migration to the UK and Israel.[4] Ireland also has a long and conflicting relationship with the Travellers, indigenous nomads whose ethnicity has been the focus of heated debates throughout the history of the Republic (Lentin and McVeigh 2006; McVeigh 2008; Loyal 2011). According to Lentin and McVeigh (2006: 129), 'ever since the turn of the 20th century, Travellers have been a dominant "other", in constructions of Irish identity'. In February 2017, the Travellers were formally recognised as an 'ethnic minority' by the Irish state, a decision that Irish Prime Minister Enda Kenny defined as 'a historic day for our Travellers and a proud day for Ireland'.[5]

Ireland's modern relationship with other ethnicities and cultures cannot be dis-cussed without reference to Irish emigration, which over the centuries has exposed millions of Irish to multi-ethnic societies. As noted by McIvor (2008: 27), 'the history of the "global Irish" includes contact with many other cultures and popu-lations'. Debates on post-colonial theory and Ireland have explored the complex relationship of the Irish with the British Empire and other colonial subjects (Graham and Maley 1999; Smyth 1999; Garner 2009, 2013). From the 1600s, the Irish travelled in the New World as 'prisoners of war and indentured labourers as well as missionaries, landowners, administrators, and soldiers' (Garner 2013: 179). Also for this reason, throughout the history of the British Empire, the 'whiteness' of the Irish was contested, both at home and abroad. In the words of Mohanram:

> [T]racing Irish embodiment historically suggests that any arguments for the naturalized comprehensions of the body, the innate, prior power and superi-ority of whiteness, fall apart in the consideration of the nature of Irish whiteness. While the early Anglo-Norman conquest of Ireland did not racialize the Irish, the discourse of racism became significant during the Reformation in Britain. It is indeed the accretive racializing and colonising of Celtic Ireland that suggests that significations of blackness are directly linked to the political and economic policies of imperial power.
>
> (2007: 170)

This has significant ramifications for contemporary Ireland, in the context of an increased diversity of the country's social and cultural landscape, and instances of racism against 'people of colour'. What I called the diverse history of Ireland helps us to better contextualise the rapid changes which Irish society has undergone over the last two decades. It was only in 1996 that the Republic of Ireland reached its migration turning point, turning officially from a country that historically exported migrants into one that imported them (Mac Éinrí 2001; Loyal 2007; Fanning 2007; Share et al. 2012). This was made possible by the so-called 'Celtic Tiger' boom, a rapid economic expansion stimulated by fiscal and other investment incentives that attracted foreign capital into Ireland, in particular from the USA (Coulter and Coleman 2003; Allen 2003). Mac Éinrí stresses that 'in the decade 1991–2000, almost half a million new jobs were added to the Irish economy, an expansion of 43% in the total labour force' (2001: 2). Ireland's economic growth could not have been possible without the contribution of a foreign labour force, even though the Irish government initially implemented programmes to attract Irish emigrants back to Ireland (Hayward and Howard 2007). In fact, a large proportion of those who immigrated during the economic boom and in the following years were returning Irish and British citizens (Gilmartin 2013).[6] Nevertheless, beside them many more nationalities found home in the Republic.

According to the national census, in 2002 the number of 'non-Irish nationals' accounted for 5.8 per cent of the population; in 2011 that percentage had increased to 12.2 per cent. In the 2016 census, the presence of non-Irish nationals had decreased to 11.6, but at the same time the number of dual citizens (the so-called 'new Irish') had increased by 87.4 per cent to 104,784 persons (CSO 2017). This shows that the recession that hit Ireland between 2008 and 2009, which caused a temporary contraction of immigration flows and a return to emigration by Irish citizens, was not followed by a decrease in the immigrant population. On the contrary, echoing the message of a moving ethnographic film by Alan Grossman and Aine O'Brien, immigrants and their families, including their Irish-born children, showed that they were 'here to stay'.[7] Today, the largest immigrant groups are those from Poland and the UK, followed by Lithuania and Romania. Among Non-EU nationalities, the largest communities are those from Brazil, India and China. Among the African immigrants, Nigerians constitute the largest group. The deep social and demographic change that has taken place in Ireland over the last 30 years is exemplified by a final figure: in 1991, only 1.1 per cent of the residents were born outside the Republic of Ireland, Northern Ireland or Great Britain (CSO 1996). In 2016, there were 200 different nationalities living in the Republic. Data on the child population of immigrants are not easy to collect and elaborate upon. For example, Darmondy et al. (2011: 3) emphasise that 'Census 2006 does not record the nationality of 13,000 children because their nationality was not stated'. Available data indicate that minors account for about 20 per cent of the immigrant population (Ni Laoire et al. 2011). What is unquestionable is that the second generation of immigrants is growing: in 2012, 24 per cent of mothers of newborn children were non-Irish nationals (Röder 2014).

Sport and the Irish

In this multifaceted context, and taking stock of McGrath's early lived experience of 'diversity' in Irish society, it is important to focus on the role of sport in relation to social changes. According to the Schoolboys Football Association of Ireland, there are approximately a hundred thousand youths playing football in the Republic of Ireland.[8] Football is the most popular sport among male youth in Ireland, followed by Gaelic football and hurling (Lalor et al. 2007; Sport Ireland 2017). Unfortunately, there are no available data on the number of 'foreign-national' children and children with an immigrant background registered to play this game.[9] Existing literature on children and young people of immigrant background living in Ireland tend to overlook sport as a fertile site for socialisation and multicultural dialogue (Gilligan et al. 2010; Ni Laoire et al. 2011; Darmody et al. 2011; National Youth Council of Ireland 2017). Moreover, studies of youth sporting practices in Ireland do not pay particular attention to youth of immigrant background and more broadly to 'ethnic diversity' (Connor 2003; Delaney and Fahey 2005; Fahey et al. 2005; Lalor et al. 2007; Woods et al. 2010). Based on a study on sport participation levels of 9-year-old children, Darmondy et al. (2016: 185–186) have found higher participation rates among children of Irish, UK and Western European origin compared with Asian, African and Eastern Europeans. The sports involvement of African children, however, is greater than that of Asian and Eastern European children. Over the last decade, sporting bodies such as the GAA (Gaelic Athletic Association) and the FAI (Football Association of Ireland) have expressed policy interest in the 'new Irish' and designed strategies to foster their inclusion/integration (Cronin 2013; FAI 2007, 2016). Nevertheless, there are critical areas which need further attention, particularly instances of racism and discrimination and the training of coaches and officials to address these issues (Hassan and McCue 2013; Mauro 2014).

Starting from the second half of the nineteenth century, across Ireland, sport has been invested in meanings strongly associated with national and cultural identity (Sugden and Bairner 1993; Bairner 2005; McElligott and Hassan 2016). This particular history still speaks to the present, despite a greatly changed global and national scenario. For instance, when talking about 'football' in Ireland one has to be aware of possible misunderstandings. As it happens, 'football' can define different sports according to the people who use the word – for Gaelic Games fans, 'football' means essentially Gaelic football, while fans of the English Premier League will reserve that word for their favourite sport. This is something that even the media find difficult to avoid. By searching the website of the leading newspaper, The Irish Times, for contents under the category 'football' one is presented with articles either about the Gaelic game and the game historically known as association football. The same research done on the public broadcaster's website (*RTE* – Raidió Teilifís Éireann, Radio and Television of Ireland) produces almost entirely results about the Gaelic sport, while the other game will usually be referred to as 'soccer'.[10]

The question of terminology conceals, understandably, a more subtle aspect of the contested relationship between sporting cultures. Since the inception of the Gaelic Athletic Association (GAA) in 1884, Gaelic Games have been associated with the Irish nationalist cause and to this day are considered one of the strongholds of the conventional representation of 'Irish culture', particularly with attention to rural Ireland (Cronin 1999; Hassan and McGuire 2016). For 120 years, Rule 42 of the GAA banned the use of GAA grounds 'for non-Gaelic Games', effectively those originating from Britain (namely soccer, rugby, hockey and cricket). This rule was relaxed as recently as 2005 to temporarily allow international football and rugby to be played in Croke Park – the principal venue of Gaelic Games and the largest stadium in the country. Association football originally became popular in Ireland among the industrial and working class of Belfast and later in Dublin (Cronin 1999; Bairner 2001; Moore 2016), and it is still in working class urban areas of Dublin that the highest number of youth football clubs happen to operate.

As noted, sporting cultures have played and still play a vital part in the cultural life of the Republic. The All-Ireland championship series of Gaelic football and hurling traditionally attract large audiences throughout the year. The major league of association football, the League of Ireland Premier Division, is far less popular.[11] Gaelic sports are still widely promoted through the school system (Fahey *et al.* 2005), although in the last three decades the international successes of rugby and football national teams have fostered great enthusiasm throughout the Republic and brought more attention and interest towards these sports (Free 2017).[12] Given its unrivalled global profile (Giulianotti and Robertson 2009), football arguably offers a more comfortable place to socialise for males with an immigrant background. By attending Saturday and Sunday morning games I could observe the changing face of Ireland, but also learn about different football styles – an experience facilitating a lively 'transcultural' encounter. Relying on the terminological use of the protagonists of my study, both youths and adults, in this book I will simply refer to football and, when necessary, to Gaelic football.

Youth sport – an orientation

In 2014, Messner and Musto published a 10-year survey of three leading sport sociology journals to evidence the limited attention paid by sport scholars to 'youth sport'.[13] They emphatically titled their report: 'Where are the kids?'. In fact, from their review it emerges that between 2003 and 2013 only 7.0 per cent of the published articles were about 'youth sport', while a further 1.1 per cent were about 'kids and sport'. According to the two authors, the reasons for this lack of attention are manifold, but they can be arguably summarised as the little attractiveness of engaging with young people's sporting practices. More often than not, scholars will study sports they are fans of, for which there is more funding available, and fewer ethical restrictions. The review focused predominantly on studies based in North America, but considering that the literature on youth sport has traditionally been more prolific in that part of the world, the data hint at a broader orientation in academic publishing and research. However, it may be argued that this trend was more recently inverted with the publication of the *Routledge handbook of youth sport* (Green and Smith 2016), which touches on a variety of themes and issues in contemporary sport studies, including physical activity and health, lifelong participation, talent identification and development, and safeguarding and abuse. Included in the same collection, there is an interesting contribution on 'Youth sport, race and ethnicity' by Fleming. He contends that, 'For though there have been some important contributions to the sports studies literature linked to ethnicity ... this element of the topic of youth sport remains relatively under-researched and therefore insufficiently understood' (Fleming 2016: 287). When it comes to football, much of the academic research has been narrowly focused on the professional game and on the experiences of adult players and elite young footballers. This gap in the study of football is highlighted in the book *Junior and youth grassroots football culture: The forgotten game* (O'Gorman 2017), which gathers together a number of original research papers on grassroots football, both in Europe and North-America.

With this backdrop, an interesting development has occurred in recent years, which relates to the specific attention being paid to how sport contributes to the settlement of migrant youth and more broadly to the negotiation of belonging in multi-ethnic social environments. A growing number of scholars from different fields (education, youth studies, migration studies, policy and sociology of sport) have endeavoured to look at sport and leisure as important venues for the formation of identity among young people, particularly youth with minority backgrounds. To confirm the resilience of the nation-state as a structural and epistemological framework in the study of processes brought about by globalisation, research on youth sport and migration reflects critical discourses that are permeated by the different declinations of the 'nation form' (Balibar 1991 [1988]). For example, studies conducted in Canada (Doherty and Taylor 2007; Stack and Iwasaki 2009) and Australia (Jeanes et al. 2014; Maxwell et al. 2013) discuss 'settlement' and 'multiculturalism', while studies conducted in European countries, such as Germany, Switzerland, Greece, Finland and Norway (Burrmann et al. 2017; Zwahlen et al. 2018; Harinen et al. 2012; Takle and Ødegård 2016) have been more interested in the contribution that sport can make to patterns of 'integration' or 'social integration' in the majority culture. The idea that sport participation may positively contribute to 'intercultural dialogue' among young people and to patterns of social inclusion of immigrant communities is supported by European institutions such as the Council of Europe and the European Union.

A defining moment in this debate has been the publication of a large report on 'Sport and Multiculturalism' by the European Commission, which highlights that sport can provide 'a crucial contribution to intercultural dialogue between young people' (Amara *et al.* 2005: 2). This sentiment is also echoed in statutory documents such as the EU White Paper on Sport (2007) and the EU Treaty of Lisbon (2007) and elaborated in more recent research conducted by Gasparini and Cometti (2010) on behalf of the Council of Europe. At the same time, over the years, studies conducted in single countries have put this belief to the test, producing evidence that sport is hardly a one-dimensional phenomenon and, in fact, it can both engender feelings of inclusion and exclusion and it can even, in some cases, further marginalise immigrant and ethnic minority communities. For example, some studies have contested the efficacy of 'sports-based interventions' to promote social inclusion (Elling *et al.* 2001; Krouwel *et al.* 2006; Kelly, L. 2011), while others have questioned the 'integrative power' of sport events targeting immigrant communities (Müller *et al.* 2008) and highlighted the mechanisms of exclusion active in organised sport (Elling and Claringbould 2005).

In their introduction to a special issue of the journal *Leisure Studies*, appropriately titled 'Migration, migrants and leisure: meaningful leisure?', Mata-Codesal *et al.* (2015), try to summarise the current debate around this topic. They conclude that 'leisure is central for processes of home-making, identity building, and meaning-making, and compels us to go beyond functionalist ideas of the role of leisure in assimilating, integrating or coping' (Mata-Codesal *et al.* 2015: 3). In fact, a growing pattern of youth research is defined by an interest in belonging and how sport may engender different forms of belonging to a new country (Kirpitchenko and Mansouri 2014). Walseth (2006) conducted a qualitative study with a group of young Muslim women in Norway to determine if playing sport created feelings of belonging to a community. She concluded that 'there is no automatic link between sport involvement and feelings of belonging' (Walseth 2006: 460). However, according to her findings, in some cases sport can be perceived as 'a place of refuge' and 'sport participation might lead to feelings of belonging that transcend traditional communities with face-to-face contact among members' (Walseth 2006: 455).

Spaaij (2015), who paid close attention to refugee youth, community sport and belonging in Australia, defines belonging 'as a dynamic dialectic of "seeking" and "granting"' (304) and as a process that is 'dynamic and situational: it can shift and change over time, be contested and plural' (305). He further identifies forms of belonging which are 'racial', taking place among youth of common African or Muslim backgrounds, or 'transnational', with youths of the African diaspora living in different Western countries, and contextual to the sport team. He recognises sport as a site for the production of belonging 'at multiple scales': to a team or club, to the immigrant community, and more broadly to the majority society. This latter dimension is of particular relevance for the purpose of this book, as among the interests and motives of my study was a desire to comprehend to what extent the cultural articulations of a small youth football club rely on discourses of 'national culture', in sport and beyond, and how migrant adolescents relate to this. As noted, intersections of sport and identity – cultural, social and national – are historically vivid and persistent in the Irish context.

On the whole, every discussion around belonging also needs to take into account structural facets which affect patterns of identification and affiliation, albeit 'at multiple scales', of migrant youth in and through sport. The question of citizenship and the degree of legal rights granted to the migrant subject are significant factors in the development of a sense of belonging. Burrmann et al. (2017) highlight that restrictions in obtaining German citizenship (as in the case of asylum seekers or other categories of migrants) limit the life agency of young people of migrant background. They contend that 'affiliation with the host country is complicated when formal membership is denied' (Burrmann et al. 2017: 193). In sports clubs, formal membership is usually not restricted, 'so that migrants can decide for themselves whether they join or not. However, these decisions are ultimately a result of the interplay of individual preferences and features of the sociocultural context' (Burrmann et al. 2017: 190). This hints at the factual circumstances that delineate and curtail the leisure opportunities of young people of immigrant background.

Across Europe and the Global North, the nation-state has become the central terrain of practices and discourses of exclusion (Agamben 1995; Sayad 2004 [1999]; Mezzadra 2006; Mezzadra and Neilson 2013). It is particularly young people, migrants and children of migrants, who are the victims of this, as they have to negotiate their inclusion into the 'national outlook' (Beck 2006) amid an increasingly hostile environment (Lentin and Titley 2011). It is not by chance that sport serves as the venue where issues of citizenship and belonging come prominently to the fore. Giardina and Donnelly (2008a: 9) contend that,

> Like the formal school curriculum or the world of cinema, youth sporting culture has become … a veritable battleground of social combatants struggling over the boundary lines of group identity and affiliation, over the very definition of citizenship and belonging.

In the Irish context, the discursive construction of 'Irishness' took a dramatic turn with the 2004 national referendum, which removed the automatic 'jus soli' principle to citizenship (Mullally 2007; Loyal 2011; Lentin 2013; Garner 2013, 2015). Children born in Ireland before that year had received Irish citizenship simply on the basis of 'jus soli', while those born later had to go through a lengthier process.[14] None of the young migrants at the centre of this book held Irish citizenship at the time of the ethnographic fieldwork. However, some of them talked about younger siblings who were 'Irish' because they were born in the country before 2004. Their precarious status – their fractional legal membership to Irish society – diminished the level of attachment they could experience for the local community. Before turning my attention to the research methods used in this study, I feel the need to better define the boundaries of my endeavour by looking at its main theoretical underpinnings.

Transcultural belonging

How do we make sense of young people's trajectories of belonging in multi-ethnic urban environments? What theoretical constructs can be employed to capture the often unpredictable cultural exchanges unfolding in young people's leisure experiences? In trying to conceptualise the patterns of identity negotiation that take place on and off the football pitch, the notion of the 'transcultural' (Mirdal and Ryynänen-Karjalainen 2004; Hoerder et al. 2005; MacDougall 2006; Ragazzi 2009) appears to be a useful concept, albeit still sparsely applied to sport studies (Mauro 2016). It arguably helps to make sense of the vitality of the performed identities (Bell 1999; Azzarito and MacDonald 2016) of young males who freely engage in the sporting field with their peers. Ragazzi adopts the term 'transcultural' in the following way:

> As a means to avoid any essential definition of 'culture' as a bounded and territorial standpoint for individuals, with the awareness that individuals invariably express cultural codes and models through a form of sociality where 'sharing' modes of experience, be they conflictual, emphatic, constructive or harmful, is always historically situated. The transcultural thus refers to both recognition of cultural difference and also a moving toward the 'other' in mutual recognition of some similar and shared cultural codes.
>
> (2009: 6)

'Transculturalism' highlights the transitory and porous nature of all cultures, including also national ones, and youth identities, immersed as they are in global cultural flows (Appadurai 2010). It stands as an alternative to well-established, but nonetheless still ambiguous and differently interpreted, paradigms utilised in the study of migration. In supporting what could be defined as a theoretical turn, Mirdal and Ryynänen-Karjalainen (2004: 3) contend that

> In contrast to the classical models of integration and assimilation, we are now seeing simultaneous local and pluralistic identities, simultaneous ethnic and transnational affiliations, and simultaneous collectivistic and individualistic attitudes.

In debates about contemporary migration patterns, 'transculturalism' should be distinguished from 'transnationalism' (Vertovec 2001, 2009; Amelina and Faist 2012) as the latter posits the nation-state at the centre of the analysis of cultural exchanges, focusing on 'patterns of exchange, affiliations and social formations spanning nation-states' (Vertovec 2009: 2). The 'transcultural' challenges this approach and, chosen as a methodological perspective, 'it obliges the researcher to analyse phenomena from various angles and thus to insist on the multipolarity, multiple perspectives, and transformative dynamics inherent in the research subject' (König and Rakow 2016: 95). It is particularly in the study of adolescents of immigrant background, born abroad or born to immigrant parents, that the 'transcultural' emerges as a relevant and appropriate theoretical construct. According to Hoerder et al. (2005: 14–15),

> More a perspective than a fixed concept or even discipline, transculturation permits us to re-read homogenized histories that construct belongings as fixed, that essentialize cultural, ethnic, national, gendered, religious, racial, and/or generational dimensions. It is young people's transcultural processes and competences that best exemplify these new understandings. Embedded in flexible and malleable settings, young people have differing senses of place, locally and globally.

During my fieldwork I had many opportunities to observe how teenagers, not only those of immigrant background but also white Irish boys, creatively engaged with definitions of cultural belonging. Football and, unsurprisingly, music (listened to via mobile phones when travelling to games or after a training session) were fertile venues for such 'transcultural' exchanges. As a global sport, which took root in almost every corner of the planet, assuming different configurations according to local and national cultures (Archetti 1999; Goldblatt 2007), football is particularly suitable to all this. Echoing the work of Bell (1999) and Back (2007), among others, belonging is interpreted here as something that is constructed through actions and experiences rather than inherited. Team sport, like music or video production, offers young people accessible contexts in which to perform fluid forms of belonging. In the next chapters, a number of ethnographic events (Jackson 2005) will provide the opportunity to explore the tangible and fruitful reality of such 'transcultural' exchanges.

However, as with every theory and assumption, it is also necessary to look critically at its potential pitfalls. For instance, if we trust that transculturalism permits us 'to re-read homogenized histories that construct belongings as fixed, that essentialize cultural, ethnic, national, gendered, religious, racial, and/or generational dimensions' (Hoerder et al. 2005: 14), are we possibly overlooking the fact that certain forms of belonging are less able to escape being essentialised in public discourses? I am referring in particular to issues of race and racialisation, which constitute the structure of black and minority ethnic people's lives in contemporary Europe (Lentin and Titley 2011; Essed 2015). As noted earlier, a further construct which can impinge on the (trans)cultural exchanges between young people is the legal framework within which their lives unfold and develop; in other words, their status as citizens, asylum seekers or migrants under specific visa restrictions.

A matter of whiteness

Differently from several other European countries, the Republic of Ireland has so far not witnessed the rise of openly xenophobic political parties (Garner 2007). This feature, albeit remarkable, does not mean that racism and discrimination are not to be found across the country. On the contrary, different reports have emphasised that 'casual racism' and racist 'micro-aggressions' constitute the daily life of immigrant communities and particularly of those of African background (Ní Chonaill 2009; Fanning et al. 2011; ENAR Ireland 2017; NYCI 2017). In introducing their report on minority ethnic young people growing up in Ireland, the National Youth Council of Ireland (NYCI) highlights that,

> One of the standard issues presenting through the interviews is the manifest and everyday experience of racism experienced by the young people interviewed. Verbal abuse is part of a daily lived experience for our young people, presenting us with a red flag to an enduring Irish cultural history of welcome.
>
> (2017: 7)

Sport is not exempt from this, and a few studies have also exposed the contradictory approaches of sporting bodies in dealing with racist and discriminatory behaviour towards immigrants taking place on and off the sporting pitch, even at youth level (Hassan and McCue 2011, 2013; Mauro 2014; Cronin 2013). But Ireland is also a country with a complex relation to British colonial history, and whose 'whiteness' has been contested and argued about in the Irish diaspora to America, Australia and Britain (Garner 2013). It is therefore important to clarify the usage of certain terms and concepts. This is the purpose of this section, which looks into the ways issues of race, racialisation and whiteness impinge on the lives of migrant youth in the sporting field, in Ireland and beyond.

These concepts, at the same time powerful and resistant social constructs and definitions of the status quo, impinge on the subjective and collective identities negotiated by young people. For instance, some of the boys of African background playing alongside white Irish boys in the Mountview side, laid claim to being 'black', overtly announcing their 'difference' and, in so doing, acknowledging their racialised position within Irish society (Lentin and McVeigh 2006; Lentin 2007). The majority of the 'African boys' in the team would generally avoid expressing their identity along racial lines, yet they were very active in denouncing episodes of racial abuse in which they were implicated or when similar incidents occurred involving other teammates of African background. The question of claiming to 'be black' or to 'be white' emerged more prominently with the second team, Insaka, where boys of different African backgrounds played alongside boys of eastern European backgrounds. Here, further patterns of racial belonging came to the fore alongside different 'shades of white' (Long and Hylton 2002), with certain 'whites' occupying marginal positions compared with others.

Burdsey (2011: 13) emphasises the 'complex and contested use of terminology in the area' and 'the myriad ways in which racialised groups themselves construct and articulate their identities'. These dynamics pose specific epistemological and ontological challenges to the researcher, who needs to closely reflect on how her or his own biography and positioning are implicated in racial discourses. In my case, one of the first steps in this reflexive process was to acknowledge my 'whiteness' (Fields 2001), and the fact that I was an adult man holding a European passport, an evident position of privilege in the contemporary global scenario of restrained human mobility. But it also meant recognising that I was the son of Italian working class immigrants (father a housepainter, mother a factory worker), that I was born in Switzerland and raised in Italy, and that I later moved to live and work abroad. These and other elements contribute to the ways I perceive and represent people who are different from me (Hall 1997).

Drawing on Critical Race Theory, my work is informed by the acceptance of 'the reality of the permanence of racism in society' (Fletcher and Hylton 2016: 92). 'Race' is interpreted as a 'sliding signifier' (Hall) or as a 'paradox' (Williams, P. 1997), a concept that, albeit lacking scientific basis, informs the way society functions, creating hierarchies of power based on a system of classification. Race is at the same time a spurious, illusory concept, and one that impinges dramatically on the lives of people – what Hylton (2018: 2) identifies as the 'lived raced realities'. Hall contends that 'racialized behaviour and difference needs to be understood as a discursive, not necessarily as a genetic or biological fact', while Appiah (2007), points out that the term 'race' can often be replaced with alternative constructs such as 'ethnicity' and 'culture'. Arguably, these latter social categories may better represent the fluid and contradictory trajectories of identity formation among contemporary migrant youth (Worbs 2006; Kelly, J. 2003; Kelly, K. 2008; Giardina 2008). Nevertheless, as pointed out by Appiah (2009: 672), 'racial identification is simply harder to resist than ethnic identification … Both in intimate settings and in public space, race is taken by so many more people to be the basis for treating people differently'.

Hylton defines the boundaries of the use of 'race' and 'ethnicity' within the field of sport studies in the following way:

> Intuitively most people understand that there is a relationship between 'race' and ethnicity which they struggle to explain fully. However, racial references tend to diverge from ethnicity as biological categories are often what is used to distinguish populations, in addition to other physical markers. Ethnicity often refers to a national subset that differs culturally rather than physically, and is regularly (incorrectly) used to distinguish numerical minorities from numerical majorities in a nation.
>
> (2009: 15)

Sport is a particularly sensitive area in which to study issues of race and racism, as it is more often than not, especially by sporting authorities and policymakers, portrayed as a levelling field characterised by meritocracy and colour blindness (Hylton 2018). However, several authors have produced evidence of how the history of modern sports has evolved and has been structured around racial lines (Cashmore 1982; Carrington 2010; Hylton 2009; Wiggins and Nauright 2016). In the UK, a substantial body of work exists around sport and racial identity formations of members of different ethnic groups, but not focusing expressly on young people. For example, Campbell (2016) traced the history of a black amateur club in Leicester, demonstrating how black clubs can be viewed as a site for resistance to prevailing prejudices (see also Williams, J. 1994). Burdsey (2006) investigated conceptions of national belonging among professional, ex-professional and amateur British Asian footballers, in particular their support for the England football team. Carrington (2008) examined the role of sport in the construction of 'black identities', joining as a participant-observer a black cricket team in the North of England. More recently, in *Race, Ethnicity and Football: Persisting Debates and Emerging Issues*, Burdsey (2011) reinvigorated the debate on racism and/in football in the British context. Included in the book is a qualitative study Bradbury (2011) conducted with five amateur clubs based in Leicester. The clubs originated in the 1960s and 1970s within 'BAME' (Black, Asians, and minority ethnic) communities and were initially focused on adults. Over the years, these clubs have shifted their interest from adults to young people, creating more inclusive environments for youth of BAME backgrounds living in the area. Bradbury drew the empirical findings of his study from questionnaire responses, semi-structured interviews with club workers and ethnographic observation. In the field of youth studies, one of the common challenges is that of giving 'voice' to the young participants, fully acknowledging them as valuable informants on their own lives (Clark et al. 2014). In an age in which 'people are increasingly observers of their own lives' (Back 2012: 18), particularly young people, it is a challenge that is both urgent and complex to undertake. This is the focus of the next section.

Time in between: adolescence

The young people at the centre of this book were aged between 14 and 18 when I first met them. They were going through that stage in life generally known as adolescence. However, according to the United Nations Convention on the Rights of the Child (UNCRC 1989) all those under 18 years of age are considered children. Is adolescence part of childhood or a stage of life in itself, with specific characteristics? There are divergent perspectives on the issue of age when doing research on young people (Hammersley 2017). As Hopkins (2010: 4) argues:

> Although some young people are also children and many young people are
> defined by the fact that they are not adults, there are young people who are

adults and embody many of the qualities and characteristics of adulthood. This diversity is probably one of the main reasons why studies of youth are characterized by a diverse range of theoretical approaches.

The adolescent lives a time 'in-between', which can be difficult to grasp for the researcher and the adult observer. Margaret Mead's (2001 [1928]) pioneering study of the transition from childhood to adulthood in the Samoa islands set the ground for many similar studies to follow. Among other things, her study contributed to transforming the idea of adolescence as an intrinsically problematic and troublesome stage of psychological development, which was prominent in social sciences at the beginning of the twentieth century (Muus 1999). However, six decades later Mead's findings were harshly attacked by Freeman (1983). He contested Mead's romantic descriptions of adolescents in the Samoas, suggesting that the North-American anthropologist had been misled by her young informants. Freeman's arguments launched what is considered as one the biggest controversies in the history of the social sciences (Côté 1994). Without taking a position in the long-lasting controversy, it is interesting to observe that it was caused by a contested interpretation of adolescents' social worlds.

In the study of identity formation and 'cultural' difference the liminal *and* central position of adolescence is particularly intriguing. Adolescence is often the time when such issues become more urgent and relevant for the young person (Perry 2002), prompting decisions to pursue peer group membership or to join activities, which are not under the control of parents or teachers (Head 1997). This is the case, for example, of the football team. Participation in sport is arguably a terrain within which teenagers can express a degree of autonomy and independence in decision-making. For according to Biesta *et al.* (2001: 111), 'sport is one of the few settings in which adults and young people engage in relationships with each other on a voluntary basis (unlike the context of school, and the context of the family)'. Parents can influence the decision of teenagers to choose one discipline – they can even apply pressure on a teenager to stay in a team if they believe, for whatever reason, that this is beneficial for her/him. But if the young boy or girl does not like that sport or, as often happens, gets disaffected at some point, there is not much the parents can do to counter that feeling and the decision to abandon the sport practice. In their discussion of leisure and youth in Ireland, Lalor *et al.* (2007: 215) write:

> Young people decide for themselves what they will do, how they will do it, as well as who they will do it with. Leisure that young people freely choose is a means through which they actively construct their personal development and identity. Leisure is also a forum through which social and cultural forces influence young people, shaping how they perceive and experience the world they live in.

All this is particularly relevant to my study, as the level of agency of teenagers exercised in their sport makes the research setting rather unstable. The situation and place where children and young people meet the researcher are among the main variables that influence the accounts that children give of themselves (Morrow and Richards 2002; Adler and Adler 2002; Bucknall 2014). As happened on a number of occasions during my fieldwork, players may leave the team anytime during the season, and not return. Also for these reasons, over the months spent doing fieldwork with two youth teams in North Dublin, I asked myself if the reading of 'discipline' and 'surveillance' adopted by Foucault (1979 [1975]) in his historical analysis of the school and other disciplinary systems, such as the prison, the hospital and the factory, can be applied to the youth sport team. Foucault analysed schooling as an apparatus of modern disciplinary power that 'succeeded in making children's bodies the object of highly complex systems of manipulation and conditioning' (Foucault 1980: 125).

Even though Foucault did not explicitly address sport or physical activity in his work, his interest in the body as a site for the workings of power has stimulated a number of scholars to utilise his theoretical frameworks in researching sporting practices (Markula and Pringle 2006; Pringle 2005; Giulianotti 2005: 102–120). Such an interpretation proved particularly useful in the analysis of a number of ethnographic events with Insaka, a team run by African coaches and composed of players of African and Eastern European backgrounds. The term 'discipline' was regularly used by the coaches, but what was the meaning attributed to it in this multifarious context? Was it just a question of the boys diligently following the manager's instructions? Or was it related to their behaviour on and off the pitch? Or was it a discourse instigated by the 'racialised' position of Insaka within the schoolboy league and by extension in Irish society? There was little doubt that the coaches attempted to enforce a 'system of conditioning' upon their players, to 'teach' them self-control and respect for the rules. However, their actions were met with different levels of resistance and opposition, something that was arguably not prominent in Foucault's analysis of disciplinary systems.

In approaching the experience of young teenagers playing football I could draw from memory on my own experience as a young player at the same age. This is a common consideration and assumption by researchers exploring youth and childhood, having themselves experienced these life stages and therefore possessing a certain level of understanding of them. However, as argued by Knopp Biklen, the use of personal memories in youth research can be a misleading approach. She writes:

> Although adults cannot 'go back' to being youth, those who study young people seem to place their recollections of adolescence into the matrix when they do fieldwork, analyse data, and write about it. Whatever happens in the process of doing fieldwork or analysing data, the effect of citing

personal memories in the written text is to authenticate the narrator's privileged speaking position.

(Knopp Biklen 2007: 252)

The apparent inequality of power relations between researcher and young participants must be carefully considered throughout the fieldwork. This is not without surprises, for according to Raby:

> With adolescence, power relations may become more complicated because teenagers are in a social position that shifts frequently between areas of dependence and independence. Furthermore, adolescents may be seen to be particularly powerful in societies that value and celebrate youth.

(2007: 47)

Participant or observer?

As noted, approaching the study of youth posits particular challenges, which are further complicated by migration patterns. By using a combination of qualitative methods I was responding to an ongoing debate in the social sciences and humanities when addressing the broad and urgent topic of migration (Grossman and O'Brien 2007; Castels 2011). The urgency for transdisciplinarity in this field of studies has been expressed by Grossman and O'Brien (2007: 2–3) when they argue that 'immigration challenges the researcher/practitioner to constructively abandon their disciplinary comfort zones, to both listen and look carefully to what is, in practice, a multifaceted and global phenomenon'. At the same time, as someone returning to university to undertake a PhD after a decade working as a journalist and a writer mainly on migration issues, I was also cognisant of bringing with me certain tools of observation and representation. To what extent would they be valued and useful in academic research? I came to the decision to adopt a flexible combination of methodological approaches, including participant observation, semi-structured interviews, and the use of the video camera, because I believed they would suit the challenge of conducting research with adolescents in the context of leisure practices, and particularly of sport (Gratton and Jones 2010). I also felt it could allow me to develop what Bourdieu defines as 'corporeal knowledge', which 'provides a practical comprehension of the world quite different from the act of conscious decoding that is normally designated by the idea of comprehension' (Bourdieu 1999: 135, quoted by Willis and Trondman 2002: 394).

One essential characteristic of methods inspired by participant observation is that questions may evolve through the course of the research (Denzin 1997; Emerson et al. 2001; Hammersley and Atkinson 2007; Crang and Cook 2007). The central objective is to achieve an understanding of the lived experiences of the protagonists. Informal conversations and observation play an important role in producing ethnographic knowledge, but the relationship between participation and observation is based on an open paradox. In Behar's (1996) view, the ethnographer aims to understand the 'native's' viewpoint while at the same time s/he does not 'go native'. Over months spent doing fieldwork, I became more and more implicated in the 'participation' act as roles were assigned to me, further blurring the already precarious boundaries between participation and observation. However, there were moments when I was sent back to a less participative position, and abruptly reminded of the fact that I could not escape my outsider's role. As noted by DeWalt and DeWalt (2010: 27), 'the balance between observation and participation achieved by an individual researcher can fall anywhere along the continuum'. Across the chapters I describe and discuss the different unanticipated roles assigned to me by gatekeepers and key ethnographic actors, such as linesman, assistant coach, guardian and driver. In so doing, I developed a role for myself that Johnson et al. (2006) might call of the 'active participant-observer', while Adler and Adler (2002) might define it as 'active membership' in the team. However, this process was always 'in flux' and never completed. The researcher's role can shift over time, and the 'identity' of the ethnographer (at the same time participant *and* observer) is never settled and it is subject to constant negotiations. Drawing on Thrin (1992), Denzin argues:

> The ethnographer works within a 'hybrid' reality. Experience, discourse, and self-understandings collide against larger cultural assumptions concerning race, ethnicity, gender, class and age. A certain identity is never possible; the ethnographer must always ask, 'Not *Who* am I?', but '*When, where, how* am I (so and so)?'
>
> (1997: xiv; the final words are from Thrin 1992: 157, italics in original)

Getting access to a youth team in Dublin as a participant-observer constituted a major task, and one that undeniably impinged on my methodological assumptions. An adult who attends young people's sports activities might provoke all kinds of questions from the adults present at games, above all the young players' parents. Fine (1987: 33) recalls how, while attending games of Little League baseball for the purpose of his research on pre-adolescent sport culture, he was often asked about his reasons for being there. 'The inquisition was friendly, but the question was asked because I was an unrecognized adult, a stranger whose presence did not "make sense" within the established community of parents'. In my case, parents very rarely attended games and related activities of the team. As we will see, this had something to do with specific patterns of masculinity among these adolescents ('We don't want our parents around') and the socio-cultural facets of the area, with working class parents or single parents either busy with other children or working weekend shifts. Other adults, club members and residents of the neighbourhood, were occasionally present at home games. Some of them were curious about my work and asked me about the reason for being there with a camera.

Researchers who interrogate youth sport practices via the method of participant-observation appear to be allowed a limited number of roles in the field, and the roles they play reflect the kind of access they are able to secure into the community they want to study. Quite often, researchers happen to be parents of young players (Fine 1987; Dyck 2000; Brown 2017) or youth workers or coaches (Giles and Baker 2008; Cuadros 2011). In some cases, they have been members of teams or athletes themselves (Sands 2002; Brownell 2006; Holt and Sparkes 2001). All these roles are, for different reasons, immediately clear and visible to the possible gatekeepers and the research 'subjects'. But what about someone such as myself, who is not a parent, relative, coach or player and furthermore, is also a 'foreigner' in the country?

Quite interestingly, I found some resonance with the role of the author of *Outcasts United* (St. John 2009). St. John, a journalist from the *New York Times*, engaged in what he defines as 'immersive reporting' (St. John 2009: 302), spending an extensive period of time with a football team of young refugees, aged 13–17, in a provincial town of the United States. It is quite likely that St. John's position as a reporter from a prestigious newspaper afforded him some credibility, thereby allowing him to gain trust from relevant gatekeepers. In my case, if I wanted to succeed in my effort to get access to a youth team in Dublin, I had to work on other 'strengths' which would help me gain the trust of the adult gatekeepers with whom I had to negotiate access to the team. One of these strengths was the novelty of the research in the Irish context. Another helping factor was the desire of the adult gatekeepers of both teams to use this opportunity to challenge public negative discourses about the locality ('Blanchardstown has a bad name') and African people in Ireland. The use of the video camera functioned as an element of attraction, or even as a passport (Rouch 2003), and over time helped to build a bridge between me and the young participants.

The work of St. John encouraged me to further reflect on the potential connections between 'deep reporting' and ethnography. It is something that has been suggested also by sociologists (Duneier 1992, 1999; Golding 2005) and social anthropologists (Marcus 2008). For example, Marcus argues that ethnographers and anthropologists 'often function nowadays like the best and deepest journalists – certainly their experiences of other places, of sites of research and reporting, are similar today' (Marcus 2008: 4). From a different perspective, that of Media Studies, Beckett (2013) notes that,

> Observation, investigation and deliberation are core functions of journalism that can fit into academic research paradigms. They can add dynamism to the often preconceived and over structured thought processes that the Academy encourages.

Les Back invites us to reflect about the challenges of conducting social research amid unprecedented levels of production of information in human society, and to 'rethink procedures and devices we use within social research' (Back 2012: 34). He contends that 'sociologists, anthropologists or those from any number of disciplines in the humanities have never had the monopoly on social analysis' (Back 2012: 19). Back draws here on Becker, who suggested paying attention to the ways in which artists, playwrights and novelists 'go about the process of telling' (Becker 2007: 20) as it 'might contain new ideas for social researchers in terms of the ways in which we convey not only the content of our research but also moral and political commitments' (Becker 2007: 20). Advocating an inter-pretivist perspective, Denzin (1997) has come to similar conclusions and, pos-sibly, moved a step further. Reflecting on the ethnographic text, Denzin (1997: 267) emphasises that, 'there are no stories out there waiting to be told and no certain truths waiting to be recorded; there are only stories yet to be con-structed'. He invites ethnographers to fulfil 'the promise of ethnography as a form of radical social practice' (Denzin 2997: 287), whose goal is not simply that of interpreting but of changing the world. Denzin's project of interpretive ethnography, influenced by cultural studies and post-structuralism, is an appro-priate and urgent instrument to critically intervene in a reality defined by con-tradictions: globalisation and neo-nationalism, electronic capitalism and new forms of labour exploitation, and finally the crisis of the liberal democracy satur-ated with nation-state ideology.

Thinking through ethics

One of my ideas about an appropriate methodological approach was that the use of the video camera would be beneficial for the progress of my study. At the same time, it obviously posed particular ethical challenges. From a practical and 'strategic' point of view, in certain situations the use of the video camera can facilitate acceptance by those observed. This might be the case, for example, with the football pitch and with sporting grounds in general. People attending games and taking part in them, especially youth, recognise visual technologies, such as cameras, as something familiar and somehow appealing, less intimid-ating than, for example, the notebook. Homemade videos of children's football games are regularly uploaded on YouTube by parents, relatives and club members. The video camera may be considered an 'obtrusive' method of research but in fact it turned out to be helpful in my research work, as, most of the time, it functioned as a possible passport (Rouch 2003) – as a tool that could help define my role in a setting previously unknown to me.

I offered to introduce the video camera into the life of a youth football team as a way to document games and significant moments, and in so doing to learn more about the dynamics at hand. My intentions, and the fact that what I was doing was purely an academic endeavour, had to be clear to everyone, both minors and adults, being aware that 'filming might affect people's lives and rela-tionships to each other' (Barbash and Taylor 1997: 44). I was prepared for different roles that might be attached to my presence, as is always the case when doing ethnography, but I could not anticipate the type and the amount of interest the camera would provoke. I came to learn that the camera can serve not only as a means of inquiry but also, and maybe even more profoundly, as a bridge between myself and my ethnographic community. It emerged that my role in the field was mostly attached to the camera. Even when I was not using it or carrying it, I was still perceived and accepted, especially by the boys, as 'the man with the camera' (Loescher 2005). The participants, both minors and adults, responded to it, and in some cases I invited them to appropriate it – to become the 'observers'.

Within youth studies, in particular when working with adolescents, there is a growing emphasis on the use of visual research methods. Drawing on her studies of young people's physical culture, Azzarito (2013: 3) stresses that 'the visual can enable young people to speak meaningfully, more authentically, and in con-textualized ways about their body experiences'. I did not embark on fieldwork with the purpose of testing the analytical potential of audio-visual media as a source of 'new knowledge', as advocated by theorists and practitioners within visual anthropology and visual studies (Banks 2001; MacDougall 1998, 2006; Pink 2007, 2012; Weber 2008). Rather, I understood the use of the camera as a helpful component of the set of methodological tools. From time to time I used the camera to take photographs of places and people in the field. In so doing, at least during the first months of fieldwork, I aspired to generate a seemingly less 'chaotic' source of material. Footage provided me with an overwhelming amount of information, which needed time to be examined and thought through (Ball and Smith 2001). By contrast, still images were immediately helpful in isolating significant details of the scene of my ethnography.

Obviously, the use of images poses stringent ethical questions. For example, how can we guarantee the respect of traditional ethical rules of conduct in such cases? What use will be made of the images? (Pink 2009). So far, these questions have not been adequately explored and there is a lack of attention surrounding the implications that the use of visual methods might have on the lives of young participants (Flewitt 2005; Thomson 2008; Papademas and IVSA 2009). In discussing visual research with children and young people, Thomson emphasises the need for 'a new ethics'. He argues:

> The ubiquity of new technologies also raises new ethical issues. Researchers working with children must always ask who owns the image – the child or the adult researcher? An individual or a team? But because new technologies offer the capacity of serial workings on images, the issue becomes even more complex – who owns the multiply manufactured image, and how is permission to be given for its reproduction?'
> (Thomson 2008: 13–14; see also Alderson and Morrow 2011)

The need for a new ethical framework in doing visual research is not limited to research on and with youth. Echoing Prosser and Loxley (2008), Clark (2012: 17) argues that 'existing institutional ethical review procedures, ethical frameworks and codes of practice are unsatisfactory for visual materials'. After obtaining permission from the families (and the boys) to carry out my study with Mountview, I discussed with my research participants ways of 'giving back' (Marcus 2010). In responding to their request, I negotiated the production of a short video about a topical game, a cup final, and its publication on YouTube. The clip was eventually uploaded on the website of the club. I followed the same route in my fieldwork with Insaka, although here I was presented with an older constituency – the boys were aged between 16 and 18 and affirmed a greater level of self-determination (Bengry-Howell and Griffin 2012).

The publication of this book presented new and, to some degree, inescapable challenges. My 'ethnographic community' had dispersed. Many of the young participants, especially those of immigrant background, had moved abroad (to the UK, Canada, France, Belgium), others had simply moved out of the neighbourhood and started independent lives, losing contact with old teammates and adult mentors. How could I claim authority on images of them taken back in the years when they were still teenagers? I could not. Nevertheless, I deeply felt that this story (their story, my story) deserved to be told and critically discussed. For doing so, the decision was taken to anonymise the names of the protagonists, and make limited and calibrated use of images, intended more as descriptive rather than analytical components of the research. In the end, this critical turn in my relationship with the young participants, and the life trajectories away from Ireland of many of them, became fruitful material for my analysis of patterns of belonging in and through sport.

The researcher and I – the meaning of biography

As noted earlier, the qualitative research process is entangled with the researcher's biography. It is not only about the reflexive acknowledgement of the role the researcher's social, cultural and ethnic background plays in framing his/her views about a social phenomenon. It is about understanding how the researcher's biography is active in producing the text. Denzin and Lincoln (2005: 21) define the 'biographically situated researcher' as an individual 'who enters the research process from inside a community. This community has its own research traditions which constitute a distinct point of view'. Gaining appreciation of the role of the researcher's body and his/her biography in the research act is particularly critical in the context of sport studies and for everyone that researches physical culture(s) (Giardina and Newman 2011a, 2011b; Atkinson 2011). Denison and Markula (2003: 9) argue that 'sport and movement experiences can be elusive, bodily, intense, and contradictory', and for Hughson et al. (2005: 175), this 'highlights the need to explore them introspectively as subjective experiences comprising holistic human significance and meaning'.

To what extent has my own immigrant background, and the fact that I lived in different countries, influenced my interrogation of issues of belonging for youth of immigrant background? There is an affinity between the concept of 'transcultural' and that of 'location' that I experienced in my fieldwork. Clifford articulates a sense of 'location' which is, at the same time, a theoretical and political stance: 'an itinerary rather than a bounded site', and something that is 'constituted by displacement as much as by stasis' (Clifford 1997: 2). Reflexivity is a key term in the context of the ethnographic methodology (Willis 1980; Pratt 1986; Marcus 1998; Berry and Clair 2011) and is particularly valuable in researching migration (Gray 2008). Ethnography cannot be non-reflexive, because the position of the researcher and the participants, and the dynamics of power at hand, will influence the type of 'distributed knowledge' (Marcus, 1995) that will be the outcome of the research. Ethnicity, gender, class and the age of the researcher, are all elements that come into play in his/her ethnographic experience and in his/her writing. This discussion is particularly relevant in the case of researchers who investigate questions of young people's identity formation, especially when ethnic and racial identification come to the fore.

On several occasions, I was made aware that my position in the field was not only determined by the fact that I am an adult man, a researcher originally from Italy – as these were the most common elements that contributed to my identification in the eyes of my participants – but also by the fact that I was a 'white' man. In reflecting upon his work with British Asian footballers, Burdsey writes:

> Ethnic differences between researchers and participants are certainly not insurmountable, but they also cannot be fully eviscerated. Consequently, we must engage in a continual process of self-reflexivity and seek to critically scrutinize and interrogate how our ethnicities impinge on the research process.
>
> (2006: 13–14)

The importance of the use of self-reflexivity in this specific field of studies has been further endorsed by Carrington (2008) and Hylton (2009). In his analysis of research approaches in studying 'race' and sport, Hylton (2009: 43) argues for 'the need to position the researcher within the research process'. With this commitment in mind, I endeavoured to make sense of a long and challenging research which has arguably altered the way I see young people, and also, to some degree, myself.

Suburban home – the 'city' and the 'community'

The location of my research is Blanchardstown, the largest residential area of what until 2015 was known as the Dublin 15 postal district.[15] This is the fastest growing urban area in the Republic of Ireland: in a matter of 10 years, between 1996 and 2006, it almost doubled its population, taking it to about 100,000 (Ryan 2009, 2010). The most intensive housing developments have taken place following the 'Celtic Tiger' economic boom (Coulter and Coleman 2003; O'Toole 2009), and pushing the boundaries of the city further towards the countryside. New estates have been built to host immigrant workers coming from a variety of countries employed by companies such as eBay and IBM, which concentrate in Blanchardstown a variety of services for the European market. But it is not only 'skilled' workers that populate the area. 'Cities are the product – the material and spatial expression – of their times', notes Stuart Hall (2006: 20), and the suburban post-industrial development implemented in this part of Dublin, defined essentially by tertiary forms of labour and production, is a clear example of what this might mean. Blanchardstown hosts the biggest shopping centre in Ireland, opened in 1996 and symbolically (and with some unavoidable irony) called 'The Blanchardstown Centre'.[16] The shopping mall appears to be the centre of life of these dispersed communities, in that all the main services and attractions are located around and adjacent to it. The Fingal County Council Hall, the District Court, a public theatre, the local FAS (Irish National Training and Employment Authority) office, two secondary schools – also eBay and PayPal have their headquarters around the 'Centre'. Workers from various countries are employed as clerks, managers, shop assistants, engineers, cleaners and security guards, creating a truly multi-ethnic and multinational landscape. This area is also home to the largest population of adolescents of an immigrant background, above all those of an African background (Gilligan *et al.* 2010).

It is not by chance, then, that the setting of my research was located in Blanchardstown. Besides being one of the most ethnically mixed areas of the whole country, it hosts a number of youth football clubs, which welcome players from a variety of national backgrounds.[17] The idea of the 'city' and of the 'community' in the eyes of my informants grew to be an intriguing subject to explore. Where do you belong? Is it the city where you live, the neighbourhood or the country where you are originally from? (Hoerder *et al.* 2005). And what role does the football team play in all of this? The majority of the young participants had played in more than one team, and some of them, especially those of an immigrant background, had played for three or even four local teams in a matter of a few years. This may tell us something about the ways affiliation to local teams and attachment to places operate, but it also leads to a broader question about the idea of 'the city' in a rapidly changing social and demographic context.

Despite the limited distance from the city centre, about 10 km, Blanchardstown is often perceived by local youth to be a different place. The 'city' lies far away; it takes between 40 to 50 minutes to go there by bus from the shopping centre. 'Where is the disco you are talking about?' I once asked Mariusz, a 17-year-old of Polish origin who was telling his friends about a night out in the city centre. I was curious about the location of his weekend gatherings. 'It's in town', he answered. 'Where in town?' was my next question. 'I don't know, they drove me there, I was in the car with some friends. I don't know much about the town'. Mariusz has lived in Dublin since the age of six. There were other examples of the boys' relationship with the geography of their city. Many of the boys of African background identified themselves as 'Blanch Boys'. The idea of being 'from Blanchardstown' as a form of collective identity was reinforced through the production of home videos, uploaded onto YouTube, that celebrate the 'Blanch Boys'. Local, suburban identities of boys of an immigrant background seem to be vital in other areas of Dublin as well: there are videos on YouTube about the 'Tallaght Boys' and even one dedicated to the 'Lucan Boys'.

Hopefully, by observing the football team I could learn about the 'truly new and challenging forms of cultural practice and identity formation that had been produced within metropolitan contexts by young people of different ethnic and cultural backgrounds' (Back 1996: 3). As soon as I entered the field, however, I understood that my scope could not be limited in the way I had imagined. By spending weekdays and weekends in one of the fastest demographically changing areas of Dublin, I was also learning about communities in the making (Williams, R. 1983), and I was doing it mainly through the means of observation of the football practice of adolescent males. Coaches, adult members of the club, players, parents and relatives would eventually become subjects in my study as well. The idea of community, of being part of a community of which the youth football club is a vital component, was a recurring term in my conversations with the chairman of Mountview FC. I was obviously interested to understand how the immigrant boys would fit into this. But how do we define community?

Community studies have a consistent tradition in Ireland, originating from influential anthropological work conducted in the 1930s in the West of Ireland by North-American scholars Arensberg and Kimball (2001 [1940]). Until recent times, the largest part of this research has focused on rural and dispersed areas (Share et al. 2012). Corcoran et al. (2010) investigated four Dublin suburban locations highlighting that, contrary to negative assumptions on suburban social fabric, feelings of belonging further arise in new suburban communities. However, there are multiple and differing definitions of community within sociological literature alone. The arrival of the internet has further complicated this field of studies. When it comes to sport, community is a powerful signifier across the island of Ireland. This is particularly true in relation to Gaelic Games, whose organisation is based around a specific territory, one's county of origin. While, for the GAA, community is strictly related to territory, there are other declinations of community based on common interests and passions but not the physical location (Crosson 2017). This is the case, for example, for fans of English clubs such as Manchester United and Liverpool or of Celtic Glasgow, in Scotland. These clubs are the most popular among football fans in Ireland.[18] In the next chapter, the relationship built by teenagers with the team they played in and the locality where the team was based will be explored through the analysis of ethnographic events and dialogue with research participants.

Notes

1 SARI is a not for profit organisation founded in Dublin in 1997. It is one of the original members of the network organisation Football Against Racism Europe (FARE).
2 From now on, simply Insaka.
3 From now on, simply Mountview.

4 According to the 2016 census there are 2557 Jews in the Republic of Ireland.
5 'Travellers formally recognised as an ethnic minority', *The Irish Times*, 1 March 2017.
6 The proportion of Irish and British citizens combined in immigration trends to Ireland was 26.7 per cent in 2006 and 43.2 per cent in 2012 (Gilmartin 2013: 96).
7 *Here to stay*, Dublin, 2006.
8 www.sfai.ie/ [accessed 2 February 2018].
9 Following FIFA regulations on the protection of minors (FIFA 2014: 22–24), national football associations are expected to keep a record of foreign national minors being registered to play in the country. However, the FAI did not make such data available for this study.
10 Searched on 12 January 2018.
11 In 2016 the average attendance at Championship matches in the All-Ireland series of Gaelic football was 13,146, a steep decline from the peak of 20,172 in 2007 (www.independent.ie/sport/gaelic-games/gaelic-football/revealed-the-attendance-figures-for-the-gaa-football-championships-are-a-cause-for-concern-35145508.html [accessed 10 January 2018]). The average attendance in the League of Ireland Premier Division in 2017 was 1,419 (www.extratime.ie/articles/19179/league-of-ireland-attendances-2017-the-story-so-far/ [accessed 10 January 2018]).
12 Over 75 per cent of second-level schools take part in Gaelic football competitions compared with 58 per cent that are involved in inter-school competitions in soccer (Fahey *et al*. 2005).
13 *Sociology of Sport Journal, Journal of Sport and Social Issues, International Review for the Sociology of Sport*.
14 Following the referendum, children born in the Irish island of Ireland on or after 1 January 2005 are entitled to Irish citizenship if they have a British parent or a parent who is entitled to live in Northern Ireland or the Republic of Ireland without residence restrictions. Other foreign national parents of children born in the island on or after 1 January 2005 must have lived in the country three of the last four years immediately before the birth of the child. In that case they can apply for a certificate of Irish nationality.
15 Following a national reform of local government started in April 2015, the Dublin 15 postal district has been incorporated into the administrative county of Fingal.
16 This 'record' is challenged by the Dundrum Town Centre, a shopping mall situated in South Dublin, opened in 2005 (Linehan 2015). Although with fewer square metres (120.000 vs 140.000), the Blanchardstown mall has more shops (180 vs 160) and parking spaces (7000 vs 3400) (Wikipedia).
17 At the time my research was conducted there were 10 youth football clubs operating in Dublin 15.
18 'Which Premier League club is most supported in Ireland?', *The Irish Times*, 21 March 2017.

References

Adler, P. A. and Adler, P. (2002). 'Teen scenes: Ethnographies of adolescent cultures'. *Journal of Contemporary Ethnography*, 31(5), 652–660.
Agamben, G. (1995). 'We refugees'. *Symposium*, 49(2), 114–119.
Alderson, P. and Morrow, V. (2011). *The ethics of research with children and young people*. London: Sage.
Allen, K. (2003). 'Neither Boston nor Berlin: Class polarisation and neo-liberalism in the Irish Republic'. In C. Coulter and S. Coleman (eds), *The end of Irish history?* Manchester: Manchester University Press, 56–73.

Amara, M., Aquilina, D. and Henry, I. (2005). *Sport and multiculturalism*. European Commission DG Education and Culture. Available from: www.isca-web.org/files/Sport%20 and%20Multiculturalism%20EU%202004.pdf [accessed 1 August 2011].

Amelina, A. and Faist, T. (2012). 'De-naturalizing the national in research methodologies: Key concepts of transnational studies in migration'. *Ethnic and Racial Studies*, 35(10), 1707–1724.

Amit, V. (2000). 'Introduction: Constructing the field'. In V. Amit (ed.), *Constructing the field*. New York: Routledge, 1–18.

Appadurai, A. (2010). 'How histories make geographies: Circulation and context in a global perspective'. *Transcultural Studies*, 1. Available from: http://archiv.ub.uni-heidelberg.de/ojs/index.php/transcultural/article/view/6129/1760 [accessed 10 October 2012].

Appiah, K. (2007). *The ethics of identity*. Princeton: Princeton University Press.

Appiah, K. (2009). 'Racial identity and racial identification'. In L. Back and J. Solomos (eds), *Theories of race and racism*. London: Routledge.

Archetti, E. (1999). *Masculinities, football, polo, and the tango in Argentina*. Oxford: Berg.

Arensberg, C. A. and Kimball, S. T. (2001[1940]). *Family and community in Ireland*, third edition. Ennis: Clasp Press.

Atkinson, M. (2011). 'Physical cultural studies [redux]'. *Sociology of Sport Journal*, 28, 135–144.

Azzarito, L. (2013). 'Introduction'. In L. Azzarito and D. Kirk, *Pedagogies, physical culture, and visual methods*. London: Routledge, 1–12.

Azzarito, L. and Macdonald, D. (2016). 'Unpacking gender/sexuality/race/disability/ social class to understand the embodied experiences of young people in contemporary physical culture'. In K. Green and A. Smith (eds), *Routledge handbook of youth sport*. London: Routledge, 321–331.

Back, L. (1996). *New ethnicities and urban culture: Racisms and multiculture in young lives*. London: UCL Press.

Back, L. (2007). *The art of listening*. Oxford: Berg.

Back, L. (2012). 'Live sociology: Social research and its futures'. In L. Back and N. Puwar (eds), *Live methods*. Oxford: Wiley-Blackwell/The Sociological Review, 18–39.

Bairner, A. (2001). *Sport, nationalism and globalization*. New York: State University of New York Press.

Bairner, A. (2005). *Sport and the Irish*. Dublin: University College Dublin Press.

Balibar, E. (1991 [1988]). 'The nation form: History and ideology'. In E. Balibar and I. Wallerstein (eds), *Race, nation, class. Ambiguous identities*. London: Verso, 86–106.

Ball, M. and Smith, G. (2001). 'Technologies of realism? Ethnographic uses of photography and film'. In P. Atkinson, A. Coffey, S. Delamont, J. Lofland and L. Lofland (eds), *Handbook of ethnography*. London: Sage, 302–320.

Banks, M. (2001). *Visual methods in social research*. London: Sage.

Barbash, I. and Taylor, L. (1997). *Cross-cultural filmmaking*. Berkeley: University of California Press.

Beck, U. (2006). *The cosmopolitan vision*. Cambridge: Polity Press.

Becker (2007). *Telling about society*. Chicago: University of Chicago Press.

Beckett, C. (2013). 'Can journalism count as a research output? British politics and policy at LSE'. *Creative Future*, weblog post, 12 December 2012. Available from: http:// eprints.lse.ac.uk/48459/ [accessed 20 December 2014].

Behar, R. (1996). *The vulnerable observer*. Boston, MA: Beacon Press.

Bell, V. (ed.) (1999). *Performativity and belonging*. London: Sage.

Bengry-Howell, A. and Griffin, C. (2012). 'Negotiating access in ethnographic research with "hard to reach" young people: Establishing common ground or a process of methodological grooming?'. *International Journal of Social Research Methodology*, 15(5), 403–416.

Berger, J. and Mohr, J. (2010 [1975]). *A seventh man*. London: Verso.

Berry, K. and Clair, R. P. (2011). 'Reflecting on the call to ethnographic reflexivity: A collage of responses to questions of contestation'. *Cultural Studies Critical Methodologies*, 11(2), 199–209.

Biesta, G. J. J., Stams, M., Dirks, E., Rutten, E. A., Veugelers, W. and Schuengel, C. (2001). 'Does sport make a difference? An exploration of the impact of sport on the social integration of young people'. In J. Steenbergen, P. de Knop and A. Elling (eds), *Values and norms in sport*. Oxford: Meyer & Meyer Sport, 95–113.

Bradbury, S. (2011). 'Racism, resistance and new youth inclusions'. In D. Burdsey (ed.), *Race, ethnicity and football: Persisting debates and emergent issues*. London: Routledge, 67–83.

Brown, S. (2017). 'Introduction: youth sport and social capital'. *Sport in Society*, published online 9 May 2017, 1–18. DOI: https://doi.org/10.1080/14681811.2017.1322755.

Brownell, S. (2006). 'Sport ethnography: A personal account'. In D. Hobbs and R. Wright (eds), *The Sage handbook of fieldwork*. London: Sage, 243–254.

Bucknall, S. (2014). 'Doing qualitative research with children and young people'. In A. Clark, R. Flewitt, M. Hammersley and M. Robb (eds), *Understanding research with children and young people*. London: Sage/The Open University, 69–84.

Burdsey, D. (2006). 'If I ever play football, dad, can I play for England or India?'. *Sociology*, 40(1): 11–28.

Burdsey, D. (2011). 'They think it's all over … it isn't yet!'. In D. Burdsey (ed.), *Race, ethnicity and football: Persisting debates and emergent issues*. London: Routledge, 3–20.

Burrmann, U., Brandmann, K., Mutz, M. and Zender, U. (2017). 'Ethnic identities, sense of belonging and the significance of sport: Stories from immigrant youths in Germany'. *European Journal for Sport and Society*, 14(3), 186–204.

Campbell, P. (2016). *Football, ethnicity and community. The life of an African-Caribbean football club*. Bern: Peter Lang.

Carrington, B. (2008). '"What's the footballer doing here?" Racialized performativity, reflexivity, and identity'. *Cultural Studies Critical Methodologies*, 8(4), 423–452.

Carrington, B. (2010). *Race, sport and politics: The sporting black diaspora*. London: Sage.

Cashmore, E. (1982). *Black sportsmen*. London: Routledge.

Castels, S. (2011). 'Methodology and methods: Conceptual issues'. In M. Berriane and H. de Haas (eds), *African migration research: Innovative methods and methodologies*. Trenton, NJ, USA: Africa World Press, 31–70.

Clark, A. (2012). 'Visual ethics in a contemporary landscape'. In S. Pink (ed.), *Advances in visual methodologies*. London: Sage, 17–36.

Clark, A., Flewitt, R., Hammersley, M. and Robb, M. (2014). *Understanding research with children and young people*. London: Sage/The Open University.

Clifford, J. (1997). *Routes. Travel and translations in the late 20th century*. Cambridge, MA: Harvard University Press.

Connor, S. (2003). *Youth sport in Ireland*. Dublin: The Liffey Press.

Corcoran, M. P., Gray, J. and Peillon, M. (2010). *Suburban affiliations: Social relations in the greater Dublin area*. Syracuse, NY: Syracuse University Press.

Côté, J. (1994). *Adolescent storm and stress. An evaluation of the Mead-Freeman controversy*. Hillside, NJ: Erlbaum.

Coulter, C. and Coleman, S. (eds) (2003). *The end of Irish history?* Manchester: Manchester University Press.

Crang, M. and Cook, I. (2007). *Doing ethnographies*. London: Sage.

Cronin, M. (1999). *Sport and nationalism in Ireland: Gaelic games, soccer and Irish identity since 1884*. Dublin: Four Courts Press.

Cronin, M. (2013). 'Integration through sport: The Gaelic Athletic Association and the New Irish'. In J. V. Ulin, H. Edwards and S. O'Brien (eds), *Race and immigration in the New Ireland*. Notre Dame, IN: University of Notre Dame Press, 157–174.

Crosson, S. (2017). 'Community games'. RTE, online article, 27 November 2017. Available from: www.rte.ie/eile/brainstorm/2017/1107/918120-community-games/ [accessed 20 January 2018].

CSO – Central Statistics Office (1996). 'National Census. Principle demographic results'. Dublin: Government of Ireland.

CSO – Central Statistics Office (2017). 'Census 2016. Population and migration estimates'. Dublin: Government of Ireland.

Cuadros, P. (2011). 'We play too. Latina integration through soccer in the "New South"'. *Southeastern Geographies*, 51(2), 227–241.

Darmody, M., Tyrrel, N. and Song, S. (2011). *The changing faces of Ireland. Exploring the lives of immigrant and ethnic minority children*. Rotterdam: Sense Publishers.

Darmondy, M., Ginnity, F. and Kingston, G. (2016). 'The experiences of migrant children in Ireland'. In J. Williams, E. Nixon, E. Smyth, and D. Watson (eds), *Cherishing all the children equally?* Dublin: Oaktree Press.

Delaney, L. and Fahey, T. (2005). *Social and economic value of sport in Ireland*. Dublin: The Economic and Social Research Institute.

Denison, J. and Markula, P. (2003). 'Introduction: Moving writing'. In J. Denison and P. Markula (eds), *Moving writing: Crafting movement in sport research*. New York: Peter Lang, 1–24.

Denzin, N. (1997). *Interpretive ethnography*. Thousand Oaks, CA: Sage.

Denzin, N. K. and Lincoln, Y. S. (2005). 'Introduction: The discipline and practice of qualitative research'. In: N. K. Denzin and Y. S. Lincoln (eds), *Handbook of qualitative research*, third edition. Thousand Oaks, CA: Sage, 1–32.

DeWalt, K. R. and DeWalt, B. R. (2010). *Participant observation: A guideline for fieldworkers*. Washington, DC: Altamira Press.

Doherty, A. and Taylor, T. (2007). 'Sport and physical recreation in the settlement of immigrant youth'. *Leisure/Loisir*, 31(1), 27–55.

Duneier, M. (1992). *Slim's table. Race, respectability, masculinity*. Chicago: University of Chicago Press.

Duneier, M. (1999). *Sidewalk*. New York: Farrar, Straus and Giroux.

Dyck, N. (2000). 'Home field advantage? Exploring the social construction of children's sport'. In V. Amit (ed.), *Constructing the field*. London: Routledge, 32–53.

Elling, A., De Knopp, P. and Knoppers, A. (2001). 'The social integrative meaning of sport: A critical and comparative analysis of policy and practice in the Netherlands'. *Sociology of Sport Journal*, 18, 414–434.

Elling, A. and Claringbould, I. (2005). 'Mechanisms of inclusion and exclusion in the Dutch sports landscape: Who can and wants to belong?' *Sociology of Sport Journal*, 22(4), 498–515.

Emerson, R. M., Fretz, R. I. and Shaw L. L. (2001). 'Participant observation and field-notes'. In P. Atkinson, A. Coffey, S. Delamont, J. Lofland and L. Lofland (eds), *Handbook of ethnography*. London: Sage, 352–368.

ENAR Ireland – European Network Against Racism Ireland (2017). *iReport of racism in Ireland*, January–June 2017. Dublin: European Network Against Racism Ireland.

Essed, P. (2015). 'A brief ABC on black Europe'. In ENAR-European Network Against Racism, *Invisible visible minority*. Brussels: ENAR, 57–76.

Fahey, T., Delaney, L. and Gannon, B. (2005). *School children and sport in Ireland*. Dublin: The Economic and Social Research Institute.

FAI – Football Association of Ireland (2007). *Intercultural football plan. Many voices, one goal*. Dublin: FAI.

FAI – Association of Ireland (2016). *Strategic plan 2016–2020*. Dublin: FAI.

Fanning, B. (ed.) (2007). *Immigration and social change in the Republic of Ireland*. Manchester: Manchester University Press.

Fanning, B., Killoran, B., Ni Bhroin, S. and McEvoy, G. (2011). *Taking racism seriously*. Dublin: Trinity Immigration Initiative & Immigrant Council of Ireland.

Fanon, F. (1987 [1952]). *Black skin, white masks*. London: Pluto Press.

Fields, B. (2001). 'Whiteness, racism and identity'. *International Labor and Working-Class History*, 60, 48–56.

FIFA – Fédération Internationale de Football Association (2014). *Regulations*. Geneva, CH: FIFA.

Fine, G. A. (1987). *With the boys. Little League baseball and preadolescent culture*. Chicago: The University of Chicago Press.

Fleming, S. (2016). 'Youth sport, race and ethnicity'. In K. Green and A. Smith (eds), *Routledge handbook of youth sport*. London: Routledge, 287–296.

Fletcher, T. and Hylton, K. (2016). '"Race", whiteness and sport'. In D. K. Wiggins and J. Nauright (eds), *Routledge handbook of sport, race and ethnicity*. London: Routledge, 87–106.

Flewitt, R. (2005). 'Conducting research with young children: Some ethical considerations'. *Early Child Development and Care*, 175(6), 553–565.

Foucault, M. (1979 [1975]). *Discipline and punish*. Harmondsworth: Penguin Books.

Foucault, M. (1980). *Power/knowledge: Selected interviews & other writings 1972–1977*. Gordon, C. (ed.). New York: Pantheon Books.

Free, M. (2017). 'From there to here': Narratives of transition, migration and national identity in Irish media representations of rugby union in the professional era'. *European Journal for Sport and Society*, 14(3), 205–225.

Freeman, D. (1983). *Margaret Mead and Samoa. The making and unmaking of an anthropological myth*. Cambridge, MA: Harvard University Press.

Garner, S. (2007). 'Ireland and immigration: Explaining the absence of the far right'. *Patterns of Prejudice*, 41(2), 109–130.

Garner, S. (2009). 'Ireland: From racism without "race" to "racism without racists"'. *Radical History Review*, 104, 41–56.

Garner, S. (2013). 'Reflections on race in contemporary Ireland'. In J. V. Ulin, H. Edwards and S. O'Brien (eds), *Race and immigration in the New Ireland*. Notre Dame, IN: University of Notre Dame Press, 175–204.

Garner, S. (2015). 'Making race an issue in the 2004 Irish Citizenship Referendum'. In F. Dukelow and R. Meade (eds), *Defining events: Power, resistance and identity in 21st century Ireland*. Manchester: Manchester University Press, 70–88.

Gasparini, W. and Cometti, A. (eds) (2010). *Sport facing the test of cultural diversity*. Strasbourg: Council of Europe.

Giardina, M. (2008). 'Consuming difference: Stylish hybridity, diasporic identity, and the politics of youth culture'. In N. Dolby and F. Rizvi (eds), *Youth moves. Identities and education in global perspective*. New York: Routledge, 69–84.

Giardina, M. and Donnelly, K. M. (eds) (2008a). *Youth culture and sport*. New York: Routledge.

Giardina, M. and Donnelly, K. M. (2008b). 'Introduction'. In M. D. Giardina and M. K. Donnelly (eds), *Youth culture and sport*. New York: Routledge, 1–12.

Giardina, M. and Newman, J. (2011a). 'What is this "physical" in physical cultural studies?' *Sociology of Sport Journal*, 28, 36–63.

Giardina, M. and Newman, J. (2011b). 'Physical cultural studies and embodied research acts'. *Cultural Studies Critical Methodologies*, 11(6), 523–534.

Giles, A. R. and Baker, A. C. (2008). 'Culture, colonialism and competition: Youth sport culture in Canada's North'. In M. Giardina and M. K. Donnelly (eds), *Youth culture and sport*. New York: Routledge, 161–174.

Gilligan, R. *et al.* (2010). *In the front line of integration: young people managing migration to Ireland*. Dublin: Trinity Immigration Initiative & Integrating Ireland. Available from: www.tcd.ie/immigration/css/downloads/In_the_front_line_of_Integration.pdf [accessed 15 May 2011].

Gilmartin, M. (2013). 'Changing Ireland, 2000–2012: Immigration, emigration and inequality'. *Irish Geography*, 46(1), 91–111.

Giulianotti, R. (2005). *Sport. A critical sociology*. Cambridge: Polity Press.

Giulianotti, R. and Robertson, R. (2009). *Globalization and football*. London: Sage.

Goldblatt, D. (2007). *The ball is round*. London: Penguin.

Golding, P. (2005). 'Telling stories: Sociology, journalism and the informed citizen'. In D. McQuail, P. Golding and E. Debens (eds), *Communication theory and research*. London: Sage, 165–177.

Goldstone, K. (2009). 'Now you see us, now you don't: Reflections on Jews, historical amnesia and the histories of a multi-ethnic Dublin'. *Translocations*, 4(1), 102–109.

Graham, C. and Maley, W. (1999). 'Introduction: Irish studies and postcolonial theory'. *Irish Studies Review*, 7(2), 149–152.

Gratton, C. and Jones, I. (2010). *Research methods for sport studies*. London: Routledge.

Gray, B. (2008). 'Putting emotion and reflexivity to work in researching migration'. *Sociology*, 42(5), 935–952.

Green, K. and Smith, A. (eds) (2016). *Routledge handbook of youth sport*. London: Routledge.

Grossman, A., and O'Brien, A. (eds) (2007). *Projecting migration. Transcultural documentary practice*. London: Wallflower.

Hall, S. (1997). *Representation. Cultural representation and signifying practices*. London: Sage.

Hall, S. (2006). 'Cosmopolitan promises, multicultural realities'. In R. Scholar (ed.), *Divided cities. The Oxford amnesty lectures 2003*. Oxford: Oxford University Press, 20–51.

Hammersley, M. (2017). 'Childhood studies: A sustainable paradigm?'. *Childhood*, 24(1), 113–127.

Hammersley, M. and Atkinson, P. (2007). *Ethnography: Principles in practice*. London: Routledge.

Harinen, P. M., Honkasalo, M. V., Ronkainen, J. K. and Suurpää, L. E. (2012). 'Multiculturalism and young people's leisure spaces in Finland: Perspectives of multicultural youth'. *Leisure Studies*, 31(2), 177–191.

Harris, N. (2002). *Dublin's little Jerusalem*. Dublin: A. & A. Farmar.

Hassan, D. and McCue K. (2011). 'Football, racism and the Irish'. In D. Burdsey (ed.), *Race, ethnicity and football: Persisting debates and emergent issues*. London: Routledge, 50–66.

Hassan, D. and McCue K. (2013). 'The "silent" Irish – Football, migrants and the pursuit of integration'. In D. Hassan (ed.), *Ethnicity and race in association football: Case study analyses in Europe, Africa and the USA*. London: Routledge, 126–138.

Hassan, D. and McGuire, A. (2016). 'The GAA and revolutionary Irish politics in late nineteenth and early twentieth-century Ireland'. In R. McElligot and D. Hassan (eds), *A social and cultural history of sport in Ireland*. London: Routledge, 51–62.

Hayward, K. and Howard, K. (2007). 'Cherry picking the diaspora'. In B. Fanning (ed.), *Immigration and social change in the Republic of Ireland*. Manchester: Manchester University Press, 43–62.

Head, J. (1997). *Working with adolescents: Constructing identity*. London: Falmer Press.

Hoerder, D., Hebert, Y. and Schmitt, I. (eds) (2005). *Negotiating transcultural lives: Belongings and social capital among youth in comparative perspective*. Toronto: University of Toronto Press.

Holt, N. and Sparkes, A. (2001). 'An ethnographic study of cohesiveness in a college soccer team over a season'. *The Sport Psychologist*, 15, 237–259.

Hopkins, P. (2010). *Young people, place and identity*. London: Routledge.

Hughson, J., Inglis, D. and Free, M. W. (2005). *The uses of sport: A critical study*. Abingdon, UK: Routledge.

Huizinga, J. (1980 [1938]). *Homo Ludens: A study of the play-element in culture*. London: Routledge.

Hylton, K. (2009). *'Race' and sport. Critical race theory*. London: Routledge.

Hylton, K. (2018). *Contesting 'race' and sport: Shaming the colour line*. London: Routledge.

Jackson, M. (2005). *Existential anthropology*. New York: Berghahn Books.

Jeanes, R., O'Connor, J. and Alfrey, L. G. (2014). 'Sport and the resettlement of young people from refugee backgrounds in Australia'. *Journal of Sport and Social Issues*, 39(6), 480–500.

Johnson J. C., Avenarius C. and Weatherford J. (2006). 'The active participant-observer: Applying social role analysis to participant observation'. *Field Methods*, 18(2), 111–134.

Kelly, J. (2003). *Borrowed identities*. Bern: Peter Lang.

Kelly, K. (2008). 'Diasporan moves: African Canadian youth and identity formation'. In N. Dolby and F. Rizvi (eds), *Youth moves. Identities and education in global perspective*. New York: Routledge, 85–100.

Kelly, L. (2011). 'Social inclusion through sports-based interventions'. *Critical Social Policy*, 31(1), 126–150.

Kirpitchenko, L. and Mansouri, F. (2014). 'Social engagement among migrant youth: Attitudes and meanings'. *Social Inclusion*, 2(2), 17–27.

Knopp Biklen, S. (2007). 'Trouble on memory lane: Adults and self-retrospection in researching youth'. In A. Best (ed.), *Representing youth*. New York: New York University Press, 251–268.

König, D. G. and Rakow, K. (2016). 'The transcultural approach within a disciplinary framework: An introduction'. *Transcultural Studies*, 2, 89–100.

Kracauer, S. (2009 [1964]). *Strassen in Berlin und Anderswo* (*Streets in Berlin and elsewhere*). Frankfurt: Suhrkamp.

Krouwel, A., Boonstra, N., Duyvendak, J. W. and Veldboer, L. (2006). 'A good sport? Research into the capacity of recreational sport to integrate Dutch minorities'. *International, Review for the Sociology of Sport*, 41, 165–180.

Lalor, K., de Roiste, A. and Devlin, M. (2007). *Young people in contemporary Ireland*. Dublin: Gill & Macmillan.

Lentin, A. and Titley, G. (2011). *The crises of multiculturalism. Racism in a neoliberal age*. London: Zed Books.

Lentin, R. (2007). 'Ireland: Racial state and crisis racism'. *Ethnic and Racial Studies*, 30(4), 610–627.

Lentin, R. (2013). '(M)Other Ireland: migrant women subverting the racial state?'. In J. V. Ulin, H. Edwards and S. O'Brien (eds), *Race and immigration in the New Ireland*. Notre Dame, IN: University of Notre Dame Press, 51–74.

Lentin, R. and McVeigh, R. (2006). *After optimism? Ireland, racism and globalisation*. Dublin: Metro Eireann Publications.

Linehan, D. (2015). '"The centre of everything": Ireland and the Dundrum town centre'. In F. Dukelow and R. Meade (eds), *Defining events: Power, resistance and identity in 21st century Ireland*. Manchester: Manchester University Press, 89–105.

Loescher, M. (2003). 'Cameras at the Addy: Speaking in pictures with city kids'. *Journal of Media Practice*, 3(2), 75–84.

Loescher, M. (2005). 'Cameras at the Addy: Speaking in pictures with city kids'. In A. Grimshaw and A. Ravetz (eds), *Visualizing anthropology*. Bristol: Intellect.

Long, J. and Hylton, K. (2002). 'Shades of white: An examination of whiteness in sport'. *Leisure Studies*, 21, 87–103.

Loyal, S. (2007). 'Immigration'. In S. O'Sullivan (ed), *Contemporary Ireland. A sociological map*. Dublin: UCD Press, 30–47.

Loyal, S. (2011a). *Understanding Irish immigration: Capital, state, and labour in a global age*. Manchester: Manchester University Press.

MacDougall, D. (1998). *Transcultural cinema*. Princeton: Princeton University Press.

MacDougall, D. (2006). *The corporeal image. Film, ethnography and the senses*. Princeton: Princeton University Press.

Mac Éinrí, P. (2001). *Immigration into Ireland: Trends, policy responses, outlook*. Cork: ICMS. Available from: www.migration.ucc.ie/irelandfirstreport.htm [accessed 23 August 2012].

Marcus, G. E. (1995). 'Ethnography in/of the world system: The emergence of multi-sited ethnography'. *Annual Review of Anthropology*, 24, 95–117.

Marcus, G. E. (1998). *Ethnography through thick and thin*. Princeton, NJ: Princeton University Press.

Marcus, G. E. (2008). 'The end(s) of ethnography: Social/cultural anthropology's signature form of producing knowledge transition'. *Cultural Anthropology*, 23(1), 1–14.

Marcus, G. E. (2010). 'Contemporary fieldwork aesthetics in art and anthropology: Experiments in collaboration and intervention'. *Visual Anthropology*, 23, 263–277.

Markula, P. and Pringle, R. (2006). *Foucault, sport and exercise*. London: Routledge.

Mata-Codesal, D., Peperkamp, E. and Tiesler, N. (2015). 'Migration, migrants and leisure: Meaningful leisure?'. *Leisure Studies*, 34(1), 1–4.

Mauro, M. (2014). 'A team like no "other". The racialized position of Insaka in Irish schoolboys football'. In J. O'Gorman (ed.), *Junior and youth grassroots football. The forgotten game*. London: Routledge, 54–73.

Mauro, M. (2016). 'Transcultural football. Trajectories of belonging among immigrant youth'. *Soccer and Society*, 17(6), 90–105.

Maxwell, H., Foley, C., Taylor, T. and Burton, C. (2013). 'Social inclusion in community sport: A case study of Muslim women in Australia'. *Journal of Sport Management*, 27, 467–481.

McElligot, R. and Hassan, D. (eds) (2016). *A social and cultural history of sport in Ireland*. London: Routledge.

McGrath, P. (2007). *Back from the brink*. London: Arrow Books.

McIvor, C. (2008). '"I'm black an' I'm proud": Ruth Negga, Breakfast on Pluto, and invisible Irelands'. *Visible Culture*, 13, 22–36.

McVeigh, R. (2008). 'The "final solution": Reformism, ethnicity, denial and the politics of anti-travellerism in Ireland. *Social Policy and Society*, 7(1), 91–102.

Mead, M. (2001 [1928]). *Coming of age in Samoa*. New York: Harper Perennial.

Messner, M. A. and Musto, M. (2014). 'Where are the kids?'. *Sociology of Sport Journal*, 31, 102–122.

Mezzadra, S. (2006). *Diritto di fuga. Migrazioni, cittadinanza, globalizzazione (The right to escape. Migration, citizenship, globalization)*. Verona: Ombre Corte.

Mezzadra, S. and Neilson, B. (2013). *Border as method, or the multiplication of labor*. Durham: Duke University Press.

Mirdal, G. M. and Ryynänen-Karjalainen, L. (2004). *Migration and transcultural identities*. Strasbourg: European Science Foundation (ESF).

Mohanram, R. (2007). *White: Race, diaspora, and the British Empire*. Minneapolis, MN: University of Minnesota Press.

Moore, C. (2016). 'Ireland – Soccer champions of the world'. In R. McElligott and D. Hassan (eds), *A social and cultural history of sport in Ireland*. Abingdon: Routledge, 38–50.

Morrow, V. and Richards, M. (2002). 'The ethics of social research with children: An overview'. In K. Fulford, D. Dickenson and T. Murray (eds), *Healthcare ethics and human values: An introductory text with readings and case studies*. London: Blackwell, 270–275.

Mullally, S. (2007). 'Children citizenship and constitutional change'. In B. Fanning (ed.), *Immigration and social change in the Republic of Ireland*. Manchester: Manchester University Press, 27–46.

Müller, F., van Zoonen, L. and de Roode, L. (2008). 'The integrative power of sport: Imagined and real effects of sport events on multicultural integration'. *Sociology of Sport Journal*, 25, 387–401.

Muus, R. (1999). *Adolescent behaviour and society: A book of readings*. New York: McGraw-Hill.

National Youth Council of Ireland (2017). *Make minority a priority. Insights from minority ethnic people and recommendations for the youth work sector*. Report, Dublin: NYCI.

Ni Chonaill, B. (2009). 'Perceptions of migrants and their impact in the Blanchardstown area: Local views'. Report, Dublin: Irish Research Council in Humanities and Social Science.

Ni Laoire, C., Carpena-Mendez, F., Tyrrel, N. and White, A. (2011). *Childhood and migration in Europe*. London: Ashgate.

O'Gorman, J. (ed.) (2017). *Junior and youth grassroots football. The forgotten game*. London: Routledge, 54–73.

Olsen, N. (2012). *History in the plural: An introduction to the work of Reinhart Koselleck*. New York: Berghahn Books.

O'Toole, F. (2009). *Ship of fools*. London: Faber & Faber.

Papademas, D. and IVSA – International Visual Sociology Association (2009). 'IVSA – Code of research ethics and guidelines'. *Visual Studies*, 24, 250.

Perry, P. (2002). *Shades of white: White kids and racial identities in high school*. Durham, NC: Duke University Press.

Pink, S. (2007). *Doing visual ethnography*. London: Sage.

Pink, S. (2009). *Doing sensory ethnography*. London: Sage.

Pink, S. (ed.) (2012). *Advances in visual methodology*. London: Sage.

Pratt, M. L. (1986). 'Fieldwork in common places'. In J. Clifford and G. Marcus (eds), *Writing culture the poetics and politics of ethnography*. Berkeley: University of California Press, 27–50.

Pringle, R. (2005). 'Masculinities, sport, and power'. *Journal of Sport and Social Issues*, 29(3), 256–278.

Prosser, J. and Loxley, A. (2008). 'Introducing visual methods'. National Centre for Research Methods, NCRM Review Papers, NCRM/010.

Raby, R. (2007). 'Across a great gulf? Conducting research with adolescents'. In A. Best (ed.), *Representing youth*. New York: New York University Press, 39–59.

Ragazzi, R. (2009). *Walking on uneven paths. The transcultural experience of children entering Europe in the years 2000*. Bern: Peter Lang.

Rivlin, R. (2011). *Jewish Ireland: A social history*. Dublin: History Press Ireland.

Röder, A. (2014). 'The emergence of a second generation in Ireland: Some trends and open questions'. *Irish Journal of Sociology*, 22(1), 155–158.

Rouch, J. (author) and Feld, S. (ed.) (2003). *Ciné-ethnography*. Minneapolis, MN: University of Minnesota Press.

Ryan, C. (2009). 'Dublin15 socio-economic profile'. Report, Dublin: Blanchardstown Area Partnership. Available from: www.bap.ie/dloads/socio_economic_profile_blanch.pdf [accessed 20 December 2011].

Ryan, C. (2010). 'Socio-economic profile of Mountview parish'. Report, Dublin: Blanchardstown Area Partnership.

Sands, R. S. (2002). *Sport ethnography*. Champaign, IL: Human Kinetics.

Sayad, A. (2004 [1999]). *The suffering of the immigrant*. Cambridge: Polity Press.

Share, P., Corcoran, M. P. and Conway, B. (2012). *A sociology of Ireland*. Dublin: Gill and Macmillan.

Smyth, G. (1999). 'Irish studies, postcolonial theory and the "new" essentialism'. *Irish Studies Review*, 7(2), 211–220.

Spaaij, R. (2015). 'Refugee youth, belonging and community sport'. *Leisure Studies*, 34(3), 303–318.

Sport Ireland (2017). *Irish sports monitor*. Annual Report, Dublin: Sport Ireland.

St John, W. (2009). *Outcasts united: A refugee team, an American town*. New York: Spiegel & Grau.

Stack, J. and Iwasaki, Y. (2009). 'The role of leisure pursuits in adaptation processes among Afghan refugees who have immigrated to Winnipeg, Canada'. *Leisure Studies*, 28(3), 239–259.

Sugden, J. and Bairner, A. (1993). *Sport, sectarianism and society in a divided Ireland*. Leicester: Leicester University Press.

Takle, M. and Ødegård, G. (2016). 'When policy meets practice: A study of ethnic community-based organizations for children and youth'. In E. M. Goździak and M. L. Seeberg (eds), *Contested childhoods. Growing up in migrancy*. Rotterdam: IMISCOE/Springer, 99–117.

Thomson, T. (ed.) (2008). *Doing visual research with children and young people*. London: Routledge.

Thrin, T. M-ha. (1992). *Framer framed*. New York: Routledge.

Ulin, J. V., Edwards, H. and O'Brien, S. (eds) (2013). *Race and immigration in the New Ireland*. Notre Dame, IN: University of Notre Dame Press.

United Nations (1989). *Convention on the rights of the child*. New York: United Nations. Available from: www.unicef.org.uk/wp-content/uploads/2010/05/UNCRC_united_nations_convention_on_the_rights_of_the_child.pdf.

Vertovec, S. (2001). 'Transnationalism and identity'. *Journal of Ethnic and Migration Studies*, 27(4), 573–582.

Vertovec, S. (2009). *Transnationalism*. London: Routledge.

Walseth, K. (2006). 'Sport and belonging'. *International Review for the Sociology of Sport*, 41(3), 447–464.

Weber, S. (2008). 'Visual images in research'. In J. G. Knowles and A. L. Cole (eds), *Handbook of the arts in qualitative research*. London: Sage, 41–55.

Wiggins, D. K. and Nauright, J. (2016). 'History of race and ethnicity in sports'. In D. K. Wiggins and J. Nauright (eds), *Routledge handbook of sport, race and ethnicity*. London: Routledge, 7–20.

Williams, J. (1994). 'Rangers is a black club'. In R. Giulianotti and J. Williams (eds), *Game without frontiers: Football, identity and modernity*. Aldershot: Arena Publications, 153–184.

Williams, P. (1997). *Seeing a colour-blind future: The paradox of race*. The 1997 Reith Lectures. London: Virago Press.

Williams, R. (1983). *Culture and society*. New York: Columbia University Press.

Willis, P. (1980). 'Notes on method'. In S. Hall, D. Hobson, A. Lowe and P. Willis (eds), *Culture, media, language*. Birmingham: Centre for Contemporary Cultural Studies/Routledge.

Willis, P. and Trondman, M. (2002). 'Manifesto for ethnography'. *Cultural Studies Critical Methodologies*, 2(3), 394–402.

Worbs, S. (2006). 'Where do I belong? Integration policy and patters of identification among migrant youth in three European countries'. In D. Hoerder, Y. Hebert and I. Schmitt (eds), *Negotiating transcultural lives*. Toronto: University of Toronto Press, 39–58.

Woods, C., Moyla, N., Quinlan A., Tannehill, D., and Walsh, J. (2010). *The children's sport participation and physical activity study*. Dublin: Irish Sports Council. Available from www4.dcu.ie/shhp/downloads/CSPPA.pdf [accessed 20 November 2012].

Zwahlen, J. A., Nagel, S. and Schlesinger, T. (2018). 'Analysing social integration of young immigrants in sports clubs'. *European Journal of Sport and Society*, 15(19), 22–42.

Chapter 2

Community, belonging and the role of the game

While sitting in the upper saloon of the number 39 bus travelling to Blan-chardstown, I kept folding and unfolding the GoogleMap printout that indi-cated the location of the football ground I was heading towards. The uncertainty of the map seemed an appropriate metaphor for the status of my pre-field knowledge (Hammersley and Atkinson 2007). On the black and white map the football ground appeared as a white spot surrounded by a laby-rinth of streets. I knew the white spot was 'my' place only because I recognised the names of two streets that I had been told defined the outer limits of the park: Fortlawn and Mountview. The initial information that I had about the people I was going to meet came through in the email sent by a Dublin North officer of the Football Association of Ireland (FAI). It said that one team at Mountview Boys and Girls Football Club fielded a good number of young players with an immigrant background and that the chairman of the club was interested in talking to me.

Some of the words that I used to introduce myself on the phone to the chair-man, Mick, echoed in my head while I was still looking at the map: 'I am a PhD student, I am originally from Italy and I am doing research on youth football and interculturalism. I would be interested in having a chat with you and telling you more about my project, would this be possible?' More or less the same words I later repeated to the coach of the Under-13 team, Willie, as he was presented to me by Mick. I was not entirely comfortable in using the term 'intercultural-ism', with its essentialist implications of cohesive cultures (Watt 2006; Halilovic-Pastuovic 2010), but I had to make myself understood and make clear in a few sentences what I was looking for. Alongside integration, intercultural-ism has a dominant presence in Irish institutional and public discourses sur-rounding immigration policies (Fanning 2007; Lentin 2010; Share et al. 2012). It can be understood as an approach that constructs 'cultural difference and ethnic minority "communities" as static and already there, ignoring intra-ethnic heterogeneities and contestations' (Lentin 2007: 611).[1] At the same time, it assumes Ireland to be a culturally homogeneous body, based on 'national dis-courses of Irish identity as white, settled and Catholic' (Loyal 2011: 240). Given the circumstances, I presumed that saying 'interculturalism' would be more effective than 'youth of different ethnic and national backgrounds' or other definitions that I had used in my first conversations in Dublin.

The field: a place with no name

The bus left me on a busy road within sight of the largest shopping centre in Ireland, emphatically called 'The Blanchardstown Centre', opened in 1996. On one side of the road there was a park, 'The Millennium Park', opened in 2001, on the other side an estate of terraced houses. I crossed the street and took a path that, according to my 'map' would lead me directly to the football ground. All the houses seemed relatively new, maybe 20 years old. They were part of the suburban development I was prepared to encounter. According to the 1996 National Census, the Dublin 15 postal district had a population of 53,221. In 2011 the population had risen to 101,032 and foreign population accounted for 23.5 per cent (the State average was 12 per cent that year). These rapid changes have been accompanied by massive housing developments that have transformed the landscape of what was, until the 1970s, a rural suburb of the Irish capital. However, lack of infrastructure and social problems have been often reported.[2]

Overlapping voices of kids and adults were audible from afar, a sign that a game was underway as I approached the football ground. The sounds of voices were somehow 'marking' the area, and this reminded me of what Les Back defines as *The Art of Listening*: 'not an automatic faculty but a skill that needs to be trained' (Back 2007: 7). Looking at the city of London, he writes:

> Sounds are, after all, the sensing of vibrations: our ears pick up the vibrations of movement. Listening to cosmopolitan London is different from looking at it, in part because race and racism operate within ocular grammar of difference. Listening admits presences in such encounters that can be missed in the visual play of skin.
>
> (Back 2007: 119)

To my surprise, the ground was not a proper football ground, but an informal pitch within the boundaries of a small park (Figure 2.1). No high fences or gates limited its access. No signs warned the visitor that these were the premises of an official football club. Behind one of the mobile goalposts, just a few metres away from the playing pitch, were placed a series of green coloured cargo-containers that served mainly as storage space. Beyond the containers a temporary metallic fence signalled the construction site of the new 'Mountview Youth & Community Centre'. In a subtle way, the uncertain boundaries of this field were telling me something about my future ethnographic practice. Metaphorically speaking, my field was not clearly demarcated but had to be 'constructed', something that has become common practice for contemporary ethnographers (Rabinow et al. 2008). For Amit,

[I]n a world of infinite interconnections and overlapping contexts, the ethnographic field cannot simply exist, awaiting discovery. It has to be laboriously constructed, prised apart from all the other possibilities for contextualization to which its constituent relationships and connections could also be referred.

(2000: 6)

The adults were almost all men, apparently in their mid-20s to early 40s, all wearing tracksuits. Many of them had on light blue tracksuit tops, with the symbol of the club printed on the front, which I recognised from having seen it on the club's web page. As for myself, wearing jeans, hiking boots, a Gore-Tex jacket and a woollen hat, I certainly stood out, but I could do nothing to downplay my difference (Winchatz 2006). I approached one man who was standing on the sideline of the pitch, watching kids, about 10 years old, playing a game. I asked him if Willie, the Under-13 team's coach, was present. He told me that he had seen him earlier in the morning. He pointed towards a section of the park where a small group of teenage boys were standing. 'Those are some of his players, but I can't see him, he probably will be somewhere around here,' he said. I decided to call Willie on the phone to announce my arrival. 'I'll be there in five minutes', he assured me. Those few minutes seemed very long, unnaturally long, and I suddenly realised that I was being observed by several eyes, among them some of Willie's team players. I was new to the situation, an outsider, and this attention towards me was understandable. Nevertheless, I felt a sense of discomfort.

Willie, when he appeared, was as a young man in his mid to late 20s. Like all the boys and men who were there, he wore his hair really short, almost com-

Figure 2.1 Mountview Park, June 2009.

pletely shaved on the sides and the back of his head. He was wearing a grey tracksuit, covered with fresh mud all along one side of his body. His hands were muddy too, and in offering me his hand he explained the reason for this: he had been helping another team's coach in training the goalkeeper. He seemed busy and with little time to dedicate to me, even though his team's game was due to kick-off in over an hour. He spoke quickly and with the strongest Dublin accent I had ever heard. I was faced with a classic anthropological challenge: learning to understand the peculiarities of the 'native' dialect. He did not ask me much about my interest in spending time with his team; perhaps he was satisfied with what the chairman had told him. But what exactly had he told him? Maybe the chairman's word was my passport to him, as the FAI's word was my passport to the chairman. But who was going to be my main gatekeeper? Mick or Willie? As Hammersley and Atkinson (2007: 49) argue, 'identifying the real gatekeeper is not always straightforward'. My main goal was to get closer to the social worlds of the young players and, in order to succeed in that, I would have to build rapport with Willie, but without Mick I would probably not have access to Willie and his team. In any case, I was encountering a common problem for researchers focusing on young people, that of having to deal with the power imbalance between adults and children in a given research setting (Clark *et al.* 2014). The main protagonists of my research – the young footballers – were initially excluded from my negotiation of access, which was undertaken essentially between adults. As argued by Leonard (2007: 137): 'Although gatekeepers do influence research with adults, their impact is much more pronounced when research subjects are minors'.

Identifying the protagonists

Willie introduced the boys to me, most of whom appeared older than their 13–14 years: 'These are some of my players', he said with little hesitation.[3] The boys did not show much interest; some busy with mobile phones, others listening to music through earphones or talking among themselves. He then made a quick comment that left me puzzled: 'We have some good players here. I hope you won't tell other teams they are so good, I don't want them to be stolen!' Then he called a young boy from the group of his players. 'This is Kevin', he said to me. Kevin seemed embarrassed and a bit annoyed to have to stand in front of me, the only player given this 'honour'. 'Hi Kevin', I said rather timidly. He looked down and, as soon as possible, returned to his friends, who welcomed him with inaudible comments and wry smiles on their faces. Why did Willie pick out Kevin? Was it for the dark colour of his skin or for his skilfulness as a player?

In his book *Interaction ritual*, Goffman explains the ways feelings of embarrassment can arise in social interaction:

> Embarrassment has to do with unfulfilled expectations…. Given their social identities and the setting, the participants will sense what sort of conduct

ought to be maintained as the appropriate thing, however much they may despair of its actually occurring. An individual may firmly expect that certain others make him ill at ease, yet this knowledge may increase his discomfiture instead of lessening it. An entirely unexpected flash of social engineering may save a situation, all the more effective for their being unanticipated.

(1967: 105)

If I wanted to break through the initial embarrassment of my encounter with Willie and the members of his team, maybe I needed what Goffman calls 'an unexpected flash of social engineering'. I thus mentioned my intention to bring the camera and film moments of games and activities of the team. Would they be interested? Would he mind? And the boys? 'No problem', was Willie's answer. A few metres away, part of the group looked on without showing approval or disapproval; the rest of the group did not appear bothered by what was going on. I had prepared myself to provide explanations about the use of the camera, anticipating that the idea of filming games could be superficially appealing to the boys, but there was no need for it, at least for now. Willie announced it was time to start the warm-up and in a matter of seconds everybody was gone, heading to another side of the small park.

Beyond a wall of bushes there was a second, bigger pitch, with regular goalposts. Greg, the secretary and oldest member of the club, who was introduced to me by Willie, briefly explained that this pitch was used for regular games played by 11-year-olds and over. I assumed that the other one was used only for small-sided games, played by younger children. Greg was not much more talkative than Willie – his answers to my questions were mainly 'Yes' and 'No', with maybe a couple of short words attached. The pitch was surrounded by a row of trees on one side and a metal fence on the other. Beyond the metal fence there was the backyard of a primary school.

I watched the game from the sideline, as everybody else was doing, since there was no reserved area for spectators and even no benches for the team's substitutes and staff. I could stay close to the coach and hear him give instructions to the team. I noticed that the team's captain was a midfielder of African origin, one of four black boys fielded in the starting team (a fifth one was among the substitutes). I could not grasp his real name: was he called Marlow? The loud tones of the voices on and off the pitch made it difficult for me to understand what was being said. It took me some time to finally learn that his name was Charlo, an Irish diminutive for Charlie. Watching the game, I got the impression that the coach was adopting a simple, straightforward tactic: pass the ball to Kevin and let him shoot. 'Shoot! Two touches and shoot, Kevin!', I could hear Willie shout. Kevin was the centre-forward of the team, a strong-built boy, and the centre of attention both for the coach and the very few people attending the match. The adults and kids whose voices had welcomed me earlier in the day had left and the Under-13's game was attended only by a few club members, all of them male and white Irish. Where were the parents of the young players? Another black boy, Philippe, played right wing, while Charlie and James played in midfield and Cheick, who was on the bench that day, was a defender. At first glance, there was no evidence of 'stacking' (Collins and Kay 2003). According to Giulianotti,

> In team sports black males are still segregated informally (or stacked) along racist lines. Stacking is defined as the placement of white athletes in central positions associated with intelligence, decision making, leadership, calmness and dependability and the location of non-whites in peripheral positions requiring explosive physical powers (especially speed), unpredictability and infrequent participation.
>
> (2005: 74)

To some degree, my fieldwork with a group of male teenagers in Dublin told a different story. Apparently, the roles of the black boys in the team were as diverse as those of the white Irish boys. From my pre-field research, I knew that this team was quite original within the context of the Dublin & District Schoolboys League, in that it fielded a good number of players of immigrant background, but their positions on the pitch appeared to contradict some of my expectations, supported by sociological literature and anecdotal evidence. My first encounter with them offered enough material to reflect upon if I wanted to understand 'how sport, which is a non-formal educational tool, contributes to multicultural dialogue between young people' (Amara et al. 2005: 1). My goal as an observer was to get through the surface, trying to understand and represent the experience of these young boys and its social meaning, while also comprehending and reflexively representing my own engagement with them.

At the end of the game, I briefly met with Mick, the chairman. Despite more or less sharing the same dress code with the other men, Mick was slightly different in appearance from Willie and Steve. He was a rather tall man in his mid to late 30s and had a cheerful expression. He was treated with special respect by Willie and every club member. His handshake felt strong, and he looked straight into my eyes. Moreover, his English seemed easier to understand to my unaccustomed ears. I had with me a letter of introduction from my institution and I was ready to hand it to him. 'It's okay, no worries', was his comment. I asked about his help in obtaining consent from the families, and he said that we had time to sort this out in the following days. In the back of my mind I could not avoid thinking about the broader social context, particularly the revelation of child abuse committed by Irish Catholic priests which had made the news headlines in the previous weeks. I knew that my interest in working with youth at this particular time would be subjected to special scrutiny by gatekeepers and people involved in the club. However, the first encounter with my ethnographic community unravelled quite smoothly.

On my way back to the bus stop I tried to make sense of the puzzling impressions and the fugitive words that I had been able to collect during my first encounter with the team and the club members. My mind was full of questions that manuals on how to do ethnographic fieldwork could hardly help to answer. My background as a journalist was not of much help either, as the long-term observational project I had in mind was very distant from anything I had experienced before. I took some notes on the bus ride to the city centre and later in the evening I wrote down some reflections in my diary, a text that I tried to keep separate from my fieldnotes: 'What role or roles did these people attach to my presence? What did the boys think of me? Will they "like" me? Too many questions!'

The football club as a 'community'

Mountview FC was founded in 1980, at a time when Blanchardstown was going through a radical transformation from a rural to a suburban area. Following the first housing projects in the late 1960s, during the 1970s Blanchardstown started to become part of the suburban landscape of Dublin (Ni Chonaill 2009; Ryan 2009), receiving a new population flow that was mostly moving out of the city, in particular from areas such as Ballymun and Finglas.[4] In that situation, the youth football club could help in bringing people together who were coming to live in a new community (Williams 1983; Cohen 1980; Hall 1993). During my time spent with club members of different generations, the word 'community' emerged as a meaningful one and it was therefore interesting to observe which role the 'newcomers', the boys of immigrant background, would play in this 'community', in the sporting community in particular. Verma and Larson (2003: 15) observe that: 'leisure provides such a context for adolescents to gain control over their attentional processes, acquire critical adult skills, and become integrated into their communities'.

There was first of all a sense of place in this idea of community, of people living in an area limited and defined by boundaries, or in Elias's words,

> a group of households situated in the same locality and linked to each other by functional interdependencies which are closer than interdependencies of the same kind with other groups of people within the wider social field to which a community belongs.
>
> (1974: xix, quoted by Brunt 2001: 80)

Generally speaking, according to Williams (1983: 76), 'community is used as a warmly persuasive word to describe an existing set of relationships'. The idea of community is also charged with symbolic values, and in pluralistic societies characterised by social and geographical mobility, the meaning of a community is less and less about 'place' and more about changing forms of loyalties and identities (Bauman 1996; Clifford 1997). In the age of globalisation people often look for affiliation and sense of community in what Appadurai (1996: 195) calls 'virtual neighbourhoods', which are 'no longer bounded by territory, passports, taxes, elections, and other conventional diacritics, but by access to both the software and hardware that are required to connect to ... large international computer networks'. In what particular ways was the Mountview (football) community related to the above-mentioned global scenario?

In one of our conversations, Mick gave me the following insight into the history of the club and the area:

> In all the communities of the Dublin 15 area, Mountview is one of the oldest clubs, it's thirty years old. Before here there were just fields. The shopping centre, everywhere fields. There was an old farmhouse up here, and a big Travellers' site over there. There have been massive changes in the area.

At this point I had learned that Mick worked as a 'community manager' for the local council, and I was also better aware of the different uses of the term 'community' in public debates in Ireland.[5] Nevertheless, his early reflections were particularly helpful in bringing me closer to the setting of my study. He further explained: 'As a football club we are basically selling a brand, a community. Kids are happy, you see them during weekdays wearing the Mountview gear. We want them to be proud, that's why we started the club-shop'. Continuing, he added:

> A club has a social value. It is a well-known fact that teenagers who are involved with sport at an early age are less likely to have problems in their adult life. They have people they can count on, coaches, fellow teammates. They are less likely to get in trouble. It's not only about the football, it's about identity, the community.

The club's constitution explicitly stated the area served by the club included 'the parish and the surrounding areas', home to about 8000 people. Interestingly, the reputation of the club at local level attracted players from different areas of the Dublin 15 district. Among the players of the Under-13 team, none of the black boys lived in the area: they were from more peripheral neighbourhoods of Blanchardstown, such as Mulhuddart, Ongar and Corduff. Just a couple of the Irish boys were living away from the Mountview area. To enable me to understand the original catchment area for the club, Mick took my notebook and drew a simple but effective map of the neighbourhood, with the football grounds, the church, the shops and the various estates stretching around them (Figure 2.2). On paper everything seemed clear, but in fact it was hard for me to understand where Mountview ended and where Blackestown, Hartstown or Huntstown started.

To get a better orientation of the suburban landscape I set out to explore the area on my bike, like a modern *flaneur* (Simmel 2002 [1903]; Kracauer

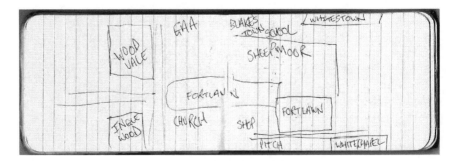

Figure 2.2 The map drawn by Mick in my notebook.

2009 [1964]). As a matter of fact, the circular nature of the streets, estates very similar to one another, and limited points of reference made my exploration difficult. I kept getting disoriented. The problematic nature of defining a rapidly growing area is common to the whole suburb (Ni Chonaill 2009), and this goes beyond its spatial dimension. Blanchardstown is a particularly multifaceted settlement in terms of social and economic landscape – neighbourhoods and areas officially recognised as 'disadvantaged' lie beside rather affluent areas.[6] Mountview, in particular, shows a high percentage of 'youth at risk', which is higher than the State overall average (Ryan 2010). There is another social element that characterises the area geographically delimited by the boundaries of the Mountview Parish. Looking at the social class categorisation of the residents, the category of those 'who have never been in paid employment, or who live in households where the head of the household has never been in paid employment' is 24.2 per cent of the population, while the state average is 17.6 per cent (Ryan 2010).

What was the Mountview sporting community made up of? There was a group of adults looking after the teams, all of whom were volunteers, and generally parents of young players. Usually, parents started to get involved in the club when their sons or daughters enrolled in the football 'nursery', targeting 4–7-year-olds, and some of them continued doing so as their children grew older. Most of the club members were men, but some women were involved in the care of the only girls' team and in fundraising activities. Each team was, in principle, taken care of by at least two adults, the coach and an assistant. Despite the fact that a number of players of immigrant background, mostly from Africa, were playing for the club, there were no immigrant adults among the club officials. During the course of my fieldwork I saw this situation slightly change. By the time I left the team, there was one father, originally from Eastern Europe ('I think he is Serbian, Yugoslavian anyway', in Mick's words), involved in coaching.

Financially, the club supported itself through a small registration fee paid by each player at the beginning of the football season, of €30, and a subscription

fee for every game played (€4 for all Under-11 teams and €5 for older teams),
paid by the boys usually before the game, into the hands of the coach. As I
observed over the months, this was common practice in youth football at this
level across Dublin. The fees covered: league registration costs; insurance;
referee match fees (€24 for Under-12, Under-13 and Under-14 team games,
paid by the home team, according to the rules published by the Dublin Schoolboys League[7]); transportation to away games (when there were no parents' cars
available, as was regularly the case with the Under-13 team, a van was hired to
take the team to away matches); and winter training, which was run on synthetic grounds owned by Fingal County. Funds were also collected through
fund-raising events organised throughout the year by a dedicated committee,
and through small sponsorship deals.

At the time of my research, Mountview catered for 13 boys' teams ranging
from Under-7 to Under-18 competing in the Dublin & District Schoolboys
League (DDSL) and a Under-12 girls' team, along with a nursery for kids under
seven years of age. DDSL is the major league in Irish youth football and one of
the three in which youth football is officially organised in the Dublin area, the
other two being South Dublin Schoolboys League (SDSL) and North Dublin
Schoolboys League (NDSL).[8] DDSL, NDSL and SDSL are among the 32
Leagues affiliated to the Schoolboys Football Association of Ireland (SFAI),
which claims to cater for 'close to 100,000 players from more than 1,000 clubs
all round the country'.[9]

The Mountview Under-13 team played in the DDSL 'A League', after having
won the lower league at Under-12 level the previous year. The fact that the
boys were made to play only with peers of the same year of birth was something
new to me. From growing up in Italy, I was used to youth football being organised in leagues that encompass boys of different ages (for example, boys aged 13
play with boys aged 14 and 15), but the young demographic of Ireland justified a
system where all youth leagues are organised on a single year of birth. I therefore
learnt that all the players in the Under-13 team were born the same year, 1995
– this being the first factual information I gathered about them. During the
season, sometimes Willie would pick up a player from the Under-12s and Mick,
manager of the Under-15s, would pick a player or two from Willie's team to let
them compete with older boys. This was thought to be beneficial for the young
players, in that they could face boys bigger and more experienced than them.

The dim dichotomy: observing and being observed

Why is this particular organisation or individual giving access to me? Do they
expect something in return? These kinds of questions need to be asked and possibly answered by every researcher engaging with ethnographic methods of
social inquiry. As said, my initial informant had been the Football Association
of Ireland, in the person of its Intercultural Officer.[10] He was the one who, with
the help of a FAI development officer in the North Dublin Area, eventually put

me in touch with the Mountview FC chairman. But was the fact that I had been introduced by the governing body of Irish football a sufficient reason for letting me 'study' a team and a club over a period of several months? Clearly, the access and the relationship built in the field could and would change over time. There is no manual for this, only the experience of the ethnographer (Duneier and Back 2006).

It soon became clear to me that there was no 'passport', not even FAI's name, which could ensure my access to the club and the team. Access could only be gained through ongoing negotiation and these negotiations were of two different kinds: one with the adults, more manageable since it involved people of my own generation, and one with the young participants, less manageable as they were all adolescents, living through a particular life phase which, for a long time, western societies have tried to 'conceptualize, define and control' (Savage 2008: xvi). In order to be allowed to observe and above all understand the social dynamics at hand I had first to go through a period of inverted observation – it was not clear for how long it would last. I was the one to be observed and questioned. For some months, the main actor of this research-dialogue was Mick. 'Which part of town do you live in?' (This was a question I was regularly asked by participants of different ages.) 'Where do the funds for your scholarship come from?' 'Is your supervisor happy with the work you are doing?' However, Mick was also eager to illustrate the various aspects of the life of the club and give me an insight into the game as it was lived and experienced in Ireland. It was a two-way 'investigation'.

Towards the end of the season, in the months of May and June, Mick started attending every game, helping Willie in his coaching duties. When Mick was present, they would share coaching duties on equal terms, both giving instructions and encouraging the players. I used to film pre-game speeches as a way to record one of the different rituals in the life of the team. Despite his longer coaching experience, together with the fact that he had also coached Willie, Mick showed respect for Willie's authority and never contested his decisions. Given the fact that Mick was also in charge of the Under-15s, and chairing the club, I wondered if the main reason for his presence was because of my presence. In fact, for most of the season Willie could not rely on an assistant coach and Mick was there to help him as, for statutory reasons, each team should be supervised by two adults. Mick used to drive his car to games, a recent model of Mercedes. He was the only club member sporting this kind of car – an evident sign of his social position. He was also distinguished from all other people that I met at the club in that he had a third level education.

Mick would often invite me into his car travelling to away games, providing an opportunity for conversation. He would take two or three young players with us, including some of the black boys. He showed a special interest in my work with the camera, a true catalytic element, as it emerged. Although I had made clear to him that I had scant experience in documentary filmmaking, he insisted to know what kind of film I was going to make. At this stage of my research I was allowing myself to be 'confused', juggling between the requirements of a doctoral programme and the interests of an author/intellectual to find the most effective way to learn about and represent particular social dynamics. 'The boys want me to do a clip for YouTube and I will try to do it for them', I explained. He had a different idea about the film-work:

> Why don't you try to give this stuff to RTE? It could be interesting having a team, I don't think they ever did something like this. The kind of documentary you are doing, is kind of 'fly on the wall', but it could be interesting for them.[11]

In this case Mick showed he had a specific idea about the contribution I could make to the club. He thought that I could bring public attention to a small and rather marginal youth football club, but in his opinion my intervention would also serve to present a different face of this part of Dublin. Local people would often complain about outsiders' perceptions of Blanchardstown, especially as portrayed in the media. For example, the first time I met Roy, one of the workers at the local Community and Youth Centre, he showed appreciation for my interest in the local community, and for the fact that I was coming from the city centre to learn about Mountview FC and the people living in the area. 'This place is given a bad name, but when you get to know the people you see they are nice people, isn't it?' he said to me. Despite its geographical extension and its multifaceted social landscape, quite often Blanchardstown was associated in public discourse with crime and social deprivation. As a matter of fact, by searching for articles about 'Blanchardstown' in the online archives of *The Irish Times* during the time of my fieldwork, seven out of the ten first results dealt with violent crimes, with titles such as 'Man held over Blanchardstown murder' and 'Man struck with machete'.[12] According to data released by Ireland's National Police Service (An Garda Síochána), between 2000 and 2008 the Blanchardstown police station registered the highest level of increase in the number of serious crimes committed in the Dublin metropolitan area.[13]

It soon became clear that, while showing positive interest in my work, Mick was also aiming to somehow 'direct' my observation. 'Kevin is good friends with Paul, why don't you point your attention on them?' he once suggested. In fact, the two boys were spending a lot of time together, and one being of Congolese background and the other white Irish, it made their relationship particularly intriguing. But both boys, at the beginning, did not show much interest in me. From the point of view of the ethnographic relationship, Mick's interest in pointing my attention at things he deemed important was understandable and acceptable. Collaboration is at the heart of every ethnographic endeavour (Marcus 1998, 2010), and any kind of 'truth' gathered through this approach is the result of a negotiation between the researcher's aims and the participants' interests.

Mick also conveyed some knowledge of documentary filmmaking in that he defined my work as 'fly on the wall'. This made me feel a bit anxious about the outcome of my 'film-work'. The question is somehow influenced by an issue that seems always to characterise ethnographic research, that of 'giving back' (Clifford 1997; Duneier 1999; Hammersley and Atkinson 2007; Marcus 2010). How does one negotiate the expectations of research participants? Conducting research with the help of a video camera can elicit interest to collaborate, yet it can also create expectations – which arguably is less the case when utilising more traditional tools of research. In adopting visual methodologies of research one has to be ready to deal with these expectations (Rose 2001; Pink 2012).

Eliciting dialogue

During my first weeks with the team I was concerned that I would not remember the names of all the boys, so I wrote them down in my notebook as soon as I was told them. Sometimes, when I could not get someone's name, I would ask the boys to write it down on my pad. The challenge seemed easier for them, since from our second meeting I was called 'Maximo'. Danny, a short winger with lively eyes, called me Maximo, probably following Willie's early distortion of my name, and from that moment on that was my name for everybody. It probably sounded more Italian than 'Max'. After a while I started to feel some affection for my 'new' name, for it was attached to the 'me-ethnographer', the 'performative-I' (Madison 2011), which was slightly different from the other 'me'. This is all part of the 'identity work' (Hammersley and Atkinson 2007: 79) which is intrinsic to participant observation. Our participants cast us into certain identities, while at the same time we tend to adapt our demeanour and appearance to the situation in order to produce knowledge about the group.

The first two months spent with the team were laden with myriad discoveries, but this exciting new experience could not distract my attention from the major challenge I was facing: how to build rapport with the young players. With the adults I could manage to do this while discussing football and being open to answering all the questions they might have about me, yet with the boys it was a different matter altogether. I was presented early with an example of the kind of task I was going to face in the coming months. My first trip with the team was for an important cup game to be played outside of Dublin. After stepping on the bus (one hired for the day, which could seat about 25 people, while the usual one was a 14-seater van) I sought to reach out to the five or six boys who were occupying the backseats, to exchange some words. 'So, are you playing in the cup today?', I simply asked as a way to start a conversation. Three boys still indistinguishable to me, all blond, sporting crewcuts and wearing tracksuits, were suddenly at the centre of the scene. The one sitting in the middle turned his head towards his teammates and repeated the word 'cup' in a strong Dublin accent: 'Cup? You mean *Cup*?' – everybody laughed. I smiled and repeated the word 'cup' trying to imitate his pronunciation, which sounded even funnier and obviously clumsy. Further laughs from the group followed. I thought this was enough to begin with and I went to sit in the front, where two adult members of the club were already seated.

As a methodological choice, I wanted to be able to let things unfold, to bear witness to the emergence of 'statements' out of my everyday interactions with the young participants. In order for this occur, I had to let conversations flow as trust began to develop between us. However, the characteristics of the setting and time limits of our meetings hindered my ethnographic work with the team. When was the best time to start a conversation with the boys? They usually reached the pitch for training or matches right on time, not much earlier. Without a dressing room available, they arrived already dressed in training gear, football boots in their backpacks or carried in plastic bags. The only place for them to hang around while waiting was the pitch itself. Some of them met 'at the shops', which were essentially a short row of stores stretched beside the site of the Community Centre under construction. The shops included: a Polish food store, of the popular Irish-based chain 'Polonez',[14] a newsagent, a pharmacy, a local food store, a Chinese take away, and a hairdresser for women. The only shops the boys would set foot in were the newsagent, usually to buy sweets, and the food store, to buy Coke and sandwiches. As noted, there was no building at the football ground, and the containers served essentially as storage space and rarely as a dressing room (there was no light inside, so the boys preferred to change outdoors, if it wasn't raining too hard).

In my quest for dialogue with the boys the camera soon emerged as an attractive technological tool, which was actually what I had hoped. It elicited curiosity from the boys, and some of them would ask direct questions. 'Would you put us on YouTube?' Philippe, a winger of Congolese background, asked me. 'Are you going to give us DVDs?' asked Danny, an Irish boy. To which I would obviously answer 'Yes'. 'One to each of us?' 'Yes'. 'Do we have to pay for that?' 'No'. 'Great!' Later, questions became more technical – 'What is that, a microphone?' 'Where is the tape?' My young participants started showing a competence in the use of visual devices. However, this was not as prominent and widespread as I had expected it to be among boys of this age. The fact that there were no parents attending the games, and nobody else taking pictures or filming but me, was a telling sign of the prevalent socio-economic landscape of the area. All the boys in the team, Irish and those of immigrant background, came from families with at least three or more children, and limited income. The African families were mostly refugees. Some of the parents were unemployed and living on social support, while quite a few were single parents (at some point I counted that seven among 15 of the boys were either living with a single parent or with a parent and the parent's new partner). Only some of the boys had an internet connection at home, and the ones who actually did have access to the internet or to a computer at home told me they had to share it with other family members.[15]

To some extent, the camera solicited an interest even in a reluctant boy such as Kevin. After a few months of silently ignoring me, he started with some insistence to ask me: 'Did you get my goal?' Since I could not film *all* his goals, for he was often scoring two or three in a single game, I once admitted I had missed what he considered one of his best goals. 'You missed it?' he asked with a perplexed expression, and then turning his head to his mates and the coach, added: 'Look, he missed the goal, we gonna sack him! We sack him!' This was surely a way for Kevin to show interest in my presence, to give me a role in the group, that of the 'cameraman', but conversations with him were quite frustrating. He was not much interested or able to articulate more than two words in answering even the most innocent of my questions, and neither did he seem curious to learn about me. As can happen with research involving children, I had to make the most of my observational tools. At this stage, there was a lot I could learn by hanging out with the team and, in the end, 'a great deal of what is important to observe is unspoken' (Foote-Whyte 1984: 83).

The serious game of belonging

To my surprise, during my first season, despite their winning record there was not much spontaneous laughter in the team. The players gathered to hear the coach's instructions and then entered the pitch with one aim in mind: to win the game or do their best to win it. This did not mean that the boys were in any way reproached if they lost a game or did not perform well, on the contrary. Willie and Mick were always encouraging them, above all when something went wrong. Among the words most widely used by the coach during the game was 'unlucky', which would relieve the frustration of the player when a challenge did not work out well, a shot off target or when a long-range pass ended up in the possession of the opposing team. A frequent expression of encouragement was 'well done'. However, for everybody, the game appeared to be a serious matter. The boys wanted to win, that only seemed to matter to them. 'We want to win', said Charlie, 'if you win everybody is happy'. As argued by Huizinga (1980 [1938]: 199): 'Play can be serious, although in our idea play is connected with non-seriousness'. It was a matter of winning, because winning gives sense to the competition. Modern sport, even when played by young people emerging out of childhood, has arguably almost completely lost its original element of 'play'. It is something that was already observed by Huizinga in the first half of the last century:

> Really to play, a man must play like a child. In the case of sport, we have an activity known as play but raised to such a pitch of technical organisation and scientific thoroughness that the real play spirit is threatened to extinction.
>
> (1980 [1938]: 199)

Gary Alan Fine came to a similar conclusion in his long-term observation of pre-adolescents playing baseball in the USA. He writes: 'Significantly, boys are frequently exhorted to "hustle" but rarely are they encouraged to "enjoy" … "Good" and "bad" play are readily defined in terms of success or failure, wins and losses' (Fine 1987: 188). Drawing upon his long-term ethnographic observation of children's sport in Canada, Dyck (2013) reads the emphasis on 'work' and 'competitiveness' from a more dialectical perspective. He contends that among the factors that make sport attractive to young athletes is the sense of accomplishment that they experience during games and competitions.

One player who seemed to deeply embrace this attitude of 'seriousness' was Charlie, the captain. The second youngest of four siblings, Charlie had joined his mother in the country at the age of eight. His little sister was the only one born in Ireland. Charlie was showing great pride in being the captain, to be the leader of the team, even though Kevin was its undisputed 'star'. On one of my first days away with the team he came straight to me, stopping before the camera and proudly showing off his captain's armband. He was not showing it to me, he was showing it to the camera. On the pitch he was controlled and took his responsibility with great commitment. He was playing in the midfield and sometimes at full-back. He and Kevin would often be praised by the coaches for their brave attitude.

Once, travelling back from a game, Mick said that Kevin and Charlie had been the best players that day, they had run and fought without rest. But then, a few minutes later, he commented about 'the black players [in the team] suffering the cold'. In fact, that day James (originally from Nigeria) and Eric (originally from DC Congo) wanted to play with a snood but Willie asked them to take it off. James was allowed to wear his gloves but not the snood. Neither Charlie nor Kevin wore a snood on this occasion, not even gloves, as this was a tacit rule within the game according to the coach. Were the two boys perceived differently, 'less' black then – an example of how their racialisation could be accomplished also through the sport practice (Ansari 2006; Adair and Rowe 2010)? Along with the rest of the team, Charlie and Kevin did not want to be considered 'sissies' by wearing gloves or even a snood. 'Don't be sissies' was a remark that could be heard at training. Being 'sissies' was essentially associated with a non-fighting spirit – to wear gloves and a snood could also count as an 'unmanly' attitude. All this echoes a polemic remark once made by legendary Manchester United manager Alex Ferguson, and certainly known to the adults in the team: 'real men don't wear snoods'.[16] Along with sissy, the word 'gay' was used by the boys to tease or mock someone. If someone was seen crying – which *almost* never happened – he was labelled as 'gay'. Crying was definitely 'gay' behaviour.

Despite the fact that the club was also proudly home to a girls' team, much of the discourse surrounding the game was explicitly male-oriented. This was unsurprising, since football in Ireland emerged under the influence of the game played in Britain, where it was historically rooted in strong, masculine, (white) working class culture (Armstrong and Giulianotti 1999). For some of the young black boys in the Mountview team, namely Kevin and Charlie, not to be 'sissies' was a way to assimilate an identity that was primarily that of the team and the game as played in the local vein, but there was obviously something else at stake. What I was observing happening in my fieldwork confirmed what Back, Crabbe and Solomos had noted in the English game. They write:

> What seems to be prevalent in the English game is a reliance on the notion that 'others', whether black, foreign or Asian, should assimilate with the normative, white coded, working class masculinity traits of English Football – unpretentious, self-deprecating, 'honest', committed, hard working, aggressive.
>
> (Back *et al.* 2001: 285)

In order to be valued as a player and a young man, a rightful member of the local 'community', the young boys attempted to appropriate some or all the above-mentioned traits. Charlie, for example, seemed to be working his way to becoming as much as possible part of the community, adhering to the rules or conventions he was presented with. In a way, given his age and complex background, he was, more than anything else, performing a belonging (Bell 1999). While many of his peers would often change club at the end of the season, he remained faithful to Mountview and to Willie, the coach who first invited him to join a team in Ireland. The first time I visited his house to meet with his mother, I noticed that one of the very few ornaments in the living room was his 'Certificate of Proficiency in the Irish Language'. The mother said he was very proud of that. When I asked her what language she spoke to her children, she said: 'It's Yoruba. But Charlie isn't good at speaking it, he understands but does not speak it, his little sister is better than him. He prefers Irish!' Charlie was also good friends with Glenn, a white Irish boy. The night before a game he would often sleep at Glenn's house.

Looking from the sideline

By way of introduction, with or without the camera, I usually asked a boy what team he supported and what made that team special to him. The choice of answers was rather limited – the Irish boys would either support Liverpool FC or Manchester United. Some of the black boys claimed they supported Chelsea or Arsenal instead. When I asked Glenn, who often wore a Manchester United jersey with his nickname printed on the back, why he supported this team, he answered: 'It is because of my uncle, he was a ManU fan'. A few months later he showed me the initials of his uncle, who died at a young age, freshly tattooed on his shin. He said he missed him. He had paid €40 for the basic tattoo, done by a friend's friend. Under Irish legislation he was too young to get a tattoo but this did not stop him.[17] Danny supported Manchester United because, he said, 'I just like them', while Charlie said he supported Arsenal and particularly liked their captain, Cesc Fàbregas.

Among the black boys, Kevin was the one who had been living in Ireland longest. He had moved with his family from Congo at the age of three, while the others had moved to Ireland at an older age. Kevin spoke in a slightly different way to the other black boys, proudly sporting a strong North-Dublin accent. He also showed more confidence on and off the pitch. His best friends during this time were white Irish boys. One was Paul, a fast right-winger, and the other was Ollie, not a regular in the team, who was also a rapper – he wrote and rapped his own lyrics to famous hip hop tunes. I first sensed that Kevin's confidence was mainly due to his ability as a player. He had been top scorer in the previous season and was the one the coach thought as his best 'asset'. 'How many goals did you score last year?' Glenn once asked him in my presence. 'Dunno', was the answer. 'If we play Major next season [Major League is the second top level league within the DDSL] he will be in the shop window', explained Willie a few times to me, meaning the boy could become a target for scouts from professional English clubs. Having spent almost all his short life time in Ireland, it appeared that Kevin could attune with his Irish peers better than the rest of the boys of African background. I had never seen him wearing blue jeans or something other than tracksuit and trainers: this was the dress-code shared by teenagers and young adults living in the area. Even though he did not feel the need to explain his behaviour, the various ways he performed, embodied and materialised his belonging were quite expressive and clear.

As the season progressed, I developed a regular dialogue with the team's substitutes. I was usually spending more valuable time with them than I was with their teammates, simply because during games I was standing on the sideline alongside them, the coach and the occasional club officials. Handling the camera, I was waiting for a good action shot and while I was doing it I held conversations with them. From this position I could also observe the interactions among the boys. Cheick was a particularly interesting character. Originally from the Ivory Coast – while the rest of the black boys were either from DC Congo or Nigeria – he shared with them the experience of being born in another country and brought to Ireland at some point in his childhood. He had been living in Ireland for five years and had two younger brothers born in the country. All the boys, apart from Eric, had younger siblings born in Ireland, who were 'Irish, because they are born in Ireland', as Cheick once explained to me, implying that they were born before 1 January 2005. The previous year, through a popular referendum, the unrestricted birthright citizenship, the 'jus soli', had been removed from the Republic of Ireland legislation. Cheick hoped that, because of his younger siblings' citizenship, he could soon also become an Irish citizen.

Among the players who were not regularly selected for the starting 11, Cheick was different. He did not show much disappointment for not being picked to play. Not 'getting enough game time' was the major reason of concern for the boys, and one that could provoke bitterness and the desire to leave the team. Some boys would openly express their disappointment, such as Darren, an

Irish boy, who I once heard saying: 'the coach doesn't know what he's doing'. Midway through my second season with Mountview, Darren left the team for this reason. But Cheick seemed not to worry, accepting the fact that there were better players than him or maybe he did not feel the pressure of making the game the centre of his life, as was the case with Kevin, whose main interest in life, as he once admitted to me, was football. Echoing Sands' (2002) approach to sport ethnography, I first had thought to engage with the players of ability, the 'leaders' of the group, such as Charlie or Kevin. I expected them to be in a better position to offer me insight into the group. However, I soon learnt it was more productive to work with the ones who appeared not to play a central role in the group and who could potentially explain it from a lateral position. It was Cheick that I dared to ask a sensitive question about the most recent recruit of the team, Eric, a tall boy of Congolese background but raised in France who had joined the team half-way through the season. It was a question that I had kept from asking the other boys, since I was afraid they would view me as a 'teacher', or just another adult trying to judge them. Our conversation proceeded as follows:

MAX: Cheick, please tell me, why do you all call Eric, 'Paki'? He is not from Pakistan.
CHEICK: Because he is, he is a gypsy.
MAX: What do you mean? His family is from Congo and he was born in France.
CHEICK: He is a gypsy.
MAX: I don't understand. Who started to call him that?
CHEICK: Dunno.
MAX: I am not sure he is happy to be called that name.

In this case, I briefly stepped out of my observer's role. I felt a moral duty to intervene, even at the risk of breaking the communication link with Cheick. Even though name-calling was generally done in the form of banter, 'to have a laugh', in this case there was a racial underpinning that I felt uncomfortable with. The story of Eric being called 'Paki' opened up a space for significant points of reflection.

The casual outsider

It is about four months since my arrival. The season approaches its end and there are games twice a week. In the months following the winter break (between December and January) many games have been called off because of the weather conditions and in order to be able to complete the season by the end of May there is no other way than play both on Saturday and Wednesday; occasionally an extra-game is even scheduled on Monday. Today is Wednesday and the team is playing one of the most prestigious youth clubs in Dublin, Belvedere. Eric, wearing the number 10 jersey, is fielded upfront along with Kevin, wearing his usual number 9 jersey. Mountview is winning easily. During the second half Willie and Mick remove Eric from the pitch. Philippe replaces him. While leaving the pitch Eric makes gestures with his hands like a rapper and, in a funny tone, looking at the coaches, shouts: 'Is it because I am black? Are you taking me out because I am black?' There is a moment of embarrassment, then Willie and Mick burst into laughter. Later Mick would recall this moment as an example of Eric's unpredictability, to being a 'character' and willing to imitate Ali G, the satirical fictional character created by English comedian Sacha Baron Cohen.

At this point, despite his skilfulness as a player, the coaches were starting to get tired of Eric's 'antics'. On another occasion, being kept on the bench for missing the last training session, Eric teased Kevin throughout the game shouting at him, in his usual jesting tone, 'Black bastard' and 'Fat Ronaldo'. Once, while travelling in the van to an away game, Eric pointed at the driver of a passing Dublin bus. 'He can't drive! He is black. Blacks can't drive!' he shouted a few times, raising laughter from his peers. On another occasion, during a summer one-day tournament, he asked me for a free ice-cream ticket. Willie called him away and told me not to give him the ticket, for he had already used the ice-cream ticket he had previously given to him and his teammates. Eric started running around the ice-cream seller shouting: 'I am black, I am hungry! I am black, I am hungry'. Everyone's eyes turned on him. One day in September 2009, at the start of the new season, he and Philippe arrived late at the training session. While the coach was instructing the rest of the group, they held a conversation with the two goalkeepers, Tom and Joe. Tom, who had just joined the team and was new to the group, asked Eric as to the reason they were so late, since they all came from the same neighbourhood, about 2.5 km from Mountview Park. 'He was in my house', said Philippe. 'Than we went to the centre', Eric said, meaning the Blanchardstown shopping centre. 'The centre is not far from you', Tom argued. 'What? It takes ages', Philippe replied. And Eric, with his usual jesting tone commented: 'Two hours. For black people is two hours'. To that Tom retorted: 'You are not black, you are Paki'.

Before Eric started using the word 'black' I had never heard it used by anybody in the team or the club. The boys of African background were, at least in my presence, simply referred by their names or when there was the need to identify them as a specific group to me, they would be labelled as 'African boys' or, a couple of times, as 'non-nationals'.[18] The black boys would avoid referring to themselves as a 'group', distinct from the rest of the team. Eric brought a different style to the team's generally moderate and shy conduct – a more stylish and eccentric one. This sometimes happened on the pitch as well. For example, his celebration when scoring a goal was louder and longer than those of his teammates. He generally liked to make jokes and cheer people up. He was not afraid of getting people's attention and often he seemed to seek it. But when approached directly by me or another adult he shied away, pretending he did not get the question being asked or had not heard it. I think Eric's use of the word 'black' deserves some attention because it is a statement of racial identification directed at the 'Irish people' *and* his teammates of African background, with whom he (at least subjectively) shared this identification.

As with other similar words that refer to alleged racial and ethnic character-istics, 'black' is a word whose meaning is neither univocal nor static. According to Hylton (2009: 18) 'the concept "black" is contested, and there have been many battles over the ownership of suitable identifiers for social groups and names that suitably describe groups of individuals in society'. Claiming to be 'black', Eric was arguably letting everybody know that he was not 'Paki'. To shout 'I am black', even though with a funny tone of voice, was for the young boy coming from France and having an African (Congolese) background a way to mark his place in the host society. Hall explains how he taught his two-and-half-year-old son 'the colours':

> I said to him, transmitting the message at last, 'You're Black.' And he said, 'No, I'm brown.' And I said, 'Wrong referent. Mistaken concreteness, philo-sophical mistake. I am not talking about your paintbox, I'm talking about your head.' That is something different. The question of learning, learning to be Black. Learning to come into identification.
>
> (2001: 205)

Eric's claim to be 'black' appears as if he were 'learning to come into identifica-tion', in Hall's words. At the same time, his urgency to claim this form of 'iden-tity' put him at risk of being cast out of the group (Alexander 2002).

Eric had joined the team halfway through my first season and had rapidly become a regular in the starting 11, proving to be a prolific scorer and a creative left-footed striker. He had lived in Ireland only for two years, after moving from France, where he was born and where part of his family still lived. As said, the family was originally from the DR Congo, the second largest African com-munity in Blanchardstown after that of Nigeria. He had been introduced to Mountview by his friend Philippe, and had not played in a regular team before. At that time, Eric was taller than most of the boys in the team; only Joe, the first goalkeeper, equalled him. Eric usually wore two earrings, one in each ear, while none of the other black boys wore one. There was one white Irish boy in the team who wore an earring. His name was John; he was the one who had teased me for the way I pronounced the word 'cup'. John left the team at the end of season to focus on boxing, his first sporting passion. 'It is that he comes from a Traveller background', Mick explained to me when I asked him why John had left the team. 'And they are big into their boxing, you know, they really enjoy it. Boxing takes preference over anything, that's the way it is. In all sorts of families like that, what the father says goes. That's what happened there'.

Over time, I observed Eric changing from a shy outsider into a lively and vocal 'insider', but this situation was not to last. I remember the very first game he played with Mountview. Before entering the field as a substitute Willie asked him to take out his earrings, which he passed on to me to keep in my jacket pocket (Willie never wore a jacket, not even in the worst weather conditions). Eric looked nervous and studious of the group's dynamics, eager to accustom himself to the general mood. The boys were focused on the game, with little evidence of joking and laughter amongst them. The only one who talked was the coach. Eric seemed not only to be carefully working his way into the group, a new member in an established football team, but also learning some rules of behaviour that were new to him. But as he started scoring goals, seven in his first three games, and getting respect from his teammates and the coach, there was a noticeable change of attitude in the boy. He became more confident and vocal, and started expressing his spontaneity in ways that would in some way disturb the group and the adults in charge of supervising it.

That's when the word 'Paki' started to be heard. At the beginning only some of the black boys would dare call him by that name, mainly as a joke, a form of banter, when they felt menaced by his spontaneity, which was somehow embar-rassing them. But to call him 'Paki' was also a way to show that he was different, that he was not like them. In fact, his skin appeared marginally lighter than his African-born mates, and according to Philippe this was the initial reason for the name calling. Eric did not seem to be bothered by the slurs, he replied in colourful ways ('Fat Ronaldo!'). Only Philippe, his closest friend, would avoid calling him by that name. Gradually, as his position in the team became less secure, the word 'Paki' could be heard pronounced not only by his black team-mates but by some Irish teammates as well. Eventually, the word became of common use within the group.

Why don't you put us on YouTube?

The idea of creating a video clip about the life of the team posed a few chal-lenges to me. First, I wanted to produce something the boys would like and be proud to be in. Second, it should be something that would ideally appeal to the whole team, and not only to a few players. With the particular exception of Eric, the boys appeared very concerned as to what the rest of the group would think of them. As noted by Head (1997: 29), 'as adolescents develop they tend to experience unease to talk to adults'. And further, 'one consequence of the deterioration of relationships with adults is a compensatory dependence on the peer group' (Head 1997: 29). Within the team, there was a tendency to conform, which was made particularly visible in the way the boys dressed and wore their hair. There was a third challenge posed by the video clip: namely, to give something back to the club, whose expectations had been expressed by its chairman. I chose to make a clip about the Cup Final won by the team in late May 2009. I first edited five minutes of footage and, one week later, I showed the rough cut to the team and the coach.

I had asked Ollie if I could use one of his songs as the soundtrack (Willie had a CD made by Ollie that he would often play in his car) but soon afterwards he left the team and did not return. The most popular music among the boys in the team, either Irish or of African background, was mainstream hip hop such as by US-American artist Chris Brown or more techno-oriented tunes. One of the 'activities' they usually engaged in before games and during unstructured time, was exchanging music tracks through their mobile phones. I once noticed Keith, an Irish midfielder whose confidence in relating to me grew over time, standing before a game with two phones, one in each hand. I asked him what he was doing and he explained to me that he was copying to his phone some of the tracks Charlie had in his. 'He has the best music', he added. This was probably due to the fact that Charlie's oldest brother was an amateur DJ, as I had previously learnt from him.

According to the kind of phone they owned, the boys would keep a selection of 70 to 120 tracks to listen to. Music was, along with football, a visible site of cultural exchange between boys of different background. For this reason, I considered it worthwhile to add some music to my video clip for the team. Even though YouTube hosts myriad amateur videos, which unabashedly use famous tunes as their soundtrack, I decided to do things the 'legal way'. My choice was therefore limited to tracks I could have access to without infringing copyright laws. To upload the clip, I created a YouTube account in the name of the club and left it with them when I finished my fieldwork. I included the clip in a 20-min DVD that I handed to every member of the team at the end of the season.

The video clip helped to establish a transient role for myself within the team and the club – that of the 'cameraman' – but, to some extent, it also contributed to projecting this multi-ethnic team as a successful representation of the local community. White Irish boys and African boys playing together, and, most importantly, winning. It seemed an ideal example of successful 'social integration'. However, as the personal trajectory of Eric demonstrates, the possibility of exclusion was not that far away and could take unexpected forms. Moreover, as will be discussed in the next chapter, patterns of belonging are complicated by issues of racialisation, state classification, and social class. Winning on the sporting pitch is just a minor factor. As noted by Bell (1999: 3), 'belonging is an achievement at several levels of abstraction'.

Notes

1 See for example, *The guidelines on interculturalism*, whose aim is to provide information for all FAS (Training and Employment Authority) staff (www.integration.ie [accessed 10 October 2012]); *Intercultural Ireland – An Garda Síochána – Your police service* (www.garda.ie/Documents/User/racial%20and%20intercultural%20english.pdf [accessed 10 October 2012]); *Intercultural education in the primary school*, produced by The National Council for Curriculum and Assessment (www.ncca.ie/uploadedfiles/publications/intercultural.pdf [accessed 12 October 2012]).

2   One of the most common criticisms of living in new estates/areas is that the houses go in first, followed by the apartments and everything else (shops, schools,

public open spaces, playing fields and public transport) lags by years if not decades. The cumulative effect of this rapidly expanding area like Dublin 15 area over the past 10 years is unsustainable.

Dublin 15 Community Council, Submission on Fingal Development Plan 2011–2016, 25 June 2009: 2, (www.dublin15cc.com/documents.html [accessed 10 December 2010]).

3 In the season 2008/2009 the Under-13 league fielded players born in 1995 or before. I started my fieldwork on late January 2009, therefore they were all in their 14th year of age.

4 These were areas in the city I most often heard of as places of origin from older members of the football club. During the 1950s and the 1960s, these areas were developed with extensive housing estates and tower blocks (in the case of Ballymun), to relocate former residents of deprived inner city areas. During the 1970s, the 'Ballymun Flats' became associated with social problems, including poverty, drugs addiction and crime (McDonald 2000).

5 Share *et al.* (2012: 79) argue that

> a rhetoric of community is alive and well and is persistently and frequently reproduced in public debates and discussions. It persists because it is useful to powerful groups in Irish society, including the state and its agents. Evocation of community, and of what 'the community' wants and needs, are an effective way to legitimise the actions of those in power and to minimise challenges from those who may be disadvantaged.

6 Within Dublin 15, the unemployed percentages vary dramatically, for example Tyrrelstown has 28.10 per cent of unemployed, while Castleknock has 5 per cent of unemployed (Conor Ryan, Blanchardstown Area Partnership, personal communication, 20 March 2018).

7 Available from www.fai.ie/images/stories/FAI_Referees_Fees__Expenses_2011–13.pdf [accessed 10 November 2011].

8 In the 2010–2011 season the number of youth clubs registered in the three leagues was as follows: DDSL, 128; NDSL, 91; SDSL, 56 [Data retrieved on 2 October 2011 from the leagues' websites]. Each club caters for different teams, so for example the NDSL claims that it 'comprises of approx. 285 teams (age 7–11) and over 300 (age 11–18)', www.ndsl.ie/index.cfm/loc/4 [accessed 2 October 2011].

9 Available at www.sfai.ie/index.htm [accessed 17 January 2018].

10 The FAI Intercultural Plan was designed in collaboration with the non-governmental sport organisations Sport Against Racism Ireland (SARI) and Show Racism the Red Card, and it ran from 2007 to 2010 (www.fai.ie/index.php?option=com_content&task=view&id=2136&IJamesd=9 [accessed 4 July 2018]).

11 Raidió Teilifís Éireann (RTE) is the public service broadcaster of Ireland.

12 Searched on 19 March 2012. During the time of my fieldwork, a young man was shot to death in the Mountview area. On another occasion, a young club member known to me was stabbed in his arm.

13 *Community Voice*, no. 119, August 2008, www.communityvoice.ie/pages/CV119/CV119n05.htm [accessed 19 March 2012]).

14 'Polonez' was started as a company in Ireland in 2003 and since then has opened 29 shops throughout the country (www.polonez.ie/en/about-us.html [accessed 25 August 2018]). Given the location of the shop, I assumed there was a number of Polish families residing in the Mountview area. However, there were no boys of Polish descent playing for Mountview FC.

15 According to the *EU Kids Online Annual Report* (Haddon and Livingstone 2012) Irish children's use of the internet at home is above average compared with their

European counterparts (Ireland 87 per cent vs EU 62 per cent). According to the *Growing Up in Ireland* Report, in 2009, 89 per cent of Irish nine-year-olds had a computer at home, see www.growing.ie [accessed 20 March 2012].

16 'Footballers who wear snoods get it in the neck from Sir Alex Ferguson', *The Mirror*, 10 December 2010.

17 The minimum age for getting a tattoo in Ireland is 18, but 16-year-olds can be tattooed with their parent's written consent. In a chapter in *The Art of Listening* Les Back offers an insight into the tattooing culture among the English working class, which mirrors my fieldwork with Mountview: 'one of the characteristics of working-class tattoos is that names of family members and lovers are often written on the skin' (Back 2007: 82).

18 'Non-Irish national' is a term used by the Irish Naturalisation & Immigration Service (INIS) to describe the residency status of people living in Ireland who are not Irish citizens or citizens of a country of the European Economic area (EEA). However, 'non-nationals' can often be heard in popular discourse; 'Non-national term a nonsense', *The Irish Independent*, 13 August 2009.

References

Adair, D. and Rowe, D. (2010). 'Beyond boundaries? "Race", ethnicity and identity in sport'. *International Review for the Sociology of Sport*, 45(3), 251–257.

Alexander, C. E. (2002). '"One of the boys": Black masculinity and the peer group'. In S. Taylor (ed.), *Ethnographic research. A reader*. London: Sage.

Amara, M., Aquilina, D., and Henry, I. (2005). *Sport and multiculturalism*. European Commission DG Education and Culture. Available from: www.isca-web.org/files/Sport%20and%20Multiculturalism%20EU%202004.pdf [accessed 1 August 2011].

Amit, V. (2000). 'Introduction: Constructing the field'. In V. Amit (ed.), *Constructing the field*. New York: Routledge, 1–18.

Ansari, H. (2006). 'Introduction: Racialization and sport'. *Patterns of Prejudice*, 38(3), 209–212.

Appadurai, A. (1996). *Modernity at large: Cultural dimensions of globalization*. Minneapolis: University of Minnesota Press.

Armstrong, G. and Giulianotti, R. (1999). *Football cultures and identities*. London: Palgrave Macmillan.

Back, L. (2007). *The art of listening*. Oxford: Berg.

Back, L., Crabbe, T. and Solomos, J. (2001). *The changing face of football: Racism, identity and multiculture in the English game*. Oxford: Berg.

Bauman, Z. (1996). 'From pilgrim to tourist – Or a short history of identity'. In S. Hall and P. du Gay (eds), *Questions of cultural identity*. London: Sage, 18–36.

Bell, V. (ed.) (1999). *Performativity and belonging*. London: Sage.

Brunt, L. (2001). 'Into the community'. In P. Atkinson, A. Coffey, S. Delamont, J. Lofland and L. Lofland (eds), *Handbook of ethnography*. London: Sage, 80–91.

Clark, A., Flewitt, R., Hammersley, M. and Robb, M. (2014). *Understanding research with children and young people*. London: Sage/The Open University.

Clifford, J. (1997). *Routes. Travel and translations in the late 20th century*. Cambridge, MA: Harvard University Press.

Cohen, P. (1980). 'Subcultural conflict and working class community'. In S. Hall, D. Hobson, A. Lowe and P. Willis (eds), *Culture, media, language*. Birmingham: Centre for Contemporary Cultural Studies/Routledge, 66–75.

Collins, M.F. and Kay, T. (2003). *Sport and social exclusion*. London: Routledge.

Duneier, M. (1999). *Sidewalk*. New York: Farrar, Straus and Giroux.

Duneier, M., and Back, L. (2006). 'Voices from the sidewalk'. *Ethnic and Racial Studies*, 29(3), 543–565.

Dyck, N. (2013). *Fields of play. An ethnography of children's sport*. Toronto, ON: University of Toronto Press.

Fanning, B. (ed.) (2007). *Immigration and social change in the Republic of Ireland*. Manchester: Manchester University Press.

Fine, G. A. (1987). *With the boys. Little League baseball and preadolescent culture*. Chicago: The University of Chicago Press.

Foote-Whyte, W. (1984). *Learning from the field: A guide from experience*. London: Sage.

Giulianotti, R. (2005). *Sport. A critical sociology*. Cambridge: Polity Press.

Goffman, E. (1967). *Interaction ritual*. New York: Pantheon Books.

Haddon, L. and Livingstone, S. (2012). *EU kids online: National perspectives*. London: The London School of Economics and Political Science. Available at: http://eprints.lse.ac.uk/46878/ [accessed 10 November 2018].

Halilovic-Pastuovic, M. (2010). '"Settled in mobility" as a "space of possibility": Bosnian post-refugee transnationalism as a response to the bio-politics of Irish interculturalism'. *Translocations: Migration and Social Change*, 6(2). Available from: www.translocations.ie/docs/v06i02/Vol%206%20Issue%202%20-%20Peer%20Review%20-%20Halilovic%20Pastuovic.pdf [accessed 8 February 2012].

Hall, S. (1991). 'Old and new identities, old and new ethnicities'. In A. D. King (ed.), *Globalisation and the world system*. London: Macmillan Educational, 42–68.

Hall, S. (1993). 'Culture, community, nation'. *Cultural Studies*, 7(3), 349–363.

Hammersley, M. and Atkinson, P. (2007). *Ethnography: Principles in practice*. London: Routledge.

Head, J. (1997). *Working with adolescents: Constructing identity*. London: Falmer Press.

Huizinga, J. (1980 [1938]). *Homo Ludens: A study of the play-element in culture*. London: Routledge.

Hylton, K. (2009). *'Race' and sport. Critical race theory*. London: Routledge.

Kracauer, S. (2009 [1964]). *Strassen in Berlin und Anderswo (Streets in Berlin and elsewhere)*. Frankfurt: Suhrkamp.

Lentin, R. (2007). 'Ireland: Racial state and crisis racism'. *Ethnic and Racial Studies*, 30(4), 610–627.

Lentin, R. (2010). '"All I have to do is dream?" Re-greening Irish integrationism'. *Translocations*, 6(2). Available from: www.translocations.ie/docs/v06i02/Vol%206%20Issue%202%20-%20Revisit%20-%20Lentin,%20edited.pdf [accessed 15 February 2012].

Leonard, M. (2007). 'With a capital "G". Gatekeepers and gatekeeping in research with children'. In A. L. Best (ed.), *Representing youth*. New York: New York University Press, 133–156.

Loyal, S. (2011). *Understanding Irish immigration: Capital, state, and labour in a global age*. Manchester: Manchester University Press.

Madison, D. S. (2011). 'The labor of reflexivity'. *Cultural Studies Critical Methodologies*, 11(2), 129–138.

Marcus, G. E. (1998). *Ethnography through thick and thin*. Princeton, NJ: Princeton University Press.

Marcus, G. E. (2010). 'Contemporary fieldwork aesthetics in art and anthropology: Experiments in collaboration and intervention'. *Visual Anthropology*, 23, 263–277.

McDonald, F. (2000). *The construction of Dublin*. Kinsale, Ireland: Gandon Editions.

Ni Chonaill, B. (2009). 'Perceptions of migrants and their impact in the Blanchardstown area: Local views'. Report, Dublin: Irish Research Council in Humanities and Social Science.

Pink, S. (ed.) (2012). *Advances in visual methodology*. London: Sage.

Rabinow, P., Marcus, G.E., Faubion, J. and Rees, T. (2008). *Designs for an anthropology of the contemporary*. Durham, NC: Duke University.

Rose, G. (2001). *Visual methodologies*. London: Sage.

Ryan, C. (2009). 'Dublin15 socio-economic profile'. Report, Dublin: Blanchardstown Area Partnership. Available from: www.bap.ie/dloads/socio_economic_profile_blanch.pdf [accessed 20 December 2011].

Ryan, C. (2010). 'Socio-economic profile of Mountview parish'. Report, Dublin: Blanchardstown Area Partnership.

Sands, R. S. (2002). *Sport ethnography*. Champaign, IL: Human Kinetics.

Savage, J. (2008). *Teenage. The creation of youth 1875–1945*. London: Pimlico.

Share, P., Corcoran, M. P. and Conway, B. (2012). *A sociology of Ireland*. Dublin: Gill and Macmillan.

Simmel, G. (2002 [1903]). 'The metropolis and mental life'. In G. Bridge and S. Watson (eds), *The Blackwell city reader*. Oxford: Wiley-Blackwell.

Verma, S. and Larson, R. (eds) (2003). *Examining adolescent leisure time across cultures. Developmental opportunities and risks*. San Francisco, CA: Jossey-Bass.

Watt, P. (2006). 'An intercultural approach to "integration"'. *Translocations*, 1(1). Available from: www.translocations.ie/docs/v01i01/watt.pdf [accessed 6 April 2012].

Williams, R. (1983). *Culture and society*. New York: Columbia University Press.

Winchatz, M. R. (2006). 'Fieldworker or foreigner?'. *Field Methods*, 18(1), 83–97.

Chapter 3

Flexible positions

Framing class, race and ethnicity on and off the pitch

During the summer after my first season with Mountview, the team underwent some changes. 'Some of the players were not getting enough game time, so I talked to the team managers of other clubs and offered the boys to change team, so they could get more game time', Willie explained to me in late August 2009. In the meantime, new players joined his team, for example the goalkeeper, Tom, recruited by Willie 'to put some pressure' on the only goalkeeper. Others, such as Junior and Patrick, contacted the coach and attended trials before the start of the season. The arrival of three new players with an African background (Hussein, of Sudanese background, alongside Junior and Patrick, who were of Congolese background), made the squad even more diverse in terms of its ethnic composition. But the ethnic diversity of the team was not limited to immigrant youth: alongside the boy from a Traveller family, in the squad there was one whose paternal grandparents were Chinese, and one whose granddad had immigrated from Italy in the 1950s.[1] A feature that confirmed that, against dominant narratives, immigration was not a 'new' phenomenon in Irish history.

At the same time, some of the old players had left, among them Cheick, one of the protagonists of my first months of fieldwork. He joined another local youth club competing in a lower league. At the same time, Eric, the 'casual out-sider', and Philippe were less involved in the life of the team and attended train-ing sessions less regularly. Their place in attack was soon taken by two of the new players, Junior and Patrick, who developed into a strong attacking trio along with Kevin. Junior had recently reunited with his family in Ireland from DR Congo. His competence in English was limited and he often relied on Patrick to help him understand what was being said. Between them, they would communicate in Lingala and French. Patrick was a smiling and thoughtful boy who had moved with his family to Blanchardstown from another part of Dublin. He had decided to join this team because, as he explained to me, 'I heard they were doing well'. He had previously played for three other football clubs, also based in North Dublin.

In a matter of a few months my ethnographic community had changed to the point that one third of its members were new. In spite of that, my relationship with some team members had improved. They were becoming more confident in dealing with me; they were to some extent getting used to my presence. This meant that it would be easier to get frank answers to my questions. I was particularly interested in understanding the importance of 'getting enough game time' as a reason to stay or leave the team. This was further a way to gain a clearer understanding of how cultural belonging is negotiated through sport practice (Biesta *et al.* 2001; Walseth 2006; Carrington 2008; Swanson 2009; Cuadros 2011). According to Crowley, 'belonging is usually taken to involve subjective and discursive dimensions of commitment, loyalty and common purpose' (quoted by Walseth 2006: 449). How does this theoretical formulation square with a player's decision to leave a team in the middle of the season because he doesn't get 'enough game time'? And how much is considered 'enough'? In this chapter, patterns of belonging among the adolescents playing with Mountview will be further explored by looking at the implications of social class and race. Finally, the conclusive vignettes will bring forward a 'different ecology of belonging' (Gilroy, 2000: 121) from the one exemplified by the policy idea of interculturalism. Young people's agency in making things happen that are not immediately readable through the lens of 'culture' and 'national cultures' will come to the fore.

The flexible team

It was October. Despite the changes in the squad's composition, the new football season played in the Major league (the second-to-top league) was going fairly well for Mountview. The first part of the season was marked by a series of victories that kept the mood high. Tom, the new goalkeeper, Charlo and Glenn were sitting on the bench in the dressing room before a game. One of the novelties was that the club had now access to the facilities of the newly inaugurated Community Centre.[2] I asked them what they thought about Darren's exit from the team. Darren had left the team after the new season had started because, according to Willie, he was not getting enough game time. 'But he cannot go to play for another club because he is signed to Mountview for this season', the coach explained to me. He said that he understood the boy was unhappy when he asked for his 'subs' (subscription money) back after a game in which he did not play. 'He was right, but it's something usually players don't do. Everybody has to pay his subs. I try to play everybody but sometimes it's hard', Willie commented. My conversation with the three boys proceeded as follows:

MAX: How do you feel about Darren having left the team?
CHARLO: He wanted to play more. He was good when he wanted to be, if he trained he was good.
MAX: Are you sad that he left?
CHARLO: I am sad for him.
'He was *shite*', someone else said (I could not distinguish who was speaking, too many people were talking loud and yelling to each other).

Despite Charlo's opinion, Darren did not seem to be missed by the group. Everybody appeared focused on winning, an observation Lever believes is characteristic of all young males' socialisation. In his view, 'virtually all male socialisation, not just sport, teaches boys to be competitive' (1983, quoted in Armstrong and Giulianotti 1997: 7). This resonates with the 'seriousness' with which the game was interpreted, that I explored in the previous chapter. Understandably, everybody in the team wanted to play. If they did not get what they considered enough game time they would easily lose interest in the team, but also in the game, and this happened more frequently as the boys grew older. As confirmed by the lesser number of teams competing in the Under-16 and Under-17 football leagues compared with younger leagues, and by other studies conducted in Ireland (Connor 2003; Fahey *et al.* 2005), teenage boys lose interest in their game as they go through their adolescent years.[3] About 19–20 players had taken part in pre-season training, in early August, but only two months later the Mountview Under-14 team faced a shortage of players.[4] In October, Willie was thus glad to welcome two new recruits (both white Irish boys). One was Reece, who was returning to Mountview after having left the team during the summer to join another local club, and the second was Shane, a midfielder from the same club.

'How is it possible that the boys leave a club to join another one when the season has already started?' I asked Willie. He honestly admitted that this was only possible because of a problem in the registration process. According to him, their club had failed to have the registration form be signed by the parents. Thus, their registration was not valid and they were allowed to join another club, even though they had already played a few games with the first one. This episode confirmed to me that player's registration procedures at youth level were not as strict as I imagined them to be. On this occasion I could not avoid recalling my own experience as a teenage player in Italy, back in the 1980s. I did this cognisant of the critical implications of the tendency of 'those who study young people to place their reflections of adolescence into the matrix when they do fieldwork, analyze data, and write about it' (Knopp Biklen 2007: 252). Memories can affect our 'ways of seeing' (Berger 1972), and in the case of the study of youth, as argued by Knopp Biklen (2007: 252), 'memory can romanticize or demonize youth'. However, I consider the use of personal memories as a reflective strategy that can help the reader to see through my eyes, obtaining a clearer understanding of how the researcher's childhood experiences can impact on the observation process.

At the time of my teenage football practice, before the start of each match the referee would enter the team's dressing rooms with the player's registration cards to call the roll. Registration cards had pictures of the players on them, and to my 13-year-old quite innocent self, they seemed a very serious matter. They appeared as a statement of the importance of the game we were playing and of our role in it. In fact, children were signed to a club for multiple years, cards were kept by the club, and transfers were a complicated matter. The system gave young people little or no mobility options, reducing their agency in their sporting practice. Arguably, things worked differently in the Republic of Ireland, in 2009. Here, the referee would usually receive before the start of the match simply a hand-written list of the players, but he would not perform a roll call or check the documentation.[5] Changes were introduced in 2012, when the FAI issued new registration rules informed by FIFA regulations on the signing and transfer of foreign underage players. With this reform, 'non-Irish nationals' became the focus of unprecedented attention. Among the new rules was that 'All player registration forms must now be accompanied by a true and exact copy of the original birth certificate'.[6] In 2014, the FAI introduced an electronic centralised registration system for the all youth leagues.

Young peoples' agency in their sporting practice is directly relevant to patterns of belonging, as changing clubs could be an indicator of their level of attachment to a team or a club. However, in the case of boys of immigrant background, changing clubs could also demonstrate the mobility of their families in a new country. At Mountview, there were players, mainly Irish, who had stayed with this club since the age of seven or eight. Long-term members were more regularly fielded in the starting 11. Dynamics of affiliation and the creation of sense of belonging also depend on the value given to the game. Drawing on her work with young female refugees in Norway, Walseth (2006: 461) argues that 'participation in sports can create strong feelings of belonging because sport sometimes is experienced as a "place of refuge"'.

Male adolescents in my study often felt the ambition to use their sport to further other ambitions. For Charlo, it arguably helped to enhance feelings of inclusion in the local community. Kevin and Junior cultivated the dream of a career in football and thought that by playing well they would attract the attention of scouts from English clubs, who have historically recruited consistent numbers of young players across Ireland (McGovern 2000; Curran 2016). Hussein wished to use his football as a way to obtain a college scholarship in the USA. The meanings attached to the sporting practice were multifarious, but what appeared evident in all the cases, was that parents played marginal roles in their children's sporting practice.

Parents: where are they?

From the first day of fieldwork, I noticed parents were quite numerous at games of children up to the age of 10, but they were largely missing from the games played by teenagers. Mick was eager to offer an explanation for this:

> We have now two parents coming down to the Under-16 games and this is very unusual. During my five/six seasons of coaching there were maybe five occasions that I had parents coming to the games. The boys they don't like it as well, even the Under-11s. It depends from the relationship with the parents. If you go to see an Under-16 rugby match in Killiney or Castle-

knock you will probably see a lot of parents. Even at football games. 'There is my son', the 'trophy' sort of thing. It's great having the parents supporting the kids, and it's also a cultural thing but kids from areas like this usually don't want them around. They are afraid of what other people would think.

There was clearly a social class element involved in the dynamics described by Mick. The fact that he picked up rugby and Castleknock as points of reference to explain parent's participation in adolescents' sport practice showed that not only the kind of game played mattered – rugby rather than (association) football – but also the geographical location of where people actually lived (Munck 2007). When I asked the boys, either Irish or of immigrant background, about their parents' interest in attending the games, they answered that their parents were busy with work or with their families. They mentioned the last time their parents attended a game, usually a cup final or an important game at the end of the season, to demonstrate that *sometimes* parents and relatives did actually attend matches. In general, they did not show interest in having parents around. Given the wider socioeconomic context of where the club was located, the limited or non-existent involvement of the parents of the teenage players appears to resonate with the findings of research on adults' volunteering in youth sport in Ireland.

According to Delaney and Fahey (2005: 24): 'Volunteering is most common among professionals. Twenty per cent of those in higher professional and managerial positions volunteer compared to twelve per cent of those in unskilled manual professions'. Thus, it could be a question of social class – lower class parents devote less time to their children's sport. Yet this is only one side of the coin. As is generally the case in youth sport practices in Ireland (Woods *et al.* 2010), all Mountview FC members were volunteers. At the time of my field-work, the club consisted of 14 teams and a children's academy and there were at least two, often three adults involved in the management and supervision of every team. To this number, other figures, such as secretary, chairman, treasurer and various informal assistants, should be added. Hence, involvement in the club's life was high and this could be witnessed every Saturday morning, when children's teams hosted their games. However, adult's participation appeared to decline as the players entered their puberty, crossing the frail line between childhood and adulthood.

To some extent, this pattern compromised the possibility of taking further one of my initial research interests. Among my aims was precisely that of investigating the ways participation in sport of male immigrant teenagers may function to enhance the social inclusion of their families. It was not difficult to obtain the permission of parents to carry out my study; their signature to the forms was facilitated through Willie and Mick and with the collaboration of the boys. However, to visit their houses and meet a few of them seemed a different matter. After some unsuccessful attempts, I finally managed to arrange a couple of appointments. Willie offered to take me in his car and I gratefully accepted his help, but I wondered if his presence was going to 'interfere' with my research endeavour. He was glad to meet some of the African boys' parents at their homes. He had never set foot in one of their houses and only briefly made contact with a few of them when collecting or taking home their sons.

When we went to visit Kevin's family, Kevin was not at home, so we met his mother, his father and his younger sister. We were invited into the living room. I immediately noticed a display case with a little souvenir of the Eiffel Tower and beside it the trophy given to Kevin as 'Best Player of the Year' of the Mountview club. It had been given to him at the Mountview FC annual pre-sentation, which had been held at the premises of the local GAA club during the summer. After a while Willie took the chance to talk openly to Kevin's father. 'Why don't you come to games sometimes? It's nice to see people when we play. When we go to play away games we see the other side full of people and ours is empty, it makes a difference.' Kevin's father recalled that he had actually attended the cup final that Mountview won at the end of the last season. He said he would try to come more often, but on Saturday he was usually quite busy with his job. He worked as a driver for a delivery company.

There is a consistent body of research showing parents' role in controlling and conditioning their children's leisure time (Fine 1987; Anderson 2003; Dyck 2003; Giardina 2005; White et al. 2008; Swanson 2009), yet there seems to be a lack of attention to the ways adolescents autonomously negotiate their leisure time and how their autonomous decisions might influence the whole family's feelings of inclusion in local and national communities. Kevin's trophy was at the centre of the room but his family had not been there when he had received it, at the club's annual presentation. None of the parents of the Under-13 team players were there that day, or if they were, they did not sit at the same table with their teenage sons, but with a younger sibling. Kevin's 'success' was not publicly shared with his family. It was therefore harder for his relatives to benefit in any way from the social capital accrued by their son (Brown 2017). With children aged 7 to 10, parents' participation was more accepted, therefore immigrant families attended in greater number their children's games. But with older boys, local habits influenced by social class distinctions hindered a more prominent participation of parents. There was a significant exception to this otherwise homogeneous pattern. It was Hussein, one of the new players.

The son of a doctor

'We've never had a doctor's son in our club. It's not that we don't want them, it's just that there aren't any. I am quite surprised the boy is here. How did he end up here?', Mick commented to me early in the new season. I was sitting in his office, the manager's office of the local Community Centre. Since the start of the new season Mick was no longer assisting Willie with his team. He had a new assistant in the figure of his cousin, Jeff, who had joined him after returning from the USA where he had lived and worked for a few years. Mick and I therefore had fewer opportunities to meet, but I tried to keep in touch with him. He was always eager to provide insights into the life of the club and about this suburban area in general. But he was also interested to know how my study progressed. That particular afternoon, I was telling him about my visit to one of the new players' home and the fact that the boy's father was a physician by profession.

This news took Mick by surprise, confirming my understanding of Mountview FC's catchment area as essentially comprising a working class population. It also showed once again that these teenage boys were inclined to leave their parents out of their sport practices. They tended to keep it to themselves, as a way to affirm their autonomy in decision-making (Lalor *et al.* 2007). According to the Player's Registration Rules, before the start of the season the club asks parents to sign their son's registration form, yet this could occur without actually meeting the parents. The boy would hand them the form and bring it back signed to the club officials. As with Willie, Mick suggested that my involvement with the team could be an opportunity for the club to get closer to the immigrant families. 'I wonder why he joined our team', Mick commented. 'Castleknock [FC] have good facilities, people there have money and parents put money in the club'.

Hussein was a 14-year-old boy of Sudanese background who had been living in Ireland for eight years. His family had previously lived in the UK. He had joined Willie's team during the summer, having previously played for Castleknock FC, based in the most affluent area of Dublin 15, where his family resided. He explained to me that the reason he joined Mountview was 'because they are doing well, they are a good team'. It probably made a difference that they were a team with a rich ethnic diversity of players, with a greater presence of boys of African background than any other team across the capital. Hussein did not confirm my assumption but said that 'It is good to have players from different countries in the team'.

My encounter with Hussein shed a light on a different perspective of social class within my ethnographic community. There was more than one element that made Hussein stand out. It was not only the fact that his family was from Sudan and not from Nigeria or Congo; or that he did sometimes sport an A.C. Roma jersey while almost all of his teammates would sport Manchester United or Liverpool jerseys. Or the fact that his father was a solitary spectator to his games. More than anything else it was the fact that he was from Castleknock and attended a private school where rugby union was, as it is generally the case in private schools in Ireland, the most popular game (Hargreaves 2007).

It also impacted on me the fact that Hussein, different from most of the boys I had met and talked to until then, was openly curious about my project and my studies. He asked me what my study was about and how I ended up doing it in Ireland. He seemed to me more mature than his age or maybe just better equipped to have a conversation with an adult. His cultural and social capital (Bourdieu 1978) was arguably different from the rest of the boys playing for

Mountview, either Irish or of immigrant background. He was himself interested in going to university, something that most of his teammates were not preoccupied with or did not express the aspiration to do. 'I want to go to university and study medicine, like my father', he explained to me after a training session, while I was waiting for the bus and he was waiting for his father to fetch him with his car (another element of distinction, for almost all his teammates would go home on their own, either walking or cycling).

Bourdieu's conceptualisation of 'habitus' is a helpful theoretical tool in defining Hussein's position within my ethnographic community. In Bourdieu's words, habitus is an 'immanent law, lex insitia, laid down in each agent by his earliest upbringing' (Bourdieu 1977: 81). Habitus is made of 'values and dispositions gained from our cultural history that generally stays with us across contexts' (Webb et al. 2002: 150). Capital and habitus are the key epistemological categories used by Bourdieu to explain people's and social classes' disposition towards a sport practice. For Bourdieu:

> The probability of practising the different sports depends, to a different degree for each sport, primarily on economic capital and secondarily on cultural capital and spare time; it also depends on the affinity between the ethical and aesthetic dispositions characteristic of each class or class fraction and the objective potentialities of ethical and aesthetic accomplishment which are or seem to be contained in each sport.
>
> (1978: 836)

Hussein was, at the same time, a member of an upper class and a migrant, but a migrant whose skin colour and origin made him, in an Irish context, 'more' migrant than others, as 'African children, and a host of others including mixed race "black" Irish, challenge the conflation of stable racial and national identities in Ireland' (Ni Laoire et al. 2011: 44). When I met him in his home, Hussein's father eagerly marked his distance from other (African, black) immigrants. 'I am not an immigrant. I came here as a hired doctor. During the Celtic Tiger there was great demand for doctors and nurses. If you go to hospitals maybe 50 per cent of the staff is made of foreign nationals', he claimed.[7] Without saying it, in quite surprising terms, he was pointing my attention to the highly racialised discourses that in Ireland have often conflated 'African' and 'asylum-seeker' in debates surrounding immigration (Lentin and McVeigh 2006; Loyal 2011a).

Returning to sport practices, my ethnographic material suggests the need to adjust Bourdieu's theoretical framework of social class and sport preferences in order to respond to the challenges posed by the markedly globalised scenario of countries such as Ireland. This is something that Giulianotti (2005: 169) further advocates, when he argues that 'sporting tastes and practices are not so conveniently class-connected, suggesting that we need to increase categorical flexibility to deploy Bourdieu's thinking within sport'. In a globalised world people move

and disconnect from their own national and ethnic milieu, distancing themselves 'not only from "official" cultural texts and their meanings, but from any
institution or text which claims to have a monopoly on meaning' (Webb *et al.*
2002: 151). Hussein's decision to play football – and to play it for a team located
in a working class area rather than the one in his more affluent area of residence
– apparently expressed his and his family's lesser affiliation to their social class
and locality. This seems to contradict what Tyler observed among immigrants
in Britain, emphasising the contrast between 'the flexibility and openness of
interethnic and diasporic identifications and the fixity of class distinctions'
(Tyler 2011: 1). At the same time, with his wish to play for Mountview, Hussein
expressed a level of agency and social creativity that is increasingly common
among young people growing up and playing sports in multi-ethnic and multi-
national cities (Giardina and Donnelly 2008; Rosbrook-Thompson 2012).

The meaning of the game

As a player, Hussein was not as skilful as Eric, nor as powerful as Kevin or a
fighter like Charlo. Overall, his approach appeared too 'gentle' for the kind of
game being played by the team. He thus ended up spending more time on the
bench than on the pitch. After a while he showed a willingness to adapt his
approach to the game in an attempt to conform to the rules of the group. This
became clear to me at a training session in late October 2009, attended by only
seven players. Willie was disappointed by the poor attendance, apparently justified by the demands of schoolwork, but did not want to let down the players
that had shown up. So he decided to arrange a training match and invited me
to join them – for the first time – in order to even out the number of players.
'Hey Maximo, do you wanna play?' he shouted in my direction. Peter offered me
a pair of spare boots my size which smelled of leather and mud. I liked that smell
– it gave me the feeling I was really participating in the (ethnographic) game, a
touch of the 'sensuous scholarship' described by Stoller (1997). I played against
Hussein and soon noticed the strength he was putting into his challenges to
impress the coach. Danny reacted angrily to a tackle by Hussein. 'If you do it
again I punch you in the face!' he yelled out of anger. Hussein did not answer
and kept quiet. Willie invited the boys to calm down and continue to play.

Over time, being diligent in attending training sessions and showing a new
attitude to the game, Hussein attracted attention from the coach. His efforts
were not in vain and before the winter break he was finally included in the first
11 for a league game. He played quite well in defence, but I could sense he was
not fully trusted by his teammates, both Irish and those of African background.
In another game he was substituted in the second half and I noticed frustration
in his face. 'What happened?' I asked him. 'Don't know, everybody is shouting
on the pitch. Willie told me to do something, the boys were telling me to do
something else. I was confused'. Willie commented that 'Hussein doesn't listen'
(to his orders). Despite these difficulties, Hussein remained passionate about the

game. 'I also like rugby, in my school that's the first sport and I like playing it, but I prefer football', he told me. During the travel to away games, Hussein was eager to hold conversations with his teammates, but the topics he seemed willing to talk about did not arouse much interest from his peers. They were topics of conversation they had little familiarity with, such as work experience in his father's clinic as part of his school curriculum or a Danish boy coming to stay for a week at his house as part of an international exchange programme, or a Green Day concert in Dublin's O2 Arena to which he had been taken to by his father.

Hussein seemed not to be troubled by his minority condition, being a 'black' immigrant boy in Irish society – he seemed to look at life's opportunities differently from his peers of African background. He was not particularly interested in using football as a way to stand out – becoming a professional footballer – or to assimilate – being accepted as one of the local boys. He was just enjoying the game and was willing to play with a successful team. More than anything else, however, he wished to go to college in the USA and he knew that being a good footballer could potentially help him reach his goal.

The DVD request

Late in February 2010 Hussein came to me with a request:

HUSSEIN: Maximo, may I ask you a favour?
MAX: Yes, go on.
HUSSEIN: Could you make a DVD just for me? I don't need much, just a few minutes showing me playing. I would need a DVD that shows that I can play football to apply to a college in the USA.
MAX: Sure, I can do that.
HUSSEIN: They can grant you a full scholarship or half a scholarship if you are good in sports, but you have to be good in the studies too. You could film me for a few minutes every game.
MAX (half jokingly): Okay, I'll try to do that, but don't tell your teammates I am doing this, they might all come to me with the same request!
HUSSEIN: Ok.

On the one hand, his initiative confirmed that his class positioning allowed him to think about mobility in a more flexible way than the rest of his teammates of African background, who were living in Ireland under an asylum scheme (which gave them limited mobility outside of the country).[8] Like many young people, Hussein worked through his identity formation in a context of global mobility, situating his sense of belonging among different countries (Sudan, his family's country of origin; UK, where he had previously lived; Ireland, where he was living; and finally USA, where he wished to move) and cultural imaginaries, not least that of football. But his 'dwelling in travel' (Clifford 1997: 26), was open to a variety of possibilities from which many of his peers were excluded. To some extent, this shows, as Dolby and Rizvi have pointed out, that 'we cannot understand the everyday experiences of young people without also looking at how global conditions of mobility are both affected by, and are instrumental in producing and reproducing, class formations' (Dolby and Rizvi 2008: 3).

On the other hand, in expressing his request to me, Hussein also revealed that he did not conform to the unwritten rules of behaviour that seemed to govern this group of teenagers. The boys were generally concerned about the group's appreciation of their actions, so they rarely took initiatives of their own, especially when these involved their relationship with adults. When they dared do it, like Eric, they were pushed towards the margins of the group or even forced out of it. Even though I had been asked before for DVDs, Hussein's request surprised me, because it was of a different kind. It showed an appreciation for a tangible benefit he could get from his interaction with me, and a very clear focus with regard to his future.

In the following weeks Hussein missed a few training sessions. According to Willie this was because of schoolwork and therefore the boy did not get many chances to play. When he played it was mainly as a substitute. But then, right after Easter, with about two months left in the season, he disappeared altogether. As said, it was not uncommon for a player to leave the team during the season. However, with him I was losing one of the most engaging participants and I was curious about the actual reasons for leaving the team. After a few weeks, I finally got the chance to visit his house again. Hussein was frank and typically articulate about his reason to quit the team: 'I was feeling I was not given much time to play, the coach was not helping the development of the players. His only tactic was to pass the ball to Kevin and Junior, that was it'. His father admitted to not being a sport fanatic himself, but said he did not influence his son's decision – he only wanted the best for his son. However, he was not entirely happy with this experience. He said he was surprised to see that when he went to attend his son's games there were no other parents present, and he did not feel at ease. Hussein was willing to join another team during the summer. It would certainly be a team closer to the city centre, because he was going to attend a secondary school there. 'What do you think of Lourdes Celtic? I know they are based in Crumlin. Is that area safe?' he asked me. Hussein did not forget his request: 'Maybe you can come next year and film me when I play for another team?'

The racist incident

With a squad of such diverse ethnic composition as the one displayed by the Under-14 Mountview team it was no wonder that the issue of 'racism' would, sooner or later, arise. Players and officials of minority background are victims of abuse not only in the big stadia of major football leagues but obviously also, which is more difficult to account for and is often overlooked, at junior and amateur level (Long *et al.* 2000; FRA 2010; Mauro 2018). During my two seasons spent with this team, only two episodes of racial abuse were brought to the attention of the team (but possibly more happened that were not talked about). The analysis of the way they were dealt by the protagonists and the adults involved, deserves some critical attention, as, on the one hand, they highlight structural deficiencies in the comprehension of issues of racism and discrimination, and, on the other hand, they potentially reveal the workings of social class divisions in youth sport.

The first episode happened at the end of a home game played with intensity by Mountview against a youth club from an affluent South Dublin area. A number of parents of the opposing team's players attended the game. They had driven their children to the game in their cars, including a few SUVs. Games against such teams were especially tense as a strong multi-ethnic team from a working class area would play against mostly white Irish teams from middle-class areas. On those occasions, two conflicting versions of contemporary Ireland faced each other on the pitch. Mountview embraced the diversity of post-Celtic Tiger Ireland to an extent that clubs from affluent areas of the town did not. This would make the young captain and his black teammates particularly proud. At the same time, Mountview would acquire an image of an area where immigrants could count, at least on the football pitch. A specific layer of belonging would come to the fore in such games – a particular form of 'neighbourhood nationalism' (Back 1996), which appeared to unite lower-class Irish nationals and black immigrants. In a way, this highlighted a shared position of otherness as, according to Loyal (2011b: 142), 'lower class Irish nationals are outsiders themselves in relation to higher ranking economic elites whose more secure socio-economic position, class codes and behavioural norms and restraints are expressions of their higher levels of economic and cultural capital'.

Immediately after the final whistle, while players and coaches were shaking hands in the middle of the pitch, I witnessed a boy falling to the ground and Eric running away, chased by an adult member of the opposition club. More people began to shout and it looked like a brawl was about to start. Confusion mounted, yet the reason for the ensuing commotion was not clear. Then I heard Kevin shouting: 'He called him nigger!' Allegedly, one of the opponents had refused to shake hands with Eric, saying to him: 'I don't shake hands with you, nigger'. That's why Eric had punched him in the face. After this, voices got loud and noisy; some adults attempted to separate the boys but there were others who were accusing the black boy of punching a member of their team. It was evident that those most emotionally affected by the event were the black boys playing for Mountview. Kevin showed his rage taking off his shoes and waving them in the air while shouting: 'This is racism! We can't accept racism!'. Charlo was also very excited, anger and frustration were evident in his facial expression. 'I cannot accept that shit', he said. Eric masked his frustration with the usual antics, showing how he used his fist to react to the abuse: 'I punched him like this!'

In a matter of minutes, the opposition team exited the ground. The referee was still there when all this happened, but claimed he did not hear or see anything; apparently, he only saw a boy on the ground and another one running away. Willie asked his team not to leave the ground and to stop outside the community centre for a brief talk. I was curious to hear what he would say in such emotional circumstances. 'What happens in the game stays in the game', he said addressing the team. 'When something is said to you keep on, don't retaliate. Show them that you can beat them on the pitch scoring goals. You go there and you trash them'. His words carried a simple message against violent behaviour on and off the pitch. Yet according to my understanding of the issue, they were somehow missing the point.

Nobody – not the coaches of both teams, or club officials present at the scene – seemed to have taken seriously the accusations of the black boys about a case of 'racist abuse'. There was no mention of the word 'racism', and no attempt was made to understand the difference between a generic insult and a racist insult. In this moment, I experienced uncertainty surrounding my role (Back 1996; Priest 2016). Should I remain separate or should I intervene? I felt the black boys expected a different outcome to the incident, since according to Charlo it was not the first time someone had made a racist insult on the pitch without adult officials taking a stance. Yet, I did nothing. I could have taken an active role in the events, for example inquiring my adult informants about the incidence of verbal abuse of a racist nature. On this occasion, I decided not to intervene because I wanted to have a better understanding of the situation before expressing my opinion.

Sportspeople and multiculturalism

A few months later, in February 2010, I was presented with a similar incident. It happened in a cup match against one of the most prestigious youth clubs in Dublin. The game was tense – the Mountview boys wanted to show the 'big' team they were better than them. About halfway through the second half – the teams were still drawing 0–0 – a row started in midfield involving Junior and a couple of players of the opposing team. I saw Kevin, the new captain for this season, running furiously towards a member of the opposition team, while Charlo tried to stop him. As it had happened in the previous incident, the boys of African background reacted with strong emotions.

'Did you hear what was said?' I asked Jeff who was standing beside me on the sideline. 'Something like "black bastard", the black boys all went mad', he answered. Languages were mixed, as Junior felt more comfortable communicating to Kevin in French and Lingala, rather than in English. Apparently nobody else but the protagonists and a few players close to them had heard the slur. The referee summoned Kevin over, inviting him to calm down, which he did, albeit reluctantly. From the sideline we could not hear if something was said about the abuse. They all went back to play. The black players, who occupied the three main attacking roles of the Mountview team, appeared frustrated but they did what the coach had told them to do: concentrate on the game and play on. Ten minutes before the final whistle Mountview scored. The mood elevated, but the players appeared nervous. With only two minutes left, the opposition team drew level and one minute later they scored the winning goal. Patrick had tears down his face, Kevin was getting very emotional again. Junior quickly left the field. Charlo was speechless. Later I approached some the boys but they did not want to talk about the abuse. They had lost – that was all that counted.

After the game I saw Willie paying the referee his fees and sharing a few words with the manager of the other team. It was just a brief salute – they did not appear to engage in serious talk about racial or verbal abuse. Willie then went back to the pitch to take down the nets, as he used to do after every home game, helped by a couple of his players (Figure 3.1). As on the previous occasion, I felt that the issue could have been dealt differently, and I wondered if I should have stepped in. Unexpectedly, on the following Monday I received a phone call from Willie. He wanted to ask me what I thought about the game. I told him I had been impressed by the way his team had played, but I admitted I was worried about the racist incident and the distress expressed by the black boys. 'I am also sorry', said Willie. 'But their coach said his excuses for anything his players might have said'. I did not feel like discussing the matter further, since I had already expressed my opinion on the matter.

Neither of the 'racist' incidents ended up in the referees' reports, because the referees said they had not heard the abuse and the club officials had allegedly not asked them to mention it. Sadly, this is what, more often than not, happens in such cases (FRA 2010; Mauro 2018). In Ireland this happens despite the

Figure 3.1 Nets.

'Good Practice Suggestions' included in the FAI Intercultural Plan, whose first objective was 'to combat racism in football'.[9] The same Plan states among its planned actions the training of referees and officials on racism and discrimination. Hassan and McCue (2011) believe that this area of intervention has not been properly addressed by the FAI and that the Intercultural Plan has remained, also for this reason, an unfulfilled promise.

At about the same time these incidents happened at Mountview games, a story of racist abuse on a youth football pitch appeared in the local news. In this case, the coach of the boy victim of the abuse had decided to abandon the game in protest and later decided to quit the club, claiming the matter had not been dealt with properly.[10] I mentioned this story to Willie, who did not know about it. He commented: 'Referees are too old and not well trained. If someone of my team does something like this [abusing another player] I'll take him out, I don't let him play'. I trusted his sincerity and knew how much he cared for his players and his team. In the end, he was the person who had chosen as captain of his team Charlo, a boy of Nigerian background, and later Kevin, a boy of Congolese background (he would choose a new captain at the start of every season). Everybody in the local community knew that Willie's team comprised boys of different backgrounds, many of whom had no previous experience of playing competitive football.

There was no doubt that he was sensitive to the wellbeing of all his players, but he probably lacked a clear understanding of this problem, and more specifically, of the ways it could be tackled inside football. It was more an institutional rather than an individual issue, as coaches and club officials were not trained in multicultural issues. At the same time, as stressed by Hylton (2018: 10), 'For those in sport an understanding of microaggressions is a crucial element in the journey to better understand how racism is reproduced and for these behaviours to be confronted more effectively'. I will return to these facets of the problem in the next chapters. The last two sections of this chapter foreground trajectories of belonging negotiation that emerged in my interaction with the young players of Mountview. They embody forms of transcultural dialogue that appear to reduce the significance of race and racialisation in this particular urban setting and within the game of football.

Embodied belongings

The Irish boys in the team sported similar fresh crewcuts: their hair shaven to blade one or blade two, sometimes with a small fringe of longer hair arranged over their foreheads at the front. The haircut contributed to constructing their own 'working class' masculine identities, which were defined on and off the pitch by a set of conventions of outlook and demeanour such as, for example, 'being strong' (not crying, not wearing gloves or jackets) and not standing out of the group. To some extent, these internalised modes of behaviour reverberate with Willis's (1977) representation of English working class male youth in his influential 'Learning to labour'. 'I go to the barber every second week', Glenn explained to me when I asked how often he would go to the barber or if he had his hair cut by a family member. 'How much do you pay?' I asked him and Ronan. 'Ten euros', Ronan said. 'I pay eight', Glenn replied with a smile. The black boys would also keep their hair very short. Charlo and James had their hair shaved by their mother or sisters, while Patrick had his hair cut by his older brother, who was a barber by profession. In such an environment, the idea that someone could sport quite long, curly hair (and especially a beard) like myself caused a sensation.[11] Despite my conscious and unconscious efforts of 'adaptation' (Hammersley and Atkinson 2007), my appearance made me stand out and on various occasions I heard comments pertaining to my appearance. Once Glenn told me: 'Maximo, you see, I am keeping my hair longer'. 'Like me?' I replied. 'Naa, like him'. He pointed at a man with very short hair, just a bit longer on the sides than what I was used to seeing.

Patrick found it difficult to adjust to this unspoken hairstyle code even after a few months with the team. One day in March he arrived at the pitch sporting his thick curly hair visibly longer on top and shaved on the sides. It was a smaller version of the 'Afro' hairstyle. This did not pass unnoticed and Patrick was immediately called 'Bob Marley' by an adult member of the club. That was the joke of the day and almost everybody, both Irish boys and those of African background, took part in it. The story would not be meaningful for my discussion had it not been for a conversation that involved Patrick, Keith, Joe and Shane, a new player who had just joined the team and did not know all his teammates yet. Shane asked Patrick if he was really from Jamaica (the country of origin of Bob Marley) like everybody was claiming. The conversation touched upon questions of national and cultural belonging involving football as an international 'language'.

SHANE: How come you are not from Jamaica?
PATRICK: I am from Jamaica.
SHANE: Naa, I am from Jamaica … change all things. Where are you from?
KEITH: Congo.
PATRICK: Same country as Kevin, same country as Junior.
KEITH: Kevin is from Nigeria.
PATRICK: … same country as Kevin.
SHANE (turning to Kevin): Kevin, where are you from?
PATRICK: My country, Congo!
KEITH: Jamaica.
SHANE: Congo.
PATRICK: Do you know LuaLua?
SHANE: Who?
PATRICK: The fella who used to play for Newcastle.
KEITH: LuaLua, who played for Newcastle.
PATRICK: Yeah, him. He is from Congo as well. We are Congolese, man … we are the best.

SHANE: Congolese.
PATRICK: Yeah.
PATRICK: You Irish, Ireland. Congo, Congolese.
JOE (in a funny tone): I don't know where is Congo. Fuck that, we are in the Congo team.

Their conversation reveals much about the 'transcultural' dialogue that the game of football engenders among teenagers. According to Hoerder *et al.* (2005) it is especially young people living in metropolitan areas with diverse populations that give rise to the 'transcultural'. They believe that 'encounters among youth from different cultural, ethnic, and social contexts produce diasporic public spheres which are neither predominantly emancipatory nor fully controlled, but emerging and therefore contested' (Hoerder *et al.* 2005: 15). The football team appears to be a site that effectively enables such encounters among young people. The boy from Congo had spent half of his life in Ireland and on another occasion had told me he would gladly play for the Irish national team, as he 'loved this country'. In this case he used a football player as an example of someone from the same origin the Irish boy might know, the Newcastle United player LuaLua. Football functioned here as a common language that everybody could understand. But Patrick was in some way also 'teaching' the Irish boys about the importance of his roots, confirming to some extent the assumption that, 'school and educational institutions are no longer the sole – or even predominant – pedagogical sites for youth' (Dolby and Rizvi 2008: 5). It was rare to hear such an open declaration of national or national belonging from a boy of immigrant background. Kevin and Charlo, for example, never revealed an interest in communicating their ethnic background, preferring to conceal it, at least in the context of their sport practice. In fact, Keith did erroneously assume that Kevin – his captain and his long time teammate – was from Nigeria and not from DR Congo. Away from the football pitch, Charlo regularly played keyboards at Sunday masses for his Nigerian congregation along with his older brothers. But within the team, he generally preferred to keep a low profile about his African roots.

It was moments such as these that I – the white adult observer – felt the generative power of younger generations who live, paraphrasing Bhabha (1996), 'in-between cultures'. Patrick, who 'loves' Ireland and would like to represent this country on the football pitch, also 'loves' Congo to the point that he is eager to explain to his friends and teammates what Congo means to him. The sporting field is a site that serves different needs: that of leisure, of sport performance, but also a site for socialisation and a place within which to negotiate sense of belonging. It is on sporting fields that young people are often eager to work their 'hybrid agencies'. According to Bhabha (1996: 58):

> Hybrid agencies find their voice in a dialectic that does not seek cultural supremacy and sovereignty. They deploy the partial culture from which

they emerge to construct visions of community, and versions of historic
memory, that give narrative form to the minority positions they occupy; the
outside of the inside: the part in the whole.

Teach me the right steps

During my fieldwork with Mountview I was able to collect several examples of
the ways the sporting practice – including time spent on the pitch before and
after games and training sessions – functions as a pedagogical arena for young
people. I am not referring here simply to the acquisition of sporting skills, but
rather moments in which young people are free to navigate autonomously and
creatively through their respective ethnic and social backgrounds, giving life to
forms of transcultural belonging, and spontaneously giving utterance to the rhi-
zomorphic principle evocated by Deleuze and Guattari. According to the French
philosophers, 'to be rhizomorphous is to produce stems and filaments that seem
to be roots, or better yet connect with them by penetrating the trunk, but put
them to new uses' (Deleuze and Guattari 1988 [1980]: 15).

The sporting practice, in this case the game of football, offers a contested site
and arguably a language through which to communicate (Biesta *et al.* 2001).
The boys create what Back defines as 'Cultural Intermezzo', a time and setting at
which 'young people interact within multicultural peer groups' (Back 1996:
245). This does not happen in a vacuum, though. In the words of Back:

> In this space a transformation in meaning can take place as symbols and
> identities are re-made. However, the content and quality of these liminal
> cultures are dependent on the social context (community discourses and
> the racial and ethnic balance of peer groups) and the pressures that are
> placed on it from outside (racial discourses and the existence of racial
> inequality).
>
> (1996: 245)

In the previous section I demonstrated how Patrick 'taught' some of his Irish
teammates something about his roots. I now turn to Ollie, a white Irish boy
who, besides playing for Mountview, produced and privately recorded rap music.
Despite being a member of Willie's team for a few years, Ollie was not a regular
in the squad. He would disappear for a month or two and then return, play a
game or sit on the bench and then disappear again. He did not seem very committed to the game, but he was good friends with some of the players, such as
Kevin and Paul. Quite surprisingly for a young rapper, he did not show interest
in dressing in a particular fashion. He usually wore tracksuit and runners like
everybody else, and sported the same haircut as his Irish peers. He told me that
his favourite rapper was Eminem but he also loved 50 Cent and other *gangsta*
rappers from the USA. Sitting on the sideline of the pitch during a game – he
was a substitute that day – he once explained to me that he had started writing

lyrics because he was bullied at school.[12] Following his father's advice, he first wrote about the experience of being bullied and learnt he was quite good at writing rhymes. He used tracks of famous rappers and recorded his voice over them on his computer, in his room. His CDs would sometimes be played in Willie's car. I asked him a few times to burn a CD with his songs for me. He promised he would, so I gave him a blank CD but he never brought it back. At some point of the season he left the team for good.

On one occasion, I witnessed Ollie teaching hip hop dance steps to some of his black teammates. They were all waiting for the van to collect them and take them to an away game. As usual, most of the boys were listening to music through their mobile phones. James started to dance to a tune they apparently all knew, but his steps appeared uncertain. Junior and Patrick tried them as well with little success, while Hussein, Charlo, and Ollie observed the scene, quite amused. Suddenly Ollie, the only white boy in the group, jumped in and showed them the right way to dance. He took the scene with the authority that Kevin would show on the football pitch. It was a surprising transcultural dialogue made real before my eyes. A white Irish boy, who had never lived outside of his country of origin, taught black boys of various African backgrounds, who had lived in more than one country in different continents, dance steps inspired by a music movement originated from African-Americans. What does this convey about 'culture' and youth identities? 'Children are the first and most ferocious students of culture', writes MacDougall (2006: 144). And further, 'they move within society as witnesses and agents, constantly re-imagining and modifying it' (MacDougall 2006: 144). Ollie was interpreting hip hop moves and passing them on to his teammates of African background who would eventually make them their own. During my time with the Mountview boys, I witnessed a good few moments such as these. As previously noted, it was often music, not necessarily football, that facilitated such transcultural exchanges: music copied from phone to phone, usually 'black' music, particularly hip hop and R&B. Yet music, as football, presents young people with imaginaries.

Imaginaries travel around the world carried by people and cultural products and they bring with themselves new and hybrid definitions of identity that can also challenge conceptualisations of 'national' culture. Salazar believes that 'imaginaries travel through a multitude of channels, including people, and provide the cultural material to be drawn upon and used for the creation of translocal connections' (Salazar 2010: 55). Ollie, James and the rest of the boys were often spontaneously experimenting with 'cultures', appropriating and giving, drawing from their backgrounds and skills, like unpredictable agents of diversity. In the next chapter I return to these questions examining the exchanges between white immigrant boys from Eastern Europe with black African teenagers. But before doing that, however, I will have to look into a tragic event that altered the setting of my study, and modified the group dynamics at Mountview and beyond.

Notes

1 The boy of Chinese descent left the team after a few weeks to focus on boxing, his main sport. I later visited the Mulhuddart Boxing Academy, where he trained, and found that about 30 per cent of the young athletes, aged 10–17, were of immigrant background, mainly from Eastern Europe.
2 A rental contract had been signed between the club and the Town Council for the use of dressing rooms and the indoor sports hall during the winter.
3 As of July 2012, in the Dublin & District Schoolboys League there were seven leagues for the Under-13s (from F to Premier), six for the Under-14s, five for the Under-15s, and only three respectively for Under-16s, Under-17s and Under-18s, www.a2zsoccer.com/Results andFixtures/NDSL11Aside.aspx [accessed 3 July 2012].
4 In the new season the team competed in the Under-14 league.
5 According to the DDSL Competition Rules (point 5): 'The players' names including substitutes must be entered in accordance with instructions on Referee's Card. The Referee's Card must be filled in before the start of the match by the official in charge of the team who shall certify as to the eligibility of his team', www.ddsl.ie/index.php?option=com_content&view=article&id=90&Itemid=97 [accessed 6 July 2012]).
6 Amendments to Player Registration Rules, DDSL, 2832, June, 2012, (www.ddsl.ie/index.php?limitstart=5 [accessed 20 July 2012]). The Rules were further amended in 2014 with the introduction of an electronic centralised registration system, www.ddsl.ie/homepage.aspx?oid=1015&ct=dl [accessed 15 August 2018].
7 According to the Health Service Executive (2008), 33 per cent of those working in the medical/dental field are from overseas as are 14 per cent of nurses and midwives (www.hse.ie/eng/services/Publications/services/SocialInclusion/National_Intercultural_Health_Strategy_2007_-_2012.pdf [accessed 1 November 2012]). The Irish health service has the highest number of foreign-trained doctors among OECD countries (*Irish Times*, 15 October 2015).
8 Refugee holders of the travel document issued by Irish Naturalisation and Immigration Service might need a visa to travel to certain countries. A refugee's children need to apply for their own document. Each document has an administration fee of €80, www.citizensinformation.ie/en/moving_country/asylum_seekers_and_refugees/refugee_status_and_leave_to_remain/travel_documents_for_refugees.html [accessed 3 July 2018].
9 According to the FAI Intercultural Plan: 'there are two distinct routes for dealing with inappropriate language and behaviour: (1) Challenge the individual directly; (2) Report the incident to the authority or person who is charged with dealing with it' (www.fai.ie/sites/default/files/atoms/files/FAI%20Best%20Practice%20A5%206p%2088831.pdf w.fai.ie/images/stories/pdf/intercultural/FAI_Best_Practice_-_Language.pdf [accessed 25 July 2018]).
10 *Dublin People*, 16 February 2010.
11 On one occasion Mick arrived at the sporting ground wearing a short beard. Apart from the oldest member of the club, none of the men had a beard. Willie commented that Mick looked like me. Mick smiled and said that he actually looked more like Ryan Giggs (the Manchester United player), who had recently started wearing a greyish beard.
12 This resonates with Eminem's personal biography, which was partly transposed into a successful film in 2002, 8 *mile*.

References

Anderson, S. (2003). 'Bodying forth a room for everybody: Inclusive recreational badminton in Copenhagen'. In N. Dyck and F. Archetti (eds), *Sport, dance and embodied identities*. Oxford: Berg, 23–53.

Armstrong, G. and Giulianotti, R. (eds) (1997). *Entering the field. New perspectives on world football*. Oxford: Berg.

Armstrong, G. and Mitchell, J. (2008). *Global and local football*. London: Routledge.

Back, L. (1996). *New ethnicities and urban culture: Racisms and multiculture in young lives*. London: UCL Press.

Berger, J. (1972). *Ways of seeing*. London: BBC/Penguin.

Bhabha, H. (1996). 'Culture's in-between'. In S. Hall and P. du Gay (eds), *Questions of cultural identity*. London: Sage, 53–60.

Biesta, G. J. J., Stams, M., Dirks, E., Rutten, E. A., Veugelers, W. and Schuengel, C. (2001). 'Does sport make a difference? An exploration of the impact of sport on the social integration of young people'. In J. Steenbergen, P. de Knop and A. Elling (eds), *Values and norms in sport*. Oxford: Meyer & Meyer Sport, 95–113.

Bourdieu, P. (1977). *Outline of a theory of practice*. Cambridge: Cambridge University Press.

Bourdieu, P. (1978). 'Sport and social class'. *Social Science Information*, 17(6), 819–840.

Brown, S. (2017). 'Introduction: Youth sport and social capital'. *Sport in Society*, published online 9 May 2017, 1–18. DOI: https://doi.org/10.1080/14681811.2017.1322755.

Carrington, B. (2008). '"What's the footballer doing here?" Racialized performativity, reflexivity, and identity'. *Cultural Studies Critical Methodologies*, 8(4), 423–452.

Clifford, J. (1997). *Routes. Travel and translations in the late 20th century*. Cambridge, MA: Harvard University Press.

Connor, S. (2003). *Youth sport in Ireland*. Dublin: The Liffey Press.

Cuadros, P. (2011). 'We play too. Latina integration through soccer in the "New South"'. *Southeastern Geographies*, 51(2), 227–241.

Curran, C. (2016). 'Irish born players in England's Football Leagues, 1945–2010: An historical and geographical assessment'. In R. McElligot and D. Hassan (eds), *A social and cultural history of sport in Ireland*. London: Routledge, 74–94.

Delaney, L. and Fahey, T. (2005). *Social and economic value of sport in Ireland*. Dublin: The Economic and Social Research Institute.

Deleuze, G. and Guattari, F. (1988 [1980]). *A thousand plateaus. Capitalism and schizophrenia*. London: Athlone Press.

Dolby, N. and Rizvi, F. (eds) (2008). *Youth moves. Identities and education in global perspective*. New York: Routledge.

Dyck, N. (2003). 'Embodying success: Identity and performance in children's sport'. In N. Dyck, and E. Archetti (eds), *Sport, dance and embodied identities*. Oxford: Berg, 55–74.

Fahey, T., Delaney, L. and Gannon, B. (2005). *School children and sport in Ireland*. Dublin: The Economic and Social Research Institute.

Fine, G. A. (1987). *With the boys. Little League baseball and preadolescent culture*. Chicago: The University of Chicago Press.

FRA – European Union Agency for Fundamental Rights (2010). *Racism, ethnic discrimination and exclusion of migrants and minorities in sport*. Vienna: European Union Agency for Fundamental Rights.

Giardina, M. (2005). *Sporting pedagogies*. New York: Peter Lang.

Giardina, M. and Donnelly, K. M. (eds) (2008). *Youth culture and sport*. New York: Routledge.

Gilroy, P. (2000). *Between camps*. London: Allen Lane/The Penguin Press.

Giulianotti, R. (2005). *Sport. A critical sociology*. Cambridge: Polity Press.

Hammersley, M. and Atkinson, P. (2007). *Ethnography: Principles in practice*. London: Routledge.

Hargreaves, J. (2007). 'Class divisions'. In A. Tomlinson (ed.), *The sport studies reader*. London: Routledge, 232–235.

Hassan, D. and McCue K. (2011). 'Football, racism and the Irish'. In D. Burdsey (ed.), *Race, ethnicity and football: Persisting debates and emergent issues*. London: Routledge, 50–66.

Hoerder, D., Hebert, Y. and Schmitt, I. (eds) (2005). *Negotiating transcultural lives: Belongings and social capital among youth in comparative perspective*. Toronto: University of Toronto Press.

Hylton, K. (2018). *Contesting 'race' and sport: Shaming the colour line*. London: Routledge.

Knopp Biklen, S. (2007). 'Trouble on memory lane: Adults and self-retrospection in researching youth'. In A. Best (ed.), *Representing youth*. New York: New York University Press, 251–268.

Lalor, K., de Roiste, A. and Devlin, M. (2007). *Young people in contemporary Ireland*. Dublin: Gill & Macmillan.

Lentin, R. and McVeigh, R. (2006). *After optimism? Ireland, racism and globalisation*. Dublin: Metro Eireann Publications.

Long, J., Hylton, K., Dart, J. and Welch, M. (2000). 'Part of the game? An examination of racism in grassroots football'. Report, London: Kick It Out. Available from: http://repository-intralibrary.leedsmet.ac.uk/open_virtual_file_path/i391n534609t/KickItOut.pdf [accessed 17 April 2012].

Loyal, S. (2011a). *Understanding Irish immigration: Capital, state, and labour in a global age*. Manchester: Manchester University Press.

Loyal, S. (2011b). 'Postmodern othering or established-outsiders relations. Understanding the reception and treatment of immigrants in Ireland'. *Cambio*, 1(2), 135–146.

MacDougall, D. (2006). *The corporeal image. Film, ethnography and the senses*. Princeton: Princeton University Press.

Mauro, M. (2018). 'Tackling racism and discrimination in grassroots sport: The case of football'. In D. Hassan and C. Acton (eds), *Sport and contested identities*. London: Routledge, 228–244.

McGovern, P. (2000). 'The Irish brawn drain: English league clubs and Irish footballers, 1946–1995'. *British Journal of Sociology*, 51(3), 401–418.

Munck, R. (2007). 'Social class and inequality'. In S. O'Sullivan (ed.), *Contemporary Ireland. A sociological map*. Dublin: UCD Press, 301–317.

Ni Laoire, C., Carpena-Mendez, F., Tyrrel, N. and White, A. (2011). *Childhood and migration in Europe*. London: Ashgate.

Priest, N. (2016). 'How do you talk to kids about racism?'. *The Conversation*. Available from: http://theconversation.com/how-do-you-talk-to-kids-about-racism-68160 [accessed 1 June 2018].

Rosbrook-Thomson, J. (2012). *Sport, difference and belonging: Conceptions of human variation in British sport*. London: Routledge.

Salazar, N. B. (2010). 'Towards an anthropology of cultural mobilities'. *Crossing: Journal of Migration and Culture*, 1(1), 53–68.

Stoller, P. (1997). *Sensuous scholarship*. Philadelphia, PA: University of Pennsylvania Press.

Swanson, L. (2009). 'Soccer fields of cultural [re]production: Creating "good boys" in suburban America'. *Sociology of Sport Journal*, 26, 404–424.

Tyler, K. (2011). 'New ethnicities and old classities: Respectability and diaspora'. *Social Identities: Journal for the Study of Race, Nation and Culture*, 17(4), 523–542.

Walseth, K. (2006). 'Sport and belonging'. *International Review for the Sociology of Sport*, 41(3), 447–464.

Webb, J., Schirato, T. and Danaher, G. (2002). *Understanding Bourdieu*. London: Sage.

White, R., Silk, M. L. and Andrews, D. L. (2008). 'The Little League World Series: Spectacle of youthful innocence or spectre of the American New Right?'. In Giardina, M. and Donnelly, M. K. (eds), *Youth culture and sport*. New York: Routledge, 13–34.

Willis, P. (1977). *Learning to labour. How working class kids get working class jobs*. Aldershot: Gower.

Woods, C., Moyla, N., Quinlan A., Tannehill, D. and Walsh, J. (2010). *The children's sport participation and physical activity study*. Dublin: Irish Sports Council. Available from: www4.dcu.ie/shhp/downloads/CSPPA.pdf [accessed 20 November 2012].

Chapter 4

The death of a black teenager

On the evening of 4 April 2010 I received the following text message from Ken McCue, international officer of Sport Against Racism Ireland (SARI): 'There'll be a gathering at 2pm tomoro at Boulevard Mount Eustace in Tyrrelstown in memory of 15yr old Toyosi Shitta-bey who died yesterday. Please inform others'. Earlier that morning I had read on the internet the news about a fatal stabbing in a Blanchardstown neighbourhood. However, the online version of the *The Irish Times* included at that time only a succinct report on the tragic event, with no details about the name, ethnic or national origin of the victim.

> Teenager dies following stabbing
> A TEENAGER has died following a stabbing in Dublin yesterday evening.
> The 16-year-old received a number of stab wounds in the Tyrellstown area at around 8.10pm yesterday. He was taken to Connolly Hospital where he died a short time later. Gardaí at Blanchardstown arrested two males in connection with the incident. They are being detained at Blanchardstown Garda station. Gardaí are appealing for witnesses to contact Blanchardstown Garda Station on 01 666700.[1]

Although the Blanchardstown area was not new to dreadful stories, this news left me shocked and it lingered in my head for the rest of the day. Right after receiving his message I called Ken. He told me that Toyosi Shitta-bey was born in Nigeria and had moved with his family to Ireland at the age of four. He also mentioned that the two men arrested in connection to the event were white Irish adults, two brothers of 23 and 38 years of age. The boy was known to Ken because he had been a member of Insaka, a football team recently founded with his help in Blanchardstown and run by two Nigerian former professional players. As later reports would confirm, football was a central interest in the life of the young boy – most of the newspapers published pictures of him in football uniform.

The story now appeared in a different light. It was not simply about the death of a teenager, but about the death of a boy of African background by the hands of two white Irish men.[2] Despite the silence around issues of race from authorities and most media, members of the African communities and Irish anti-racism organisations immediately raised the question of a possible racial motivation in the killing of Toyosi.[3] The boy was a schoolmate and good friends of some of the players of the Mountview team I had been following for the past year.

In this chapter I first focus my attention on the implications this story had for my ethnographic inquiry into the football practice of adolescents of immigrant background living in the Dublin 15 district. At a time when I was about to conclude my fieldwork with Mountview FC, I found myself presented with the unexpected opportunity to follow another team, Insaka, with which the young victim had started playing football. I could then examine some of my research issues from a different perspective – that of a team composed only of immigrant players and run by immigrant coaches – while exploring new questions that would arise from this setting. Among the issues addressed in the discussion that follows are the challenges of setting up and running a team focused mainly on boys of immigrant background and the various ways in which cultural belonging is constructed within such a team.

Toyosi Shitta-bey: death of a 'Blanch-Boy'

The week after the tragic death of the boy, Mountview FC planned a trip to England to attend a Manchester United game. The Mountview officials had been working on this for a while with the aim of bringing as many young players as possible. For most of the young players, this was their first time at a Premier League game. I asked if I could join them and Mick said the board would have to discuss it, because only coaches and club staff were supposed to take part in the trip. Willie argued I could act as his 'third assistant coach', a fictitious role but revealing of my position within the sporting community of the club. My name was eventually added to the list as one of the adult mentors.[4]

I had been looking forward to the trip and was excited by the opportunity to spend a few days away with many of the participants in my study. However, when the day arrived my mood was low. The same day the game between Blackburn Rovers and Manchester United took place, and all the Mountview group including me were sitting in the stands of Ewood Park, the Blackburn Rovers FC stadium, in Dublin around two thousand people were marching in memory of Toyosi Shitta-bey and 'for a tolerant society, free of racism' (Figure 4.1).[5] I wondered if I should have been there instead.

Looking at it from an ethnographic point of view, my participation in the trip, and the kind of role I was assigned to play, made me feel more an 'insider' than an 'outsider' in the group. Towards the end of the first football season spent with Mountview I had been informally asked to do certain tasks that were normally assigned to club members. For example, a few times I was linesman. Other times I was asked to help the coach writing the players' list. However, it was only in preparation for the Manchester trip that I fully realised the extent to

Figure 4.1 The rally in memory of Toyosi Shitta-bey, 10 April 2010, Dublin (www.indymedia.ie).

which my 'participation' role might have overtaken the 'observation' role. Moreover, I was invited to spend the night before our departure at Willie's house, so I did not have to take a taxi in the middle of the night to be there at the departure time of 6 a.m. Despite all this, I was overwhelmed by a sense of confusion and bewilderment. It seemed unlikely to me that the boys would enjoy a weekend away in the name of football while one of their peers who was so passionate about the game had just lost his life in such tragic circumstances.

On the morning of the departure from the parking lot beside 'the shops' only Charlie, out of the seven black players in the team, turned up. I knew that some of them were keen to participate, as they had expressed their interest to me. Apparently, their families had not paid the fee on time. But there was also the question of the legal status of the boys. Almost all of them were living in Ireland under the asylum scheme, which restricted their mobility abroad. Charlie's mother had unsuccessfully submitted a visa request to the British Embassy for her son. The club stepped in to help and eventually the boy was allowed to take part in the three-day trip. On the bus, and for most of the time during the trip, Charlie wore a T-shirt with Toyosi's face and his dates of birth and death. The T-shirt had been printed by Toyosi's friends and had been worn by many of them, both male and female, black and white, Irish and immigrants, on the day of the funeral. I would get used to seeing it worn by the Insaka players on different occasions. This emotional trace of the tragic event travelled with us to Manchester.

On the ferry, I tried to talk about this with some of the adults, as a way to ease my inner tension and to get a better understanding of the story, but there was reluctance to address the question. One man, however, was not afraid to speak in a defensive tone about the two brothers who had been arrested, claiming that some details of what had happened were still not clear. I listened to his words but I could not pay attention. To me, the story did not need many details to be understood. A 15-year-old boy had died following an altercation with two adults. Moreover, there were elements to support the suspicion his death had been racially motivated: the man accused of manslaughter (later upgraded to murder) had previously been convicted for a racist attack that had taken place in the Dublin city centre in 2001. Out of respect for the sub-judice rule, this fact was not mentioned in any journalistic report about Toyosi's death, but it was widely shared on social media.[6]

If, by assigning me the role of mentor, I was made to feel part of the group, and of the community, after talking to the man on the ferry I was made to feel like an outsider again – someone who cannot understand everything, how things *really* happened, because he is not from this place. I was promptly sent back to my observer/ethnographer role. This was a disjointing feeling, because it presented me with the recurring issue of belonging, something that resonates with my own biography. I was somehow made to feel like one of Sebald's emigrants (Sebald 2002), witnesses of the fragility of sentimental attachment to places and nations. Ethnography can produce strong feelings of participation, and unsettling emotions, in a way that is impossible to pre-determine.

After returning from the Manchester trip I attended a few more games of the Mountview team but I could sense that my time with them was over. 'When does the fieldwork terminate?' I had been asking myself for a while. There is an obvious element of necessity in this decision: the fieldwork had to be completed within the limits of the doctoral programme, leaving me time to write the thesis. But this is only part of the answer. In fact, the ethnographer has to consider if his/her presence in the field is still accepted or indeed whether s/he has become too familiar to the setting, and if there is more to learn and understand. From the researcher point of view, as argued by Hammersley and Atkinson, the decision to leave the field is not easy, for 'there is always something new to discover, unforeseen events to investigate, unpredictable outcomes to follow, and so on; but the line has to be drawn somewhere' (Hammersley and Atkinson 2007: 91).

In my last weeks with Willie's team I never heard anyone mentioning Toyosi, but I could observe a definite change in the behaviour of most of the black boys. Hussein departed before Easter (soon after Toyosi's death – was there a correlation?) and did not return. Patrick cried following a small argument with the assistant coach – this indicated an unusual loss of control, as crying was a taboo in the group. Junior had a surprisingly angry reaction after being substituted during a match: he left the ground without saying a word, walking home before the end of the game. Charlie became closer to James; they would arrive at the pitch and leave it together, something that did not happen before. James left

Mountview during the summer to join Insaka, the first team Toyosi had played for. All these changes appeared to me to be influenced by the circumstances of Toyosi's death – they somehow altered the conditions in which the teenage boys of African background practised their football. Partly for this reason, after the trip I felt I could not progress further with my research. A line had been drawn before my eyes by an unexpected event. Ethnographers may experience a sense of relief when they leave the field, because it means they can focus on the writing and speed up the completion of their project. But in my case, relief was mixed with a feeling of perplexity and inner confusion.

From one team to another – a serendipitous journey

When I decided to attend the gathering in memory of Toyosi, which took place just two days after his death, I did not know that that was going to be the first step of a new stage in my research. That afternoon, getting on the bus to Tyrrelstown, I was reacting like other Dublin residents, both Irish and non-Irish, who were touched by the story and were willing to express their grief, as many did, attending the gathering, the funeral and the rally. However, there was something related to my research which I could not avoid thinking about. The boy had lived in Blanchardstown, he was of immigrant background and had been a passionate football player. Had the boy not had any of these traits, would it have made a difference to me? Was I so overwhelmed by my research endeavour to the point of not honestly accepting the fact that I was going to Tyrrelstown *also* out of sheer curiosity about the location, the people, the events?

I now realise that the not-forgotten journalist in me somehow influenced my decision to go – to see if there was something I could learn from this story. Journalists are often portrayed as cynical observers of reality. This is how they emerge out of Waugh's classic novel *Scoop* (2000 [1938]), and the title of reporter and writer Richard Kapuscinski's book of reflections on journalism, *A cynic doesn't suit this profession* (Kapuscinski 2000; translation mine), sounds openly provocative in this regard. I am not claiming here that scholarship per se excludes cynicism, the truth could not be further from this claim. But certain non-journalistic forms of writing and knowledge production allow for reflexivity and self-criticism – something journalism is not renowned for (Beckett 2013). The process of writing ethnographies as 'partial truths' (Clifford 1986: 18), for example, is among other things an exercise in reflexivity. To honestly look at my background and to the ways it might affect my researcher's gaze is part of the exercise as a reflexive practitioner (Bourdieu 1990) – an exercise which helps to clear the view for the writer as well as for the reader.

At the gathering I met with Ken. About 300 people had turned up. As we silently walked through the circular streets of this new settlement, the most recent development in Blanchardstown, I thought how strange it was I had never set foot there before.[7] It seemed an experiment in urban planning: parallel series of neat two-storey terraced houses separated from the narrow street by flowerbeds. Toyosi had lost his life on the street, a few metres from the houses, and now at that place there were flowers, written messages and a Shelbourne FC's scarf (Shelbourne was the club for which Toyosi was playing at the time of his death). We met Elisha, a young SARI (Sport Against Racism Ireland) volunteer and college student originally from Zimbabwe. Ken had introduced me to him early in my research, and he had been a helpful informant about issues of youth sport, immigration and racism in Ireland. We had been regularly in touch for a while but less after I started my fieldwork with Mountview. We met again on this tragic occasion. Ken updated me about Insaka. He asked me if I was interested in attending one of their games, so he could introduce me to the manager, or to visit the team at their training ground. He believed it was important to document the life of such an original team and to show support for the boys, who, according to him, were experiencing racism on and off the pitch. I said I would, for I felt it was important to do it. And not only for the progression of my study.

The 'squatted' pitch and the regulated game

Insaka trained in a half-built all-weather pitch located in Ongar, on the northern fringes of Dublin's suburban landscape. Beside the pitch there was a construction site. On the other side of the road from the pitch there was a big field where two little horses ran, apparently free, maybe abandoned.[8] Bordering the field and the road was an unfinished housing development – its residential access way partly paved and with a long string of street lamps with no lamps in them. Both the unfinished pitch and the housing development vividly narrated the epilogue of the Irish property boom, defined by O'Toole (2009: 101) as 'the loudest in Europe, if not in the world'. During the boom years, from 1996 and 2006, most of the growth took place in the areas around Dublin, especially in Fingal County, where Blanchardstown is located. When the recession started to hit hard, and buyers disappeared, many developers left houses and everything that came along with them unfinished. Some companies simply went bankrupt. The 'ghost estates' soon became a new trait of the Irish urban and suburban landscape and in 2010 it was estimated that there were more than 620 'ghost estates' and thousands of empty houses throughout Ireland (O'Callaghan et al. 2014). Paradoxically, the unfinished pitch where Insaka trained was located in a part of town where lack of facilities and infrastructure was an ongoing problem.

The pitch was surrounded by high fences, but there were several holes through them. Debris of different kinds occupied the area before the main 'entrance' to the pitch: plastic bottles, pieces of wood, a heap of dirty sand, a plastic flush toilet, some odd shoes (Figure 4.2). The artificial pitch had a number of burned spots. There were no goalposts. It seemed probable that local youth had broken into the pitch and made it theirs, for different uses.

Figure 4.2 The entrance to the all-weather pitch. Ongar, June 2010.

The training had not begun, the coaches had yet to arrive, but the young players were already there, some lying on the ground and chatting or listening to music from their phones, others joyfully kicking a deflated ball. As I would learn in the following months, the pitch was not only used by Insaka as their training ground but was, more than anything else, a place of gathering and refuge for local youth, regardless of their diverse origins. Often, after the Saturday training session, while the team members were leaving the pitch, other younger boys would arrive there with their own ball and start a game. During the summer, twice a week, a varying number of teenage boys gathered at the pitch for the Insaka training. As a matter of fact, they would spend more time there than that dedicated to the training session – sometimes arriving early and often leaving late. This meant I could use this extra time to engage with the players and to get to know them better. It was so that I came to know Ciprian and Adrian, two Romanian boys, Benni, from South-Africa, Mariusz, from Poland, Fredy, from Angola, and Yano, born in Germany from Angolan and Congolese parents. This spontaneous appropriation of public space by teenagers, and its use to play football or simply to hang out together, can be seen as an act of freedom from the control of the adults. In Sennet's (1990: 195) words:

> A game of basketball played among loading docks is not like a game played in the family driveway. Kids in an urban playground cut themselves off in play from ties to their home and family; they shun the nice places adults made for them. In these places a conscious fiction is also at work. Kids at the 'hot' playground behave as if they were parentless, totally free agents.

To some extent all kids play with each other by behaving in this way, but city kids find places where they behave without challenge as though fiction were fact, that there was no reality before right here, right now.

The level of spontaneous socialisation taking place at the 'squatted' pitch reminded me also of the football games that recur in Pier Paolo Pasolini's novels and short stories.[9] For Pasolini, football played in improvised pitches, on streets or vacant lots, by improvised teams, was an expression of a popular culture, in particular of working class youth and of the *lumpenproletariat* that was rapidly vanishing under the pressure of massive consumer culture.[10] Nowadays 'street football' is not so commonly seen in western European cities anymore. In the last 20 years, there has been a decline in unsupervised games paralleled by 'the increasing professionalization, the seriousness and the organization of youth sport' (Connor 2003: 68; see also Lusted and O'Gorman 2010; Ellis and Sharma 2014). 'Street football' – a definition that encompasses a variety of styles of football played in informal situations – has even become a regulated game put at the centre of an international 'sport-based intervention programme aimed at combating social exclusion of homeless people' (Magee and Jeanes 2011: 3).

As noted in the previous chapters, much of the discussion about children and youth sport practices highlights the role of adults – be they parents or coaches/educators – as regulators and controllers (Fine 1987; Anderson 2003; Dyck 2003; Simpson 2005; Smith and Green 2005; Giardina 2005; Swanson 2009) and according to Dyck (2003: 58), 'playing fields and other venues of community sport have in certain respects been designated as extensions of domestic space'. Within these environs, he argues, 'operate notions of socialization that tend to view children as vulnerable and incomplete persons who need to be moulded, directed and completed by parents and other tutors' (Dyck 2003: 58). The 'squatted' pitch in Ongar prompted a diverging reality, one where adolescents claimed an urban space for themselves and eventually 'let' adults make use of it. Both the young players and the Insaka club officials could be considered 'intruders' in this abandoned place, but to some extent the adults would be the real intruders, because they were entering and making use of a place informally owned by young people. In the hands of these teenagers, against an unsettling backdrop, belonging assumed uncanny forms which demanded new analytical attention.

A different role for the ethnographer

During the summer months, Insaka trained regularly twice a week. On the one hand, as James used to say, this was a way 'to keep the boys busy', since most of them did not have the possibility to go on holiday or leave Ireland to visit their families in their countries of origin. There were usually between 20 to 30 young players from different African national backgrounds (Nigeria, DR Congo, Angola, South African, Ivory Coast) and several Eastern European ones

(Poland, Romania, Russia, Kazakhstan, Lithuania). On the other hand, James and his assistant Zuby made clear to me that this was not merely 'play': throughout the summer sessions they would select the players who would form the squad for the new season.

As happened with my previous fieldwork, I soon started wondering who would become the central characters of my research. One was probably going to be Ken, my main gatekeeper. James and Zuby, with their fascinating personal biographies, also attracted such attention. James had played professionally in Germany and Ireland, while Zuby has spent his brief career in Nigeria and Poland. Finally, I would have to single out some of the young players. Most of them were friendly with me and showed an interest in the camera, asking me questions about what I was doing and why I was doing it. The catalytic effect of the camera (Rouch 2003) proved evident again. I explained that for the purpose of my study I intended to film moments in the life of the team, including matches, training sessions, and interviews. They were all aged between 16 and 18, older than the Mountview players, and displayed more self-confidence. They seemed less inhibited in asking me questions and generally in dealing with adults. Nevertheless, I was aware of the fact that their interest in me would fade at some point and I would have to negotiate a different kind of relationship. I was intrigued by the white boys' participation in a team composed mostly of Africans. At the same time, I tried to create a dialogue with all the players, to see how the group worked as a group and above all if, given the novelty of the team and the precariousness of the setting, they truly worked as a group at all (Alexander 2002).

The way I was introduced to the coaches, under particular circumstances, put me in a different position than the one I had found myself at Mountview. The first time I attended an Insaka away game, in late April 2010, Zuby had thanked me for being there: 'Thank you for coming, thank you', he said. This confirmed my perception that, in this case, there was more at stake than a research project. My presence at the game as a white, educated, non-Irish man, with a video camera, was probably deemed of particular value. My adult gatekeepers were expecting me to document the daily challenges that a team like theirs was facing. The two coaches were also pleased to have some recognition of their work. The fact that I had a camera with me certainly helped to build rapport, since, as noted by Crang and Cook (2007: 107), 'it is also the case that a researcher carrying a camera can take on what, for many, is an acceptable and understandable role of the person who "documents" things'.

An article published in *Metro Eireann*, gave me an insight into the life of Insaka and helped me make better sense of Zuby's special welcome. In its title the article made explicit mention both of the recent death of Toyosi Shitta-bey and racism. This is how the story was presented:

> According to manager of Insaka FC James Igwilo, one of its players was racially abused by a member of the opposing side during an under-18 NDSL

game last Sunday against Ratoath Harps. Igwilo, a former professional footballer from Nigeria, told Metro Eireann that his team of mostly African-
born players are regularly on the receiving end of racist remarks from the
opposition, though 'not in all games'. The manager said feelings among his
teenage players are running high in the wake of 15-year-old Shitta-bey's
killing.[11]

'Is this team for everybody?'

The club was run and funded by James, Ken, acting as honorary secretary of the
club, Zuby, and Kennedy, a friend of James who had also played professionally in
Germany before migrating to Ireland. Usually, after the training, I would follow
them to a Nigerian restaurant located in an industrial area alongside other commercial activities run by immigrants. This was one of the various locations through
which my ethnographic journey with Insaka would take place. From the beginning
my ethnographic endeavour appeared multi-sited and multi-locale (Marcus 1995,
2009; Gille 2001; Falzon 2009). At the same time, my fieldwork was often made of
'travel encounters' (Clifford 1997). The act of travelling, of moving from one site
and another, from a not-so-distant home of the ethnographer to where the participants lived and operated, and the act of travelling with them from one site to
another of their cultural activity (running the team), became key elements of my
research practice. In Clifford's words, 'The materiality of travel, in and out the
field, becomes more apparent, indeed constitutive of the object/site of study'
(Clifford 1997: 68). My research sites included the Ongar pitch; the county-owned
and -rented ground where Insaka played its official games, located in another Blanchardstown neighbourhood; the Nigerian restaurant, called KKK; the houses of
some of the protagonists; the many locations of away games, in and out of Dublin;
the SARI office in the Dublin city centre; and obviously the cars and buses I would
regularly travel in along with my participants.[12]

    In KKK we would eat Nigerian dishes, cooked the Igbo way, since the owner
shared this ethnicity with many of the men I happened to meet there. We
would drink beer imported from Nigeria. One brand of beer was Star, a popular
Nigerian lager, and another one was, to my bewilderment, Guinness. One of the
first times I was with them at the restaurant James handed me his bottle of
Guinness and invited me to read the label. It was produced in Lagos, Nigeria's
largest city and its former capital, and had a higher alcohol content than regular
Irish Guinness (7.5 per cent against 4 per cent). 'The biggest Guinness brewery
is in Lagos, not in Dublin', he said with a large smile. In fact, Nigeria happens
to consume more Guinness than Ireland, but to find the most famous Irish stout
beer imported from Africa to Dublin seemed an example of the unpredictable
translocated connections created by migration. To James, the bottle of Guinness reminded him of Nigeria, while to many people around the world Guinness
is strongly associated with 'things Irish' – what better example of the surprising
'social life of things' (Appadurai 1986) in the era of globalisation?

KKK was most of all a place for football fans. A big TV screen was hung high on the wall at the centre of the room and, at weekends, Premier League games were broadcast throughout the day. It was here, sitting at a table with food and beers, with the pervasive background noise of broadcast matches and the piercing look of Muhammad Ali supervising the scene from a big poster hung on the wall, that the men running Insaka had their meetings. My presence with the camera was easily accepted, so I took advantage of it shooting what I initially regarded as video-fieldnotes (Postma and Crawford 2006). On one of these occasions, towards the end of my first season, I captured a rich discussion about the motto 'All Africa' that originally accompanied the name of the club. 'Should we leave it or take it out?' was the question being discussed by James, Zuby, Ken and Kennedy. This was a revelatory moment because I was witnessing the tension between the idea behind the team and what actually came out of it. Insaka means 'a place to gather' in Bemba, one of the languages spoken in Zambia. It was first adopted as a name for a football team by Ken, who had invited an 'All Africa' representative (meaning of the African immigrant communities living in Ireland) to take part in one of the first editions of the annual SARI Soccer Fest.[13]

More recently, Ken had supported James's desire to start a youth team with the aim of nurturing 'African talent' and they had given this team the same name. Insaka AFC was eventually registered in the Under-18 North Dublin Schoolboys League. Unfortunately, a team composed mostly of African boys and some white immigrants appeared not to be appreciated by the local authorities and the main Irish football body. In a meeting James and Zuby held with Fingal County Council and FAI representatives, they were invited to change the profile of their team, to try to make it more 'open', this being the word they reported to me that was used. Insaka had initially asked for a meeting with the County Council to seek financial help or the use of a training pitch in the area; they were denied both requests and they were invited to reconsider the nature of their project. For training, they had no other option than to 'adopt' the Ongar discarded pitch. The discussion at KKK took place the weekend after that meeting. The following excerpts of the discussion explain the question under consideration:

KEN: Did you see the team playing next door to us? They are called Pro Italia, but nobody ever complains to them.[14]

KENNEDY: But they are all Italians, we are not all Africans.

KEN: No, they are not all Italians, they have Spanish and Irish playing for the team. But how come nobody has a problem with 'all Europeans'? And then, the fact that is called All Africa it doesn't mean that only Africans are playing, a style of football. The problem we are facing is that they say 'look all those African are playing' but we can prove we have Polish, Romanians – we can also have Irish playing in our team.

ZUBY: You see the game we play against these teams, it is very clear that is something else, it's total football. Based on that I am suggesting that we should take out the 'All Africa', so that when we have a meeting with the FAI they cannot say it's All Africans. It's equal, it's for everybody.

JAMES: We are not removing the 'All Africa' because of the FAI. Maybe at the end of it they won't give us any help.

KENNEDY: Don't you think that 'All Africa' prevent us from getting some things?

KEN: What about the Polish and Romanian kids? It hasn't stopped them to participate … It's because of the type and quality of football that those kids want to play. They don't see the all thing around 'All Africa'. But if you want to take it out from the letterhead it's okay.

JAMES: Most of the players when they call me they ask: is it for everybody? That's the first thing they ask. Because they say they've heard it's only for Africans … And when I'm looking for sponsorship they ask me 'Is this only for Africans?' 'No.' 'And why you say is only for Africans?' I say it's just the brand name but it is open for people … What I'm trying to say … it doesn't matter, it might be all Africans that will be in the team, that is our main target, and they will be the greatest percentage because that is the only people who play the kind of football we are introducing.[15]

This above discussion reflected an ongoing issue during the 14 months I spent with the team and one that was interpreted in different ways by the protagonists. Eventually, the 'All Africa' motto disappeared from under the club's name, but the question about the identity of the club remained open. Before discussing some of the boys' experience with Insaka, I want to examine the different expectations of the adult informants.

It's not only about football

James and Zuby were both originally from the south-eastern state of Abia and, before moving to Europe, had both played for the most successful Nigerian club, Enyimba FC. However, James had represented Nigeria at junior level, and this was something that gave him enduring status in Nigerian football. This also helped him acquire a special position within the immigrant communities in Irish society, for he was nominated among the 12 'Ambassadors of Dublin Sport 2010', chosen to represent the city in the year Dublin was designated 'European Capital of Sport'. After representing his country at the Men's Under-17 World Cup in Ecuador, in 1995, he was signed by a German club, MSV Duisburg, competing in the second top division of German football. His brief career was affected by injuries, and it ended in Ireland, at the height of the Celtic Tiger. Zuby had been recruited by a Polish club and enrolled in a football academy in Warsaw. He played for a few clubs in Polish lower professional leagues, before leaving the country and focusing on coaching.

James and Zuby were driven by the ambition to build a successful team out of a group of teenagers mostly of African backgrounds, and to gain recognition in

Ireland as competent coaches. Ken had a slightly alternative, but com-plementary, view of the mission of a team such as Insaka. Ken was a long-time vocal advocate for minority rights and anti-racism campaigns in Irish society, and in 1997 he had co-founded Sport Against Racism Ireland (SARI). The organisation promotes a variety of projects, from large-scale events such as the annual SARI Soccer Fest to educational programmes in schools. Highlighting SARI's work resonance with a Critical Race Theory approach, Hylton underlines that

> SARI's work is not just about what happens in the stadium but also about wider issues than sport, on the street, which sometimes takes SARI into highly charged or politically sensitive arenas with immigration depart-ments, the police, and law courts: for SARI, individuals suffering racism need support whether within or beyond sport.
>
> (2009: 244)

It is precisely for this reason that I deemed Ken's role within Insaka particularly interesting. He wrote the introductory notes on Insaka's website, expressing the spectrum of expectations for the club: he wished it to be not simply a youth sport club but a cultural project whose aim is 'to promote youth participation in democratic structures and foster active citizenship in Irish society through culture, sport, education and work'.[16] But how did the implementation of such ambitious socio-political statements work in the face of the daily struggle of a small youth club to endure financially?

One of the collaborative roles I found myself performing with Insaka was that of 'postman'. Ken would often hand me letters for the club that he had received at his inner city address, the club's official address; he would ask me to bring them to James in Blanchardstown. Before handing them to me he would explain or show me their content in detail, so I was made aware of nitty-gritty organisa-tional matters in the club's life. As noted, forms of research collaboration such as this were not unusual during my time with Mountview and Insaka. Marcus (2010: 268) believes that 'working, committed collaborations' are among the key features of fieldwork today. Such collaborations also reveal different power dynamics. According to him:

> One gets caught up in the events of ordinary local life, as always, but one finds there reflexive subjects who stimulate a politics of collaboration neces-sary for ethnography to proceed in a way quite different from the way anthropologists have in the past enrolled subjects in their projects.
>
> (Marcus 2010: 268)

The letters regarded issues such as the annual league registration fee (€360) or the rent for the pitch to be paid to the Fingal County Council (€735, not including pitch line-marking, which cost €140 and had to be done every three or four games because lines would disappear in less than a month). From the beginning, it appeared clear to me that the funding of the club was a problem as big as building a successful team. If it had been quite easy to register a new club in the league, to make the club financially sustainable was a different matter. The club was funded directly by James, Ken, Zuby, and Kennedy, and by the 'subs' paid the young players before every match. However, this source of funding was not fully reliable, as there were often players who did not or could not contribute.

To support the team, Ken arranged a few sponsorship deals. One was with an Irish charity initiative, 'Rebuilding Pakistan', which had been started by members of the Irish-Pakistani community and other Irish organisations to help the victims of the 2010 floods that had left about 14 million people without a house. The logo of the campaign was printed on the front of the new club's kit. The fact that the logo had a crescent at its centre aroused some curiosity in the young players. The day they were presented with the kit, Fredy, the 17-year-old captain, made a sarcastic comment. 'Who came up with this idea?' he said coming towards me and Ken, while the team was getting dressed in the parking lot. 'Was it you?' he ironically asked Ken, who smiled. 'What's the problem?' Ken asked back. 'We are Christians, not Muslims', replied the boy before walking back to his mates. By saying this, Fredy overlooked the fact that in team there were also players of Muslim background, such as the centre-forward Kelechi, whose family was originally from Northern Nigeria. 'Hey, where is your armband, captain? I want to see it, don't wear it upside down, I want to see United Against Racism and to be able to read it', shouted Ken in a joyful tone. This and other episodes made me believe that the boys were only dimly aware of or interested in the club's cultural mission expressed by SARI's involvement. After a while, the players got used to the 'Rebuilding Pakistan' jersey, and the question was not raised again.

Throughout the season, Insaka used two other sets of jerseys which had been provided by Glentoran FC, a historical Northern Irish football club based in a Unionist area of East Belfast. The partnership with Glentoran was something that made Ken particularly proud, as it epitomised an anti-racist approach which holistically addresses different forms of racism and discrimination present in Irish society. As noted by Alana Lentin (2004: 154), 'The connection between racism and the sectarianism brought about by colonialist legacies has contributed to a specifically Irish understanding of the interrelation between various types of discrimination'. At this stage, the relationship with Glentoran consisted not only of the use of their kit but also in visits to Belfast to play friendly matches and the participation in cultural events related to sport and social inclusion. However small it might be, the Insaka-Glentoran partnership was a significant message sent out to the people on both sides of the border. As such, the Insaka-Glentoran partnership was praised also by the Irish Football Association (IFA), based in Belfast.[17]

From the point of view of an observer looking at the intricacies of Irish history, this was a remarkable example of intercultural dialogue between the

North and the South, across the enduring tensions between Catholics/Nationalists and Protestants/Unionists. A Northern-Irish club supported a Republic of Ireland youth team run by African coaches fielding only boys of immigrant backgrounds. In the North Dublin Schoolboys League it did not pass unnoticed that Insaka were wearing jerseys with the colours, and above the symbol the name, of a Northern Irish team. On one occasion, before the beginning of a home game, the referee asked Ken (often club and match officials would approach him first instead of the black coaches, assuming he was the person in charge of the team), if it was a 'Unionist club' jersey they were wearing. Ken smiled and said it was Glentoran, 'the famous Belfast club which was once sup- ported by a young boy called George Best'. How far was this North–South part- nership appreciated by the boys? Most of them admitted they knew little about the history of 'The Troubles', most had not been to Northern Ireland before, and when I travelled with them to Belfast the questions they asked were about the club – How good are they? Are they all professionals? How big is their stadium? – rather than inquiring about the social and political conflicts that had given the city world fame during the previous decades.

As long as you win

In my conversations with the young players I was particularly curious about their motivation in joining Insaka and not one of the other more established youth football clubs operating in the area. Further, what kind of belonging to the local and national community could they develop playing for a team made of and coached by 'non-Irish nationals'? The question of national identities and affiliations in the context of sport, especially in football, assumes particular relevance in Ireland. There is ample literature which deals with sport and pol- itics of identity within and across the two state entities of the divided island (Sugden and Bairner 1993; Cronin 1999; Bairner 2005; Agnew 2010; Free 2010). Scant attention has been given to date, to the potential of young boys and girls of immigrant background who could be recruited by the Republic of Ireland and Northern Ireland national teams (Hassan and McCue 2013; Mauro 2014, 2016).

Once the season started, the white players were usually the first to reach the training pitch. This helped me develop a dialogue with them. Ciprian, one of the two 17-year-old Romanian boys playing for the team, admitted that when he first saw Insaka training in a local park he thought it was only for Africans. Our conversation took place in the Ongar pitch on a Saturday morning, waiting for the training to start. Ciprian and Adrian sat in front of me. Ciprian stressed he had been told about the team by Benni, a schoolmate of South-African back- ground. He explained:

> Benni told me to come down, they were making a team, they were going for trials. I went with some friends, we were just messing because we knew it

was just Nigerians. I asked James, he said it was only Africans, no white people, but now he would say 'no, no I didn't say so' [he laughs]. But then I came here and got into the team and I brought Adrian.

Ciprian had played before for two other local teams. Adrian added other elements about the reasons that attracted them to Insaka:

ADRIAN: It's proper, a proper team. James is good, they keep the ball down.
CIPRIAN: It's proper football.
ADRIAN: They keep the ball down, not like Irish football, they just bang the ball and that's it.
CIPRIAN: Kick it up and that's it.

Mariusz, a 17-year-old boy of Polish background had played for a number of teams before joining Insaka. 'I changed every year. I wanted to do better', he said. He had been invited to join by Fredy, they were in the same school. 'He said they needed a player like me. I like it here because the coaches have great experience and you can learn from them'. Vujadin was a 16-year-old boy originally from Bosnia. He had left his country with his family when he was a child, escaping the Yugoslavian wars, and they were eventually granted asylum in Ireland. He had an experience similar to Mariusz's, having played for three teams before this one and having also been invited by his schoolmate Fredy. 'The last team I played with was disbanded and I had to leave. I like it here because you can learn a lot from James'. For Benni, the reason for joining Insaka was a different one. Growing up in South Africa, his favourite sport was cricket, but since migrating to Ireland with his mother he had not found a cricket team to play with. He said:

Cricket is not that big in this country, they don't support it that much. So I started playing football. It's not working perfectly, it's okay, I am not that bad at football and I'm not that good at football, but you improve with this team, the team it's actually good. Some of them go to my school, some of them I grew up with and my mum knows the coach.

Lukas, originally from Lithuania, was the last player to join the team, and being only 15 he was its youngest member. He was a goalkeeper and James assured him he would certainly improve from playing with older guys. Insaka had an abundance of players in all positions but they were in dire need of a regular keeper, a problem worsened by the lack of goalposts at the training pitch. Lukas had previously played with two other local teams, and he left the last one because, he said, 'I did not get along well with my teammates'. It was possibly for this reason that he liked Insaka. 'There are no Irish here', he commented, 'it makes it more friendly'. However, after one season he went back to his old team.

Jonathan, a 17-year-old boy of Angolan and Congolese background talked about his experience with Insaka in peculiar terms. As with the rest of his mates he had previously played for other clubs, four in total, and eventually had joined this one because other friends did the same. Despite all the problems the team had to face to survive, Insaka was doing well, they were top of the league and this was the most important thing to him. He commented:

> Usually [in previous teams] there were two or three black people and the rest would be white but here it's the other way around. But in the end it's the same, it's just football, as long as you win you don't care, so I don't care who I play with as long as you win.

Jonathan's words are paradoxically challenging. Is it really so that in the final analysis of the story 'it's just football'? Carrington (2010: 4) is critical of 'dominant assumptions about the neutral, benign nature of sport', which can often be found in policy statements by sporting bodies and organisations.[18] He argues:

> It is sport's assumed innocence as a space [in the imagination] and a place [as it physically manifests itself] that is removed from concerns of power, inequality, struggle, and ideology, that has, paradoxically, allowed it be filled with a range of contradictory assumptions that have inevitably spilled back over and into wider society.

If one examines Insaka as a youth club and as group of young people who happen to be all of immigrant background it appears that the reality is just the opposite of what Jonathan's words suggest. For most of the boys it made a difference that they played in a team composed mostly of friends of the same racial background or immigrants like themselves (Rosbrook-Thomson 2012; Long *et al.* 2014). And they chose to play with this team precisely for this reason, because they did not feel 'at home' in other teams. At the same time, some of the black players claimed they had been victims of racial abuse on the football pitch, when they played for other youth clubs. To some extent, this mirrors Bradbury's findings of his study of youth football in Leicester, UK, where he notes: 'BAME [Black Asian and Minority Ethnic] clubs were conceptualised as sites that enabled collective safeguards against the prevalence of racism in the local game' (Bradbury 2011: 74). Fredy argued that 'to play with Insaka is easier because we are of the same culture'. Considering that there were about 10 nationalities represented in the team, was being 'not Irish' enough to share the same culture? Despite the efforts undertaken by the members of Insaka, both players and officials, white Irish boys did not join the team, even though some of them occasionally attended training sessions, invited by schoolmates.

Taking the discussion to another level, that of a youth club run by African coaches competing in an Irish schoolboys' league, it could be argued that Insaka was made to be different by the structural position of its protagonists within the broader context of Irish society. Drawing upon Marx's ontological dialecticism, Andrews and Giardina write:

> It could be argued that people make their own working, leisure, political, religious, and indeed sporting lives but not in the conditions of their own choosing. Rather, they do so under the constraints and opportunities of the particular social location that their working, leisure, political, religious, and sporting lives represent, reproduce, or challenge.
>
> (Andrews and Giardina 2008: 396)

Following this line of thought, one has only to ask, why did Insaka end up training on an abandoned and precarious pitch – something both the sport and civil authorities were aware of and openly allowed?[19] This can be interpreted as an act of resistance and what Hylton (2009: 115) defines as 'informal antiracism'. According to him, 'sport can be used as a site of resistance', and 'often sport acts as an arena in which groups can restate their identities and positions of power that are being negated by racism in other areas of their lives' (Hylton 2009: 115). For Giulianotti (2005: 53), 'resistance' defines 'how subordinate groups challenge domination through cultural practices'. In a sense, this is precisely what Insaka was doing: it was challenging dominant social and racial relations in organised sport and society. In the next chapter I will elaborate further on this, but in the closing sections of this chapter I turn my attention to questions of belonging among the white teenage players. I do so analysing an 'ethnographic event' (Jackson 2005) that showed the potential of the use of the video camera as a means of inquiry when working with youth.

The catalytic role of the camera

Jackson defines an 'ethnography of events' as an ethnography

> [T]hat seeks to explore the interplay of the singular and shared, the private and public, as well as the relationship between personal 'reasons' and impersonal 'causes' in the constitution of events. As such, it approaches everyday life from an existential point of view – as a series of *situations* whose challenges and implications always ramify beyond the socio-cultural.
>
> (2005: xxvi, emphasis in original)

Even though the life of a football team is highly ritualised through the repetition of necessary actions (training drills, travelling to games, manager's speech, getting dressed/undressed, playing a match, etc.), I often had the perception that my fieldwork with Insaka could be framed as a succession of momentous events. Events would occur, and like lanterns on a dark and busy road would illuminate elements of insight I had been seeking to neatly grasp for a while.

The two Romanian boys, Adrian and Ciprian, were among those who regularly attended training sessions. Their position within the team was particularly intriguing. They were always together but open and friendly with everybody. One of the revelatory moments in my ethnographic relationship with them arose one Saturday morning, during my first summer with Insaka, while waiting for the training session to start. As usual, Adrian, Ciprian and Mariusz, their Polish teammate, were among the first to arrive and were sitting on the pavement near the training pitch. Holding the small video camera in my right hand, I sat on the pavement with them. The boys were talking about the forthcoming football World Cup and then the conversation rapidly moved on to the summer holidays. Adrian was about to head to his native Romania for two months and Mariusz was going to Poland. He had previously commented that he had been living in the country for only three years and was 14 when he and his younger brother joined his mother in Ireland. I entered the conversation and after a while, out of curiosity, hearing Adrian's strong North Dublin accent, I asked him if it had been difficult to learn English.

MAX: Alex, was it difficult to learn English?
ADRIAN: Yeah, it was, but only the first six months, then it was all right.
MARIUSZ: Man, you are only here three years. When you speak it seems like you're raised up. Proper accent and everything.
CIPRIAN: Like a knacker accent.[20]
ADRIAN to MARIUSZ: How long have you been living in Ireland?
MARIUSZ: Since I was five. See now when I come back to my country, man, I don't know where to go, what's happening around me.
ADRIAN: I know everything man.
MARIUSZ: Yeah but you are only three years.
ADRIAN: Plus, I'm used to go every fucking holiday.
CIPRIAN: …and you are fucked up because you didn't go to school and you don't know anyone.
ADRIAN: What you mean? You can still know people.
CIPRIAN: You see, when I went last time I didn't go for the last five years and…
ADRIAN: Man, if you keep in touch on fuckin' Yahoo messenger, any of them fuckin' shit … You can still … You don't have to know people man, you only have to know bitches, that's it!
Everyone laughed. The conversation then moved back to the World Football Cup.

Arguably, had the camera not been there this conversation would probably not have taken place. Despite the fact that the three boys had been playing in the same team for various months, they did not know much about their respective histories of migration. My curiosity tangibly elicited theirs, instantiating the catalytic effect of the camera. They instinctively referred to the country where they were born as 'home'. However, having spent a large part of their lives in

Ireland they felt more 'at home' here: they somehow belonged here (hooks 2009). The fact that they played for what might be regarded as an 'African team' conveys more about the fluid ways they worked to negotiate their own identity and their sense of belonging in a multicultural urban environment. The non-African members of Insaka maintained that they joined this team mainly for the style of football it played, or for the fact that the coaches were former professionals and so they could learn something from them, or simply because some schoolmate or friend invited them. But my previous ethnographic field-work with Mountview – a football club with a strong identification with the local Irish working class community – suggests that Insaka attracted these boys and their friends of African background for other reasons. It was less a struc-tured and more loose kind of involvement compared with that of other local Irish teams. And then, as hinted by Lukas, if you play among 'foreigners' you don't have to be reminded of your background.

Adrian took the chance to 'perform' a character – that of a 'tough' boy who makes use of laddish language, including lingo acquired from African-American rap, who, on later occasions, would avoid performing. Ciprian talked less, leaving the 'stage' to the other two. This made me also reflect on a more basic question: how is the use of the video camera furthering the aims and objectives of my ethnographic research on youth, sport and cultural belonging? MacDou-gall underscores the argument that in working with images rather than words, 'we are in a different experiential world – one not necessarily inferior to reading a text, but to be understood differently' (MacDougall 2006: 270). According to Weber (2008: 44), images 'can make us pay attention to things in new ways' and 'can be used to capture the ineffable, the hard-to-put into words'. In my case, the use of the video camera enabled me to look at the situation in a different way, unpacking and 're-packing' a series of material details that were fundamental elements of narratives of cultural belonging – for example, Adri-an's exhibited accent, the tattoo with his mother's name that covered his right forearm, together with the chain necklace that he wore. Was he macho or 'mommy's boy'? Maybe both or possibly neither. And then, the car which Mariusz leaned on, an old Fiat Punto (that he drove locally without having a full driving licence), or indeed the way the boys were dressed or undressed on this sunny and surprisingly warm day. And finally, the location where we were sitting, one of the most recently built estates on the fringes of Dublin.

From football to hip hop (and return)

In the weeks following that encounter, I developed a closer relationship with Adrian and Ciprian. I was interested in having a deeper understanding of their backgrounds, to better situate the role that sport and leisure played in their lives, and for doing that I felt training sessions and Sunday games were not enough. I expressed to them my interest in visiting their families. Adrian's answer was 'yeah', but from his expression I felt it was merely an act of courtesy.

Ciprian remained silent, his silence confirming my impression that the sport practices represent an 'autonomous territory' of teenagers. I interpreted his silence as a
self-evident question: 'what has my family got to do with my football?'

When our conversations turned to music, I perceived this could be a pertinent reason to move away from the sporting pitch. As had been the case with
Mountview, most of the times the young players of Insaka were listening to hip
hop: North-American rappers such as Lil Wayne were quite popular, but some
boys also listened to modern African music and reggaeton, a genre that origi-
nates from the Caribbean and combines hip hop, dancehall and salsa. When I
asked Ciprian what music he was listening to he said it was Romanian rap. This
struck me as unusual since I knew he had been living in Ireland for most of his
life and had only been back once to his country of origin. But, even more surprisingly, Ciprian was not only listening to Romanian rap but also writing songs
in Romanian, recording them and putting them on YouTube. And he was doing
this with Adrian: they were a hip hop duo. I asked whether I could observe
them rapping, and possibly film the session, to which they agreed.

I met Ciprian at his home, located in a neighbourhood of semi-detached
houses in a peripheral neighbourhood of Blanchardstown. He invited me into the
living room, where the television was showing a Turkish soap opera subtitled in
Romanian. Above the faux fireplace was placed a framed picture of him and his
mother on the day of his graduation. Ciprian was the third of six siblings but the
oldest of the four living in the house with the mother. The father had returned to
Romania. Ciprian told me that the house did not have an internet connection,
which we needed to watch their YouTube clips – so we headed to Adrian's place.
A 10-minute walk through a monotonous landscape of terraced houses took us to
the home where Adrian lived with his younger brother, mother and stepfather.
Here I was introduced to the mother, a woman in her late 30s who had worked in
various countries before settling in Ireland and finally reuniting with her sons,
who during previous periods of migration had remained in Romania. She spoke to
me in fluent Italian, having spent some time in Italy working in hotels and later
working in Italian restaurants in Dublin. Soon the boys invited me to follow them
upstairs, where the computer and the landline connection were located.

Sitting on the bed of an unadorned sleeping room I showed them a couple of
clips of the team, which Adrian uploaded on the computer. The two boys were
amused by seeing themselves on screen – they laughed and made comments
about each other. The conversation then moved on to rap music. I had several
questions in mind – for example, 'what do you rap about?', 'why don't you do it
in English?' – but I tried to keep quiet, to let things emerge at their own pace. I
didn't want to fall into the interview-trap. And, second, I wanted to make the
most of the presence of the camera, to be able to capture something of the atmo-
sphere of this encounter: the size of the room, the basic furniture, the empty
walls, the postures and gestures of my protagonists, their silences and sights.
They all seemed to me elements of their social landscape that could reveal more
of the place and the stories that inhabit it.

Adrian, his younger brother Darius, and Ciprian introduced the song whose YouTube clip was showing on the computer's screen. The lyrics were sung and written both by Adrian and Ciprian. It was an opportunity to explain to me also the kind of topics they addressed in their songs, even though they did not seem entirely in agreement. According to Adrian: 'The song is about the way out, yeah. Everything about the government, how people have to work hard to live'. Ciprian expressed disagreement and turned towards him: 'Stop lying man, it's not about the government, it's about us'. The discussion also involved Darius, who had done some rap tunes with his brother and was somehow part of the group. They finally agreed that they rapped about 'poor people in Romania' and about 'problems'. 'That's what we like to rap about', concluded Ciprian. They then played the clip and Adrian started rapping along with it. At the end of the song Adrian further explained why they didn't rap in English. He said: 'if you rap in English you have to rap about guns, weapons, killing each other, and have money, basically'. Adrian and Ciprian believed that nobody would be interested in their rap anyway, so they did it in Romanian.

At a later moment Ciprian took his explanation further, arguing that rap music is something he does for himself, and that he is not interested in getting people's attention. He also explained that Romanian was the language he felt most comfortable using, since he spoke it at home and with his closest friends. 'If you are Romanian, speak Romanian', he said. 'If you don't have the right accent when speaking in English, people will pick at you', he added, mentioning that he had been the target of racist abuse at school because of his origin, with Irish peers calling him 'gypsy'. The boys' reflections made me think of Stuart Hall's reasoning surrounding the multicultural question in modern European societies and the role of culture and art. He argues:

If you want to learn more, or see how difference operates inside people's heads, you have to go to art, you have to go to culture – to where people imagine, where they fantasise, where they symbolise. You have to make the detour from the language of straight description to the language of the imaginary.

(Schwarz and Hall 2007: 152)

Adrian and Ciprian produced rap music in Romanian while coming of age in Ireland. What does this convey about their sense of cultural belonging? Quoting their own song's title, there seems to be 'no way out' of a multiplicity of belongings, which as in every migration experience, mirrors a multiplicity of gains and losses. It appears that their personal migratory experiences 'are tied into a cultural web of ongoing discourses of belonging, separation and achievement' (Salazar 2010: 64). Discourses originating in Romania – in the form of the hip hop national canons they are inspired from, which are obviously influenced by African-American hip hop but also rap made in other European countries – are elaborated in Ireland, and percolate back to Romania and the whole world through the internet. Through rap they draw their own 'narratives of location and dislocation', problematising 'the status of identity' (Hopkins, 2010: 139). On one hand, by using the Romanian language, they appeared to embrace the idea of stable and homogenised national cultures of immigrant communities which inspires interculturalism in Ireland (Halilovic-Pastuovic 2010). Yet, on the other hand, by using this language to produce underground rap which speaks critically of Romanian society and the government, they overtly position themselves at the margins of the same idea.

The transcultural dynamics surrounding their music production and football practice elicited my fascination even further. Adrian and Ciprian had first started rapping with a Nigerian schoolmate. They even recorded a song together that unfortunately got mislaid. And now they publicly shared their own videos on Facebook, getting comments in English and Romanian from friends living in different countries. On Facebook they also published pictures of their football team that I had sent them or that they had taken themselves. There was even a picture of me, taken by Ciprian during a Belfast trip, with the title 'camera man' (Figure 4.3). Myself, as the observer, I was observed and photographed. All the

Figure 4.3 The researcher as 'camera man' on Facebook, January 2011.

pictures he had taken with Insaka were on the Facebook page of the team, where players would often post comments.

Learning from the learners

My engagement with the young players was a process of continuous learning. I soon understood that I could learn something about my research questions, what actually motivated my presence in the field, and also about unanticipated ways through which the boys understood and represented their lives. In adopting a flexible methodological approach, I was responding to the challenges posed by my young participants, whose interest to have a dialogue with me demanded constant negotiations. My access to their lives, although necessarily temporary, was never secured. The fact that I was most of the times holding a camera, would allow me to move more quickly, to get where it would be more difficult to be without the attraction of the camera. But this was not without risk and frustration on my side. At the same time, I was aware of growing interest in incorporating visual methodologies in research with young people (Loescher 2005; Thomson 2008; Azzarito 2013; Back and Puwar 2012). Emphasis is usually placed on the potential for collaboration in the production and discussion of images. This is facilitated by the fact that new digital technologies have made it easier and cheaper to work with visual media.

Intrigued by their music, I proposed to Adrian and Ciprian that they collaborate in a video I was producing about the SARI Soccer Fest. It was a documentation of the day, with interviews and some footage of the games, that I made mainly to show appreciation of SARI's work. Adrian and Ciprian agreed to collaborate and offered to record a version of one of their songs to be used as a soundtrack. They explained to me that the song was about poor people, street life, nasty policemen and such things that are often the focus of hip hop music, in Romania as elsewhere. Surprisingly, Adrian proposed to record a different version, with a 'brighter' musical theme, and they invited me to their 'studio' to attend the recording. I was satisfied with the suggestion and trusted the boys and their enthusiasm. The studio was located at the Blanchardstown Youth Centre and it consisted of a room provided with an Apple computer with editing programs, a sound mixer and a keyboard. There were also other computers with different programs and an internet connection. Local youths who were under the age of 18 could access the facilities for free.

The way they worked on their music was similar to that of Ollie, the rapper in the Mountview team. They searched the internet for 'good beats', and added their lyrics. There was a creative element of appropriation and recombination in what they did – a dialectic that is a fundamental characteristic of rap music (Frith 1996). This seems to me a good metaphor for the challenges undertaken by adolescents of immigrant background, who have to deal with multiple patterns of identification (Worbs 2006) and whose quest for identity 'is subject to adaptation and assimilation to and within a "host" choice' (Head 1997: 56).

Through their use of technology, they were also affirming a sense of their autonomy, 'of their right to make their own choices and to follow their own paths –
however illusory this may ultimately be' (Buckingham 2008: 17). Some 'beats'
used by Adrian and Ciprian were actually taken from well-known artists but
through their intervention became something else. Ciprian was eager to explain
to me their creative work:

> I just get beats from internet and write my own lyrics. There're lots of
> rappers, and you find yourself in some songs, in a beat, but it's better to
> make your own song and just make it about yourself and listen to it. It's
> better that way, I think, but everyone is different. That's me.

Our video received good feedback and SARI asked to post it on their website.
Ciprian and Adrian said they were happy with the video but, strangely enough,
they did not show much enthusiasm about its diffusion. After a couple of
months since its publication on the web, SARI's director sent me an email
regarding the lyrics of the song used as soundtrack for the video. Apparently,
there was a problem with its language. A member of the Romanian immigrant
community had questioned the lyrics, and asked if they were in accordance with
'SARI ethics'. I was forwarded a translation of the parts of the soundtrack that
had troubled this person.[21]

My first reaction to the email was one of embarrassment. According to this
translation, the lyrics included expletives, also of a sexist nature, and this understandably made the organisation uncomfortable. Maybe I had been a bit naive
in my collaborative effort and should have insisted the boys get a translation of
their song before using it. For these reasons, I had no problem if SARI took the
video down from their website. But why did Adrian and Ciprian let me to use
this song? Maybe they thought the language was 'typical' of urban hip hop and
since it was in Romanian nobody would understand it. However, at the same
time, I was somehow excited by this unexpected turn of the story. It looked to
me as a sort of rhizomatic development of my initial interest in sport. I deemed
it a rich ethnographic event. Through my intervention more people had been
introduced to the boy's music and, following this controversy, some had learnt
what they had to say about their lives divided between Ireland and Romania.
And then, despite part of the content (the troubling lyrics lasted just 70 seconds
of the five-minute video), their song worked well with the images. I did not
want to let Adrian and Ciprian down after the work they had done, and could
not really blame them for giving me the song. I had to find a compromise solution. SARI's director asked me if I could edit a shorter version of the video to
send to an international philanthropic organisation that was to decide whether
to support SARI. Hence, I agreed to edit this short version leaving out the parts
of the lyrics that had caused controversy. The original version remained on
YouTube, while SARI published and sent out the short one.

Notes

1 Saturday 4 April 2010, www.irishtimes.ie (accessed 10 April 2010).
2 Paul Berry (38) was initially charged with manslaughter, and his brother Michael (23) for the possession of a hockey stick. The charge for both was later upgraded to murder. Paul Berry was found dead the morning the trial was to begin and Michael was later acquitted. 'No one will ever be jailed for killing of schoolboy', *The Irish Times*, 13 December 2012.
3 See the column written by Ronit Lentin (professor of sociology at Trinity College Dublin) in *Metro Eireann*, 'Why is everyone afraid of the R word?', 15 April 2010. *Metro Eirann*, is 'Ireland's first multicultural newspaper'.
4 The cost of the trip, including the ticket for the Premiere League game and the entrance ticket to the Alton Towers Park, a popular amusement park, was €325, but €100 was paid by the club through lotteries and subscriptions. So I paid €225.
5 According to *The Irish Times*, about 1500 people took part in the rally. 'Supporters say "never again" at emotional Toyosi rally', *The Irish Times*, 12 April 2010. Other sources spoke of 2000 participants, see www.sari.ie/ss/new-newsitem-2/ [accessed 3 April 2012].
6 'Six charged with in connection with Pearse Street assault', RTE news, 18 May 2001, www.rte.ie/news/2001/0518/stabbing.html [accessed 14 August 2018].
7 The residential development was launched in 2001, the Tyrrelstown Town Centre was completed in 2005 (Wikipedia – accessed 10 August 2018).
8 Horses had traditionally been a popular gift to children and teenagers of working class households. Danny, the Irish winger of the Mountview team, told me he used to have a horse and he kept it 'in the fields', meaning in empty land beyond the boundaries of the city. He recently had to sell him because he did not have money to feed him anymore. Other boys in the team also had horses, of their own or of their family. Abandoned horses in the Dublin area became a problem after the recession ('Nearly 350 horses abandoned in Dublin last year', *The Irish Examiner*, 7 June 2010).
9 See, for example, *The ragazzi* (2007) and *A violent life* (2007), both based in post-WWII Rome periphery. Pasolini's passion for and interest in sport has been investigated by Piccioni (1996).
10 In the USA, 82 per cent of the children play organised soccer exclusively, and 89 per cent prefer organised games to pick-up games (Ellis and Sharma 2014: 366).
11 'Slain teen's former team condemns "racist abuse"', *Metro Eireann*, 22 April 2010.
12 I once inquired about the origin of the name of the restaurant, which reminded me of the Ku Klux Klan. The owner offered a candid answer: 'This is my kitchen, with mine and my wife's names, both starting with a K'.
13 The SARI Soccer Fest takes place since 1997 in Phoenix Park, Dublin, in the second week of September.
14 Pro Italia is a senior team that at the time of the fieldwork was based in North Dublin competing in the Amateur Football League (AFL).
15 Thanks to the use of the video camera I was able to save much of the original language used by the protagonists, including vernacular expressions that define Dublin's new linguistic landscape (Kallen 2010). As noted by Duneier, 'The meanings of a culture are embodied, in part, in its language, which cannot be grasped by an outsider without attention to the choice and order or words and sentences' (Duneier 1999: 339).
16 The website is no longer online.
17 www.irishfa.com/news/item/6233/glentoran-academy-in-united-through-sport-events/ [accessed 7 December 2011].
18 For example, the 'Football for Hope' programme funded by FIFA, www.toolkitsport development.org/mega-events/html/resources/22/22736AF1-DF5C-4F96-B3B5-F9380 155F698/FootballforHope_E.pdf [accessed 2 March 2018].

19 On one occasion, a sergeant from the Blanchardstown Garda station paid a visit to Insaka at their 'training ground', meeting the players and talking to the coaches. Ken handed him a T-shirt of the UEFA Respect campaign, pictures were taken and later published on the website of the club.

20 The word *knacker* was originally associated with being a member of the Irish Traveller community (Dolan 1998: 133), which rates at the bottom of the social respectability scale. Nowadays, in Irish slang, it's generally used to mean a despicable person, or to describe someone who is perceived to be from a lower social class.

21   To live in Romania is like shit/One way out of it is to go robing/The frustrated cops are arresting us/As the politicians fill their pockets and venish/Stupid is the one that sais 'Money don't bring happiness'/Withouth money you are like a hore with no pimp/Who get's f***ed by everyone but no one is paying/I'm in a maze and don't know how to get out of it/I wasn't born to rob but I have to rob/The life is bitter/A way out of it is to share with your pal's the 'smiles from the cigarette' (more than likely reffering to drogs/to get high).

Note: Spelling errors in the original.

References

Agnew, P. (2010). 'Football and evolving national identity'. In P. Dine and S. Crosson (eds), *Sport, representation and evolving identities in Europe*. Oxford: Peter Lang.

Alexander, C. E. (2002). '"One of the boys": Black masculinity and the peer group'. In S. Taylor (ed.), *Ethnographic research. A reader*. London: Sage, 91–112.

Anderson, S. (2003). 'Bodying forth a room for everybody: Inclusive recreational badminton in Copenhagen'. In N. Dyck and F. Archetti (eds), *Sport, dance and embodied identities*. Oxford: Berg, 23–53.

Andrews, D. and Giardina, M. (2008). 'Toward a cultural studies that matters'. *Cultural Studies Critical Methodologies*, 8(4), 395–442.

Appadurai, A. (1986). *The social life of things: Commodities in cultural perspective*. Cambridge: Cambridge University Press.

Azzarito, L. (2013). 'Introduction'. In L. Azzarito and D. Kirk (eds), *Pedagogies, physical culture, and visual methods*. London: Routledge, 1–12.

Back, L. and Puwar, N. (2012). 'A manifesto for live methods: Provocations and capacities'. In L. Back and N. Puwar (eds), *Live methods*. Oxford: Wiley-Blackwell/The Sociological Review, 6–17.

Bairner, A. (ed.) (2005). *Sport and the Irish*. Dublin: University College Dublin Press.

Beckett, C. (2013). 'Can journalism count as a research output? British politics and policy at LSE'. *Creative Future*, weblog post, 12 December 2012. Available from: http://eprints.lse.ac.uk/48459/ [accessed 20 December 2014].

Bourdieu, P. (1990). *The logic of practice*. Cambridge, UK: Polity Press.

Bradbury, S. (2011). 'Racism, resistance and new youth inclusions'. In D. Burdsey (ed.), *Race, ethnicity and football: Persisting debates and emergent issues*. London: Routledge, 67–83.

Buckingham, D. (2008). 'Introducing identity'. In D. Buckingham (ed.), *Youth, identity, and digital media*. Cambridge, MA: The MIT Press, 1–22.

Carrington, B. (2010). *Race, sport and politics: The sporting black diaspora*. London: Sage.

Clifford, J. (1986). 'Introduction: Partial truths'. In J. Clifford and G. M. Marcus (eds), *Writing culture. The poetics and politics of ethnography*. Berkeley: University of California Press, 1–26.

Clifford, J. (1997). *Routes. Travel and translations in the late 20th century*. Cambridge, MA: Harvard University Press.

Connor, S. (2003). *Youth sport in Ireland*. Dublin: The Liffey Press.

Crang, M. and Cook, I. (2007). *Doing ethnographies*. London: Sage.

Cronin, M. (1999). *Sport and nationalism in Ireland: Gaelic games, soccer and Irish identity since 1884*. Dublin: Four Courts Press.

Dyck, N. (2003). 'Embodying success: Identity and performance in children's sport'. In N. Dyck and E. Archetti (eds), *Sport, dance and embodied identities*. Oxford: Berg, 55–74.

Dolan, T. P. (1998). *A dictionary of Hiberno-English*. Dublin: Gill & Macmillan.

Duneier, M. (1999). *Sidewalk*. New York: Farrar, Straus and Giroux.

Ellis, J. M. and Sharma, H. (2014). 'Can't play here: The decline of pick-up soccer and social capital in the USA'. In D. Hassan (ed.), *Ethnicity and race in association football: Case study analyses in Europe, Africa and the USA*. London: Routledge, 74–93.

Falzon, M. A. (ed.) (2009). *Multi-sited ethnography*. London: Ashgate.

Fine, G. A. (1987). *With the boys. Little League baseball and preadolescent culture*. Chicago: The University of Chicago Press.

Free, M. (2010). 'Migration, masculinity and the fugitive state of mind in the Irish emigrant footballer autobiography: The case of Paul McGrath'. *Estudios Irlandeses*, 5, 45–57.

Frith, S. (1996). 'Music and identity'. In S. Hall and P. du Gay (eds), *Questions of cultural identity*. London: Sage, 108–127.

Giardina, M. (2005). *Sporting pedagogies*. New York: Peter Lang.

Gille, Z. (2001). 'Critical ethnography in the time of globalization: Toward a new concept of site'. *Cultural Studies Critical Methodologies*, 1(3), 319–334.

Giulianotti, R. (2005). *Sport. A critical sociology*. Cambridge: Polity Press.

Halilovic-Pastuovic, M. (2010). ' "Settled in mobility" as a "space of possibility": Bosnian post-refugee transnationalism as a response to the bio-politics of Irish interculturalism'. *Translocations: Migration and Social Change*, 6(2). Available from: www.translocations. ie/docs/v06i02/Vol%206%20Issue%202%20-%20Peer%20Review%20-%20Halilovic%20 Pastuovic.pdf [accessed 8 February 2012].

Hammersley, M. and Atkinson, P. (2007). *Ethnography: Principles in practice*. London: Routledge.

Hassan, D. and McCue K. (2013). 'The "silent" Irish – football, migrants and the pursuit of integration'. In D. Hassan (ed.), *Ethnicity and race in association football: Case study analyses in Europe, Africa and the USA*. London: Routledge, 126–138.

Head, J. (1997). *Working with adolescents: Constructing identity*. London: Falmer Press.

hooks, b. (2009). *Belonging. A culture of place*. New York: Routledge.

Hopkins, P. (2010). *Young people, place and identity*. London: Routledge.

Hylton, K. (2009). *'Race' and sport. Critical race theory*. London: Routledge.

Jackson, M. (2005). *Existential anthropology*. New York: Berghahn Books.

Kallen, J. L. (2010). 'Changing landscapes: Language, space, and policy in the Dublin linguistic landscape'. In A. Jaworski and C. Thurlow (eds), *Semiotic landscapes: Language, image, space*. London: Continuum, 41–59.

Kapuscinski, R. (2000). *Il cinico non è adatto a questo mestiere. Conversazioni sul buon giornalismo (A cynic doesn't suit this profession. Conversations on good journalism)*. Roma: E/O.

Lentin, A. (2004). *Racism and anti-racism in Europe*. London: Pluto.

Loescher, M. (2003). 'Cameras at the Addy: Speaking in pictures with city kids'. *Journal of Media Practice*, 3(2), 75–84.

Long, J., Hylton, K. and Spraklen, K. (2014). 'Whiteness, blackness and settlement: Leisure and the integration of new migrants'. *Journal of Ethnic and Migration Studies*, 40(11), 1779–1797.

Lusted, J. and O'Gorman, J. (2010). 'The impact of New Labour's modernisation agenda on the English grass-roots football workforce'. *Managing Leisure*, 15(1–2), 140–154.

MacDougall, D. (2006). *The corporeal image. Film, ethnography and the senses*. Princeton: Princeton University Press.

Magee, J. and Jeanes, R. (2013). 'Football's coming home: A critical evaluation of the Homeless World Cup as an intervention to combat social exclusion'. *International Review for the Sociology of Sport*, 48(1), 3–19.

Marcus, G. E. (1995). 'Ethnography in/of the world system: The emergence of multi-sited ethnography'. *Annual Review of Anthropology*, 24, 95–117.

Marcus, G. E. (2009). 'Multi-sited ethnography: Five or six things I know about it now, problems and possibilities'. In M. A. Falzon (ed.), *Multi-sited ethnography*. London: Ashgate, 181–196.

Marcus, G. E. (2010). 'Contemporary fieldwork aesthetics in art and anthropology: Experiments in collaboration and intervention'. *Visual Anthropology*, 23, 263–277.

Mauro, M. (2014). 'A team like no "other". The racialized position of Insaka in Irish schoolboys football'. In J. O'Gorman (ed.), *Junior and youth grassroots football. The forgotten game*. London: Routledge, 54–73.

Mauro, M. (2016). 'Transcultural football. Trajectories of belonging among immigrant youth'. *Soccer and Society*, 17(6), 90–105.

O'Callaghan, C., Boyle, M. and Kitchin, R. (2014). 'Post-politics, crisis, and Ireland's "ghost estates"'. *Political Geography*, 42, 121–133.

O'Toole, F. (2009). *Ship of fools*. London: Faber & Faber.

Pasolini, P. P. (2007 [1955]). *The ragazzi*. Manchester: Carcanet Press.

Pasolini, P. P. (2007 [1959]). *A violent life*. Manchester: Carcanet Press.

Piccioni, V. (1996). *Quando giocava Pasolini (When Pasolini played)*. Arezzo: Limina.

Postma, M. and Crawford, P. I. (2006). *Reflecting visual ethnography. Using the camera in anthropological research*. Leiden & Hojibjerg: CNWS Publications & Intervention Press.

Rosbrook-Thomson, J. (2012). *Sport, difference and belonging: Conceptions of human variation in British sport*. London: Routledge.

Rouch, J. (author) and Feld, S. (ed.) (2003). *Ciné-ethnography*. Minneapolis, MN: University of Minnesota Press.

Salazar, N. B. (2010). 'Towards an anthropology of cultural mobilities'. *Crossing: Journal of Migration and Culture*, 1(1), 53–68.

Schwarz, B. and Hall, S. (2007). 'Living with difference'. *Soundings*, 37. Available from: https://grand-union.org.uk/wp-content/uploads/Living-with-Difference-Interview-Stuart-Hall-.pdf [accessed 4 September 2018].

Sebald, W. G. (2002). *The emigrants*. London: Vintage.

Sennet, R. (1990). *The conscience of the eye. The design and social life of cities*. New York: W. W. Norton & Company.

Simpson, B. (2005). 'Cities as playgrounds: Active leisure for children as a human right'. In P. Bramham and J. Caudwell (eds), *Sport, active leisure and youth cultures*. Brighton: Leisure Studies Association, 86.

Smith, A. and Green, K. (2005). 'The place of sport and physical activity in young people's lives and its implications for health: Some sociological comments'. *Journal of Youth and Studies*, 8(2), 241–253.

Sugden, J. and Bairner, A. (1993). *Sport, sectarianism and society in a divided Ireland.* Leicester: Leicester University Press.

Swanson, L. (2009). 'Soccer fields of cultural [re]production: Creating "good boys" in suburban America'. *Sociology of Sport Journal*, 26, 404–424.

Thomson, T. (ed.) (2008). *Doing visual research with children and young people.* London: Routledge.

Waugh, E. (2000 [1938]). *Scoop.* London: Penguin.

Weber, S. (2008). 'Visual images in research'. In J. G. Knowles and A. L. Cole (eds), *Handbook of the arts in qualitative research.* London: Sage, 41–55.

Worbs, S. (2006). 'Where do I belong? Integration policy and patters of identification among migrant youth in three European countries'. In D. Hoerder, Y. Hebert and I. Schmitt (eds), *Negotiating transcultural lives.* Toronto: University of Toronto Press, 39–58.

Chapter 5

A team like no 'Other'

Those who have played competitive football know that in every team there will likely be someone who can't control his/her temper and ends up collecting yellow or even red cards, much like a good striker collects goals. Often youth leagues award a 'Fair Play Cup' to the team that, during the season, has showed the 'best' (meaning less confrontational and problematic) behaviour on the pitch and that has therefore obtained the lowest number of yellow and red cards. This is ascribed to the practice of discipline on the sporting pitch. Players are expected to abide by the rules of the game, including referee's decisions, but they also have to respect other rules of discipline, those imposed by coaches and managers, whose regime of power is at work within the team or the club. In this regard, Foucault's analysis of discipline in schools, factories, military camps and prisons (Foucault 1979 [1975]) can be, to some extent, adapted to sport practice, especially when young people are involved – as training can also be thought of as 'a means of producing useful, docile individuals' (Malcolm 2008: 70). Huizinga (1980 [1938]) observed how modern sports were born in nineteenth century England precisely through the systematisation and regimentation of the play element in traditional games.

Sometimes these different regimes of discipline can collide, as in the case when a team is told by its manager to 'play hard' on the opponents, being aware that by doing so they will probably be sanctioned by the referee. Even though the link between discipline and sport appears sufficiently clear, its interpretation by the protagonists of the game can take unpredictable trajectories. Discipline might even be used as a screen word, a word with which to cover what the protagonists really mean by using it. I regularly heard James and Zuby speaking of 'discipline' at Insaka's training sessions and at Sunday matches. They would talk to their players either individually or in group, asking them to improve their discipline, or complaining about their lack of discipline. 'The most important thing is discipline', James told his players at a summer training session right before the start of the season. However, despite all this talk, something was missing in my understanding of discipline. Its *true* meaning was slipping through my hands like a wet ball. What did they mean by 'discipline'? Was it just a question of the boys diligently following the manager's instructions? Or was it related to their behaviour on and off the pitch? Perhaps both?

As argued in this chapter, the affirmation of 'discipline' in the context of a team managed by African immigrants and largely composed by boys of African background was sensibly instigated by the racialised position – following Fanon's argumentation that 'not only must the black man be black; he must be black in relation to the white man' (Fanon 1987 [1952]: 109) – of Insaka within the schoolboys' league and by extension in Irish society. 'Race' is intended here mainly as a cultural and social construct favoured by state regulations (Goldberg 2002, 2015) that, in Ireland as in other European countries with immigration, creates different types of migrants/persons who are entitled to various levels of rights, sometimes even full citizenship, but still being racialised (Agamben 1998; Mezzadra 2006; Lentin and McVeigh 2006; Loyal 2011; Mezzadra and Neilson 2013). Moreover, as evidenced by the Irish case, the racialisation of the migrant subject in European countries (Balibar and Wallerstein 1991), which generally targets migrants from poorer countries, is magnified when it comes to 'people of colour', particularly those originally from Africa (McGinnity et al. 2006). As we will see, Insaka's discourse on discipline was also motivated by the perceived need for learning to deal with racism on and off the football pitch. This has obvious implications for patterns of inclusion in and through sport. Finally, following a series of key ethnographic moments I return to a central point of my study, that of the negotiation of cultural and national belonging by young footballers of immigrant background.

A matter of discipline?

The discourse on discipline that surrounded much of the club officials' talks appeared in a particular light on a Sunday morning in March 2011. Insaka were playing a Cup match at home against a team they had previously beaten in a League match. The winners would be allowed to play in the cup final, which would award the second most important trophy for clubs at their level (the first being the league title itself). Insaka were looking forward to the first title in their short history and all the team members were eager to accomplish this result. For this game, the league had sent a young and athletic referee who appeared at odds with the slow middle-aged referees I had frequently seen taking care of youth matches around Dublin. As was often the case, the Insaka players were tackled hard by the opposition, a tactic that sometimes in previous games had annoyed the more temperamental of them, provoking their reaction. More often than not, referees did not sanction such type of rough game. Today, however, the referee was so competent that nobody could complain. The game was played by both sides quite correctly and it ended in a draw. In extra-time, tension arose between some of the players, and the referee was prompted to send off two of them, one from each side. Eventually, Insaka won and the players celebrated the victory running around the pitch like they had won a proper title and not just the right to play a final. All the tension they had accumulated was let out in the celebration and most of them forgot or did not bother to shake hands with the members of the other team, as was common practice at the end of each game. A few minutes later, while the Insaka players were getting dressed on the side of the pitch and James and Zuby were talking to them about the game, they were joined by the manager of the other team. He reached the group and approached the only white club official, Ken, asking permission to speak to the boys, while the two African coaches remained silent. This is what he said:

> The key to be a really good team is discipline. You are a very good footballing team but, remember, that goes out of the window if you don't have discipline. You are the best footballing team that's out there but to keep your discipline is absolutely key [to success]. Well done.

Why was he doing this? What motive lay behind his speech? In the end, two red cards had been shown, one to his own team, so he might be considered part of the problem. And what about the Insaka coaches' role – was it not diminished by this unusual intervention of the opponent's manager? James and Zuby did not appear to share my bewilderment regarding the man's initiative. As soon as he left, Zuby told his players: 'You see? This is what we always say to you. Discipline, it's all about discipline'. To me, it felt like that the Insaka players were on this occasion treated like children who had to learn how to behave. They can be a good 'footballing team', the 'best that's out there', but they have to improve their behaviour. Stuart Hall (1997: 262) defines the 'infantilization of difference' as 'a common representation strategy for both men and women', particularly meaningful when referred to the racialised representation of black masculinity. Probably without meaning it, unconsciously, the Irish coach was making use of strategies of representation and stereotyping that are diffused, in Ireland as elsewhere. Earlier in my fieldwork, during a digitally-recorded interview, a youth coach with a prominent Dublin youth football club, who was also PE teacher in a secondary school, made some 'revealing' observations on black youth.[1] He said:

> Nigerians are generally troublesome. I would not say this in public, but in my experience black and troublesome, he will be Nigerian. Part of the problem is that black kids don't understand the team ethics, they just play for themselves. They tend to be more athletic, physically fit, but they tend to be lazy. They don't chase back for the ball.

This type of statement can be better comprehended if read alongside Hall's words:

> The problem is that blacks are trapped by the *binary structure* of the stereotype, which is split between two extreme opposites – and are obliged to *shuttle endlessly between them*, sometimes being represented as *both of them at the same time*. Thus blacks are both 'childlike' and 'oversexed', just as black

youth are 'Sambo simpletons' and/or 'wily, dangerous savages'; and older men both 'barbarians' and/or 'noble savages' – Uncle Toms'.

(1997: 263, emphasis in original)

At this stage, Insaka was predominantly a 'black' team, since some of the Eastern European players had left and there was only one white player in the starting 11, the goalkeeper, Lukas, while Ciprian was among the substitutes. Therefore, the manager's speech was directed at what might be seen as an 'African team'. Would the manager have dared to address a team different from this one without embarrassing himself and that team's staff? It was arguably the structural position of the two teams that made such an uneven dialogue possible: on one side Insaka, a new team composed almost entirely of boys of African background mentored by African adults; on the other, a well-established (white) Irish team. As noted, there were probably different parameters of discipline at work here. In the eyes of the opponent's manager, Insaka were not only playing *differently* but also behaving *differently*, therefore they needed to change, to improve their 'discipline'. This was something that, to some extent, also James and Zuby would like to see happening. But their idea of discipline concealed another issue, related not simply to the game and to the respect of its rules but to the wider position of 'Africans' in Irish society, and to their image in the eyes of the Irish people (Lentin 2007: Ní Chonaill 2009; Fanning *et al.* 2011). All this was arguably influencing Insaka's mission and everyday work. When, later that year, Insaka played the league cup final (Figure 5.1), Kennedy, who acted as assistant coach that day, clearly expressed his sentiments about the role of the team in helping to 'clean' the name of an entire community. Before the start of the game he addressed some black boys, friends and relatives of the Insaka players, who had come to support the team. He said:

We should try to keep our best behaviour. We should omit any foul language against the referee or any person in charge of this game. We should try to be good ambassadors of Africa. We should not be here to mess ourselves up. We already have the bad name so we have to try to clean it.

Kennedy's speech added another meaning to the recently founded team. He pointed at the need to behave well in order to 'clean the name' of the African community. Set alongside the recurrent discourse on discipline within the team, his words emphasised the racialised position of African immigrants in the schoolboys league and in Irish society. At the same time, his words also served as a possible strategy to tackle a problem previously encountered by Insaka – that of racial abuse. James and Zuby were particularly worried that during each game things could get out of hand, that their players would react and start a brawl, as indeed had happened in the weeks following Toyosi's death. As noted in the next section, all the talk about 'discipline' could therefore be read through the lenses of racism, either perceived and manifested, and of strategies

Figure 5.1 The Cup Final, May 2011.

of 'resistance through sport' (Hylton 2009: 115–119) carried out by the ones who are at the receiving end of abuse.

It's in the game

In Chapter 2 I discussed the contested evidence of racism on the football pitch as it emerged during my fieldwork with Mountview. I dedicated special attention to the ways the adults in charge of the game dealt with this issue, considering the implications of their decisions for the victims of abuse. My new ethnographic material allowed me to expand on the discussion on racism in youth football and to address it from a different perspective, that of a team 'structurally' positioned at the receiving end of abuse.

Among the pitches I visited with Insaka there was one that was situated outside the first and largest 'Direct Provision Centre' for asylum seekers in Ireland, Mosney, located approximately 50 km north of Dublin. Mosney had been originally built as a holiday centre and it functioned as one through the 1990s; in 2000 it was turned into a reception centre for asylum seekers with a capacity of about 800 places.[2] The club that was using the pitch had nothing to do with the centre; it was simply a local club that was entitled to use a portion of the vast fields surrounding the fenced area of the centre. While travelling to the game, Vujadin told me that he had lived for about three years at Mosney. It was the first place his family had moved in after arriving in Ireland from Bosnia. Another Insaka player said his mother had lived there for several months before getting refugee status and being allowed to reunite with her family. Loyal (2011) describes the Direct Provision Centres as 'total institutions': 'disciplinary and exclusionary forms of spatial and social closure that separate and conceal asylum-seekers from mainstream society and ultimately prevent their long term integration or inclusion' (Loyal 2011: 106; see also Loyal and Quilley 2018). The Direct Provision regime was introduced by the Irish government in 2000, and, according to official statistics, since 2008 nine out of ten asylum applications were turned down in the Republic of Ireland, the highest level of refusals in the EU.[3] Asylum seekers are not allowed to work or to travel abroad while their application is processed, and they have to rely on a personal allowance of €21.60 per week.[4] In the original plan, asylum seekers should not spend more than six-months in these centres, but the average stay is four years (Lentin 2016). At one of the Insaka trainings I met a young man who had spent eight years at Mosney before being granted refugee status. This was the background story to the game Insaka was going to play a few metres from the Direct Provision Centre's main entrance.

Half-way through the first half of the match, Vujadin, playing as centre-half, had a confrontation with the centre-forward of the opposition team, a black boy of African background. The referee decided to send both of them off, but this did not calm down the players on and off the pitch. Vujadin appeared particularly nervous and Zuby asked him to have a walk to calm down. There were only fields around us, and the imposing presence of the high-fenced Direct Provision Centre. At some point James decided to replace Joshua, a defender originally from the Ivory Coast, who seemed to be particularly nervous. He said he removed him from the game fearing he could get booked or even sent off. Joshua was not happy to have to leave the pitch, and looked agitated. He shouted that he had been racially abused by a player of the other team. It was an emotional moment and I saw James was worried. Despite all the problems his team was regularly facing he attempted to always keep a smile on his face, often eliciting laughter in his players via telling them jokes. But this time his face was serious, like he felt the message he had to share was a crucial one.

Joshua expressly referred to what happened to Toyosi, to the racial motivation for his killing: 'That's how it all started with Toyosi and now he's doing it, only a few months after that and now's he's doing it', he said pointing at an opponent. James tried to calm him down, but it was not easy. In fact, their heated conversation made manifest the challenges the team faced – the kind of problems they were presented with on and off the pitch. Joshua made clear his point: 'We are meant to kick out racism from the football'. To which James replied: 'If you can't control your anger forget about football'. A few minutes later James rejoined Joshua, who had calmed down and was now ready to listen to what he had to say to him. At this time James offered a brief and momentous insight into his understanding of racism in football. 'There is no way you can't see it. It's in the game', he said. And then, 'But you can't kill anybody here, you can't kill, that's it. The better for you is to know that these things can happen in the game'. Joshua listened attentively to what his manager had to say and did not comment.

After James had spoken to Joshua there was still tension in the air. Other Insaka players were angry with the player who, according to Joshua, had abused him. 'That's the way they do it', Adrian, the Romanian boy, explained to me. 'They do it when the referee can't hear it'. As I have previously discussed, if the referee does not hear the abuse it is unlikely that he will mention it in his report, even though someone asks him to do so. Consequently, there will be no record of the incident, and no space for it in official statistics about racism in football.[5] The Insaka officials often lamented the lack of attention of sporting bodies on this problem, and the limited understanding of match officials. James felt that Insaka were often being treated by the League as the 'problem' rather than the victims of racial abuse. The question of racism in football was further discussed after the game. While travelling in James's car back home with three Insaka players sitting in the backseat, I asked James how he felt about Joshua's abuse. James took the chance to explain again to his younger players how they should deal with racism within football. He said:

> They are trying to wind you up, it's normal, it's in the game. When they say 'fucking black' ignore them, it's fine, they can't say it again, they feel you don't care. But when they say it and you reply that means that you are angry because of that and they continue saying it.

James's approach to the problem was apparently a passive one (King 2004), in the face of institutional inaction to tackle it (Hassan and McCue 2013). Play on. It's in the game. Play your football. It will happen again. Try to be the best player. Discipline, I came to understand, had much to do with learning to cope with racism. However, there were moments when someone could not take it anymore, as was the case of Joshua, normally a jolly and friendly boy. As it happened, this was the last game Joshua played with Insaka. I was later able to reach him to find out what motivated him to leave the team. He told me he was busy with his hip hop band and did not have time for football anymore. He did not mention the racist episode among his reasons to quit football, but, as I learned during my long-term work with youth of African background living in Ireland, they rarely felt at ease discussing with an adult, especially a white researcher, issues related to racism.

This is similar to what Ni Laoire et al. (2011) found in their study of the migration experiences of children and young people of African background in Ireland, and to what emerges from the more recent report of the National Youth Council of Ireland (NYCI 2017: 14). Ni Laoire et al. (2011: 46) comment that, 'In many cases the children and young people sought to brush off and even deny their experiences of racism'. I wonder what the reason was that motivated the silence on such issues of the black boys I had spent months with. Was it simply the critical truth that a 'white man' can't understand this problem? Drawing on his work with young people in South London, Back provides a helpful observation:

While it is profoundly true that whites cannot fully comprehend the experiential consequences of racism, we do experience the transmission of racist
ideas and formulas. This is an important distinction in research within mul-
tiracial contexts. The question that is raised is what one does in situations
where racist ideas are communicated to the researcher – to say nothing in
response to them points to the legitimization of these ideas through silence.

(1993: 213)

Some of the young participants in my study were curious about my place of birth
and I used this as an opportunity to instantiate a tentative dialogue on issues of
racism and discrimination. I would mention my parent's migration experience
in a German-speaking area of Switzerland, where I was born and where I spent
the first years of my life. I told them that Italians (and, I must say, particularly
Southern Italians, which was not the case of my family) experienced open forms
of racist behaviours, both in their employment and in their everyday interaction
with the local population (Frigerio and Merhar 2004). I explained that I was
forced to became an 'illegal immigrant', and to live separated from my parents,
unknown to the authorities, because the law did not allow migrants on seasonal
working permits, like my father, to keep their children with them (Frigerio and
Buergherr 1992; Mauro 2005).[6] Unfortunately, but not surprisingly, even these
stories could not 'unlock' certain topics. There is arguably an element of age and
maturity involved, since I did not encounter such a level of resistance in talking
about racism in most of the adults of African background I happened to work
with during my research.

To some degree, what I could learn about the lived experiences of racism I
learnt making the most of my participant-observer's position, which allowed me
to collect 'evidence' of the problem. In this regard, my approach echoes the one
followed by Duneier (1999). Drawing on his ethnographic work with black
street book vendors in New York, he argues:

My continual presence as a vendor provided me with opportunities to
observe life among the people working and/or living on the sidewalk,
including their interactions with passersby. This enabled me to draw many
of my conclusions about what happens on the sidewalk from incidents I
myself witnessed, rather than deriving them from interviews. Often I simply
asked questions while participating and observing.

(Duneier 1999: 12)

However, in my experience, the process of knowledge production through participant observation appears less linear. I think it is important to critically situate
our own observational endeavour by constantly questioning the reasons why a
research dialogue is possible (Denzin 1997, 2007). Even if I am only 'observing',
my role in the field is never neutral. The world that I describe cannot stand
outside the politics of representation (Hall 1997; Denzin and Lincoln 2011).

Despite my multifaceted background, in the eyes of most my young participants I remained an adult white man, an Italian (an EU citizen), a friend of Ken, a researcher, who for some reason was interested in their lives, including their experiences of racism. How much was I allowed to learn and represent?

The challenge of teaching 'common sense'

Both James and Zuby admitted to have experienced racism in their careers in Europe, and for this reason they did not want their players to react aggressively if they received abuse of any kind. On one hand, theirs was an educational effort that should be read bearing in mind the fresh memory of a young footballer who had lost his life after an altercation which was probably racially motivated. They both feared something like that could happen again. This was confirmed to me by what I witnessed on a Saturday morning in November 2010, at a training session in Ongar. The pitch was overwhelmingly occupied by boys of African background training under two African coaches. At some point we heard a yell coming from outside the fenced pitch, and the boys stopped playing. The shouting came from a young white hooded man. With one hand he waved a bottle of some spirit, with the other he showed the middle finger. He was clearly drunk, and repeated his insults so that everyone could hear them: 'Fucking niggers!', he yelled. Most of the boys stood still, dumb, but Eddy, an 18-year-old originally from Congo, made a few steps towards the fence saying something back to the man.

The moment they saw him reacting this way, James and Zuby started shouting and rushed to stop him. They were not shouting at the man on the other side of the fence, they just ignored him. They shouted, with voices full of emotion, at Eddy and the rest of the boys. They told them to forget about the man and to focus on what they were doing – training. However, since Eddy did not seem to immediately follow their order, James told him to leave the pitch and go home. This was a form of punishment, an expression of the micro 'disciplinary system' (Foucault 1979 [1975]: 177) James and Zuby attempted to inculcate. Their role gave them the power to decide not only what team to play on Sunday games, but also to implement rules of behaviour at training sessions. They gave orders and sanctioned those who did not abide by them. To some extent, they did believe that their use of 'discipline' could produce 'subjected and practised bodies, "docile" bodies' (Foucault 1979 [1975]: 138). Unfortunately for the coaches, things were not that simple for a team such as Insaka. As soon as James realised that the boy could *really* leave the ground and maybe decide to go and confront the drunken man, he ordered him to go back on the pitch and play. He had to revert his original ejection order, for the good of the boy and the group. In this case, discipline had to be negotiated and compromised – something that Foucault's historical analysis of regimes of discipline arguably did not take into account, and which appears particularly problematic in the study of children and youth institutions (Deacon 2006; Gallagher 2010, 2013). As noted by Dyck (2008: 4):

The likelihood of encountering a wider range of pragmatic problems, opera-tional inconsistencies, and analytical alternatives pertaining to discipline seems to increase significantly when one strays beyond the bounds of textual certainty through engagement in ethnographic inquiry.

In the meantime, the drunken man had left the scene, his bottle hanging loosely from his hand. The training resumed and Zuby reached the side of the pitch where I was standing. He appeared shaken by the incident and made a brief comment: 'These boys, they don't have common sense'. It was clear enough to me that the main reason of concern for James and Zuby was the safety of the group and the individuals. The fact that most of the players were 17, some already 18, old enough to claim autonomy in decision-making, and felt reas-sured by being part of a group of common African background, did not make things easy for the adults in charge of the team. Nevertheless, they would gener-ally accept the coaches' decisions. When they were in serious disagreement with them they would simply leave the team. In my understanding, the discourse on discipline was much about teenagers being able to control their temper, both on the football pitch and off it. Sometimes, this was a problem not limited to the black players in the team, as evidenced by the red cards received by some Eastern European players.

Differential whiteness

Historically, sport has often been considered a great social leveller, a colour-blind space where merit and talent are rewarded regardless of differences in racial, ethnic and social backgrounds (Fletcher and Hylton 2016). However, sport is a cultural domain where ideas about 'race' are actively constructed and re-constructed (Carrington 2010; Hylton 2009) and where 'whiteness' still defines the norm among sport institutions (Burdsey 2011). In general terms, whiteness can be considered as 'an exclusive social category produced through history' (Ware and Back 2002: 27). In the case of Insaka, these issues took par-ticular facets, as black people were in charge of the team and black players were the majority. The white players represented what Fletcher and Hylton (2016: 89) define as 'different shades of white', occupying marginal positions in Irish society among those who appear phenotypically white. A further layer of com-plexity was added by the fact that the Irish themselves, in their migration, had experienced racialisation and the challenge of 'becoming white' (Ignatiev 1995). Hylton (2009: 73) contends that 'whiteness is something that affects us all in ways that enhance or negate our social, cultural and economic capital as it works dynamically with classed, gendered and raced beings'.

Ciprian had told to me that 'there were no whites in the team' before he joined Insaka. Jonathan argued that this team was different because there were 'more blacks than whites'. Emphatic statements which assume a clear demarca-tion along phenotypical lines. However, as indicated by the story of Eric being called 'Paki' while claiming to be 'Black', terms of identification such as 'black' and 'white' have a contested and historically situated nature (Ignatiev 1995; Roediger 2002; Garner 2013). In my fieldwork, I was interested in terms of self-identification used by the boys themselves, but, at the same time, I was attentive to critical declinations (verbal and non-verbal) that could emerge in my interactions with them and between them.

When training was delayed, as often happened after the summer, young players and their friends would arrive and sit on the artificial turf in small groups. Maybe two white boys would be sitting together a few metres away from a larger group of black boys. Cliques along racial lines spontaneously emerged until the moment one 'mediator' would join. There were a few natural mediators in the team: one was Fredy, who had invited some white schoolmates to join Insaka; another was Kelechi, who, not knowing anybody before joining the team, apparently liked to make friends with everybody, regardless of their ethnicity. A third mediator was Ciprian, who was the first Eastern European to join the team and stayed with them even when he lost his place in the starting 11. As said, the Insaka training sessions were often attended by boys who were not in the team. One of them was Almat, originally from Kazakhstan. He was a friend of Mariusz, the Polish boy, but was he considered 'white'? Probably away from this context, by the white majority he would have been visually perceived to be 'Asian' or 'brown', but being a friend of the Polish boy and hanging out with white boys, and not being African, he was apparently made to be 'white'.

Football would often serve a common language to break spontaneous barriers. For example, on a few occasions I witnessed the boys discussing who was the best player, Messi or Ronaldo. Ronaldo was overwhelmingly more popular within this team. In the eyes of many of the teenage boys, both of African or European backgrounds, the one thing that made Ronaldo more interesting than his rival Lionel Messi was his spectacular body, in particular his sculpted 'six pack'. Within this group, the most popular sport practice after football was the gym. Almost all the boys would proudly admit they would go to the gym on a weekly basis.[7] On one occasion, Yano showed his 'six pack' comparing it to that of Ronaldo, and Mariusz did the same. Which one was 'better'? On another occasion, a discussion on 'how to mark skilful players like Ronaldo' involved most of the players in the team. Fredy showed how this should be done, then Vujadin (the tallest in the group) came in and demonstrated his way of marking technical players, emphasising that the defender has to let the player 'feel your presence'. With words, and above all with their own bodies, they re-enacted skills or 'techniques of the body' (Mauss 1973) they had learnt from their coaches or watched on television and the internet. To some extent, the boys, either black or white, were performing a belonging (Bell 1999) – belonging to a common game they all loved to play. Such interactions created transcultural spaces of socialisation among these youths of diverse ethnic and social backgrounds. But they were temporary, precarious spaces, which could vanish as easily as they appeared. They would be made to last a little longer if the team won – as success on the pitch could compensate for the lack of recognition and stability of the team/club, and foster a sense of togetherness across different positions of 'otherness' in Irish society.

The 'racial' composition of Insaka fluctuated and towards the end of my second season with them the team was predominantly 'black'. Over time, Insaka had become more 'African', as it was meant to be from its inception. A number of black boys had also left Insaka during the previous months. This was normal, bearing in mind the observations about the characteristics of teenage sport participation addressed in Chapter 3. But it was the disappearance of the white players that attracted my attention and aroused my curiosity. Did cultural and ethnic differences mean something particular in the context of what I have described as the 'discourse on discipline' articulated within Insaka? To be more precise: how did discipline apply to the 'white' players – who were, in the eyes of their opponents, uncritically rendered homogeneous on the basis of the colour of their skin, as the African boys were through their 'blackness', despite their many different origins and cultural and ethnic backgrounds?

In one occasion Zuby shared with me his view that the white players were 'more disciplined' and were a good example for the African boys. He pointed out that the Eastern Europeans were more regularly attending trainings. He further believed that a difference in attitude was the main reason Mariusz and Vujadin had left the team. While James considered boys of African background better suited for the kind of game he had in mind, and would not be upset at the prospect of running an 'All African' team, Zuby appreciated the importance of having boys of other (white) backgrounds. Early in my fieldwork, I had witnessed an African boy who was sitting on the bench comment that the coach 'shouts to all the players but not to the whites'. At the time I thought it was the bravado of a young man frustrated for not getting 'his game', but over the months I learnt that this was something that worried Zuby. That comment was a rare exception and the boy who made that comment soon left the team.

As the number of players in the squad fluctuated, the same happened to the team's results. In a way, the mood in the team, and the quality of personal relations, depended on the results. The game at Mosney, where Vujadin was sent off, ended in a draw, and it was followed by a series of disappointing results. In one of the following games, even Mariusz, usually a composed and quiet player, was shown a red card. In one training session in February, I took the chance to ask him what was happening in the team. I meant the players being sent off, the tension between teammates on the pitch and an unusual discussion with the coaches after a game Insaka lost at home. He said: 'It's always like this, when you start to lose games people start going mad, if you win everybody is happy'. Like Jonathan and Charlie, he seemed to have a clear vision of what being in a football team means. He was apologetic about his reaction, which resulted in his first red card ever. 'That player was cheating on me and the ref did nothing', he commented. Following his suspension, Mariusz lost his place in the starting 11 and that was when his commitment declined. He was soon gone, not to return.

Vujadin left the team at about the same time, but I felt it was not simply lack of game-time or poor results that justified his decision. On a few occasions he had lamented with me and some teammates the 'lack of organisation' and 'punctuality' in Insaka. This was not only affecting training sessions, but also Sunday morning rendezvous. To leave Blanchardstown for away games the team would usually meet at 9 am in the Blanchardstown Shopping Centre parking lot. Taking their players to away games was one of the most difficult tasks for the team's administrators. On those days, Zuby and James were often late, as they would spend time on the phone, calling friends, asking them to drive some of the boys to every destination they were supposed to go to play. Delays were normal, and organisational problems were evident. A few times James asked the players – those who were already 18 years old – if they could come in their mother's cars. Some did so. On a couple of occasions, a van was rented by Ken to take the group to a particularly distant destination. When the team won, problems were minimised. But when something began to go wrong, that was the time when issues emerged. 'I can't stand this lack of organisation', commented Vujadin in the weeks following the Mosney incident. 'I don't like to play in a team like this, it's already 9.30 and coaches are not here', he added. The lack of organisation reflected the precariousness of the club's existence, and this arguably did not create great expectations for the young players. They liked it anyway because it was different from any other team they had played before – it was more fun playing 'ball to feet', and, above all, it was quite successful. However, after a few negative results and a couple of incidents, due especially to bad refereeing, some players started losing affection and commitment. In the end, for some, it did not seem worth the effort.

The Cup Final: in memory of a friend

The results of the team were inconsistent for a while, but in the spring they improved and the last part of the season was very positive. Their expectations of success were gratified by the opportunity to play for the League Cup. The Cup Final was played in the training centre of the North Dublin Schoolboys League in front of about 300 people (an unusually large audience for this league). A minority of the crowd was made of young members of the African immigrant communities and some family members of the players. Some former Insaka players of African background turned up to support their friends. The game was supervised by a referee and two official linesmen. Everything conferred importance to the event, magnifying its ritualistic language and meaning (Archetti 1999). James made sure that the players' behaviour and performance were at their best, underlining in his dressing room speech that 'if you win, all the eyes will be on you'. They played against a team made up of all white Irish boys. Despite the hard tackling by the opposition, the Insaka players kept their composure and played well throughout the game, winning 3–0. The referee controlled the game and the team's discipline was, as the coach commented afterwards, 'exemplary'. The end of the match celebration lasted several minutes, with the players carrying James around the pitch and screaming their joy.

In the days before the final I had discussed with some of the boys the idea of making a short video about the upcoming match, responding to an expressed desire of theirs. I edited a five-minute clip following the pattern of my first video for Mountview. I interpreted the video as an act of giving back and a little tribute to all the people involved in the club. During the celebration, right after the end of the game, Jude was wearing the T-shirt in memory of Toyosi. As soon as he showed it he was joined by his teammates (Figure 5.2). He looked in the camera and shouted: 'This is for you Toy! This is for you!' They were later presented with medals and the trophy, and the T-shirt was displayed in front of them, placing it at the centre of the scene. Friends, relatives and other people were watching, so Kennedy took the opportunity to say a few words, holding the T-shirt in his hands, while someone was holding the UEFA Respect campaign flag underneath it.[8] 'We want to dedicate this trophy to one of us who was a player in the Republic of Ireland and who suddenly lost his life last year', he said, followed by clapping hands and the emotional screaming of the boys.

The sporting event and the trophy Insaka had just won were charged with a special meaning that went beyond the fact that Toyosi was a football player and had started playing with Insaka. For the players and their adult mentors, this was an opportunity to talk 'to the public' about his story – a story that, until his sudden death, was very similar to those of his friends playing for Insaka. During the trophy's presentation all the young players celebrated in front of my camera and their friends and relatives' cameras with the same hand gesture, similar to the one that signifies 'okay': the thumb and index fingers are connected to form

Figure 5.2 In memory of a friend.

a circle, while the other fingers are held very straight in the air. 'What does this mean?' I asked Lio, a 17-years-old winger of Nigerian origin. 'It's a Blanchards-town thing, you know. Representing Blanchardstown', he answered. Their feeling of belonging, not or not only to the team, but to a community of young boys polarised along the 'colour line' (Du Bois 2008 [1903]) was interwoven with the sense of belonging to a locality, of being from a certain part of town. As Hopkins notes, 'For many young people, their sense of identity and com-munity is shaped by where they live, the territorial affiliation they hold and the tensions that exist between them and groups of young people from neighbouring communities' (Hopkins 2010: 119). Often these forms of behaviour are inter-woven with other forms of identification, such as religion or ethnicity. The idea of 'representing Blanchardstown' is a form of 'neighbourhood nationalism' (Back 1996: 56), which seems to particularly appeal to boys of different African back-grounds who also stick together away from the football pitch. This pattern of belonging emerged quite spontaneously, but what about belonging to a larger 'community', that conceptualised as the 'nation'? This is what I will turn my attention to in the final sections of this chapter.

Would you play for Congo or Ireland?

Football is increasingly interpreted as one of the main sites for the projection and representation of ideas of the 'nation' (Armstrong and Mitchell 2008). Dine and Crosson (2010: 2) contend that 'sporting practices and representations con-tribute significantly to the social construction of identities'. Therefore, the choice of which national team to support or to wish to play for is, for immigrant youth, of symbolic importance – a choice that also has social and cultural implications (Poli 2007; Rowe 2018). During my time with Insaka I could at times notice someone training in an Angola jersey. Almat was often seen in a Kazakhstan jersey and Benni in a T-shirt with the colours of South Africa's national flag. Of course, there was always someone who would wear football shirts of teams such as Manchester United, Chelsea or Arsenal, but the national teams' shirts arguably carried a different meaning, imbued with questions of national identification and a broader sense of cultural belonging.

'Would you play for Ireland or Congo?' Ken once bluntly asked one of the players, who had spent half his life in Ireland, as a way to engage him in a dis-cussion that we were both quite interested in to develop. The boy looked back and smiled. 'Congo', he uttered after a few seconds, but he did not seem as intrigued by the topic as both of us were. In defining national and cultural affili-ations in the era of globalisation, Appadurai (1996) uses the term 'ethnoscape'. According to him, 'the landscapes of group identity in the 20th century need a new definition, the groups are no longer tightly territorialized, spatially bounded, historically unselfconscious, culturally homogeneous' (Appadurai 1996: 210). Today, migrant youth are often at the foreground of these intersections, for they find themselves in-between cultures (Bhabha 1996), navigating through different forms of belonging that are framed and influenced not only by the places they happen to travel to and reside in, but further by digital means of communication, in particular online social networks, and corporate branding targeting youth with the aim of creating 'follower-type consumers' (Boden 2006; Rinehart 2008). With this in mind, in the case of adolescents of immigrant background, the concept of 'transculturation' emerges as a particularly relevant theoretical construct. It is precisely this concept that Hoerder *et al.* (2005) adopt to depict immigrant youth living in Europe and North America's sense of cultural belonging. At the same time, Back and Sinha (2012), drawing on their work with young migrants in London, alert us of new hierarchies of belonging produced within a neo-liberal and globalised world. 'For migrants, tension exists constantly because their footing on the ladder of inclusion is neither stable nor clear but contingent and always subject to scrutiny' (Back and Sinha 2012: 149).

At the Ongar training pitch, conversations such as the one elicited by Ken occurred more than once. Given their age, and the league they were playing in, it was quite unlikely that any of these young players could be selected for a national team. There were no immediate practical implications about which national team one may choose to play for. Nevertheless, this topic provided a fruitful terrain for the expression of feelings of national and ethnic belonging (Seiberth *et al.* 2017). On that particular day, I decided to continue the conversation with the boy who claimed his 'sporting allegiance' (McGee and Bairner 2011: 438) for Congo; his name was Tony. He was not a member of the team, but would often attended training sessions and was well known to me. We were sitting on the synthetic grass and he was putting on his training boots. We were soon joined by another boy and later by two more. I first asked Tony about his manifest interest in playing for 'Congo', despite having spent most of his childhood in Ireland.[9] Martin entered the conversation saying that he would prefer playing for Ireland and not for his native Nigeria. His tone was playful, with some cussing, but his point was firm. The conversation continued between the two boys, both aged 17.

MAX: What country would you like to play for?

TONY: I want to play for my country, Congo.

MARTIN: I'd play for Ireland, fuck you and your country.

TONY: That's why I want to make a few videos and send them down there.

MAX: Why do you want to play for Ireland?

MARTIN: I want to play in the European Cup, the Africa Cup of Nations is shite.

TONY: Think about it, if you go to Ireland they won't treat you like a star. If you go to Nigeria you get all the attention you want.

MARTIN: I don't want attention.

TONY: What do you want?

MARTIN: I just want to play ball.

TONY: That's if you play ball, though.

MARTIN: Okay.

TONY: They are racist, they don't want black people like you.

MARTIN: Yes they do.

TONY: Barely. Nigeria are better than Ireland.

MARTIN: They are shite.

TONY: They have better players than Ireland.

MARTIN: They are shite, they couldn't even beat North Korea.

TONY: That's because they have a shit coach. If they had someone like Trapattoni, what do you think?

MAX (talking to two other boys who sat down, probably attracted by the conversation): And what about you?

ERIC: I want to play for Congo. Ireland they won't put you on.

GABRIEL: No, if you are good enough they would.

ERIC: Congo for life.

TONY: Play for Africa, man.

Tony wants to play 'for Africa' because that's where he comes from, and he thinks that 'black' immigrants won't be considered for the Irish national team. Martin apparently shows a feeble affiliation to his place of birth and declares his interest to play for the 'best team', or at least the one that is going to play in the most important competitions, namely the European Football Championship instead of the Africa Cup of Nations. In their discussion they significantly overlook the fact that they were both living in Ireland as refugees and did not possess Irish citizenship. Therefore, their choice for which country to play for was limited. While Tony's stance is a little surprising, as it confirms the conventional link between country of origin and sporting nation, Martin's stance is less predictable. But if Martin's opinion is read in the context of diasporic youth's dynamic and fragmented identities (Dolby and Rizvi 2008), it does not appear that surprising. The question of which nation to support or even belong to also depends on the structural positioning of the protagonists. Do these young people have a choice? And is this choice equal? And why should one bother which sporting nation one chooses if the individual bears two or more nationalities, a feature of many young people with an immigrant background?

In early 2011, the French Minister of Sport, Chantal Jouanno, launched an official inquiry after the news emerged that the technical staff of the French Football Federation (FFF) had discussed the possibility of excluding from national youth academies those players (expressively referring to those of Black African background) who might, later in their lives, opt to play for the nations of origin of their parents or ancestors. According to Mediapart, the news website that published the leaked verbatim account of that meeting, the manager of the men's national team, Laurent Blanc, was well-disposed towards a change in the selection criteria of youth talent aged between 12 and 13 'to favour those who he described as having "our culture, our history"'.[10] In May 2018, at a friendly match played by Italy's men's national team, a banner was unfurled that read: 'My captain has Italian blood', a racist reference to the possibility that the captain's armband could be worn by Mario Balotelli, son of Ghanaian immigrants. The Minister of the Interior, Matteo Salvini, commented that he hoped the manager would choose the captain 'not for sociological, philosophical, and anthropological reasons', implying that Balotelli would not be the best choice.[11] These are just two examples of the role that football, as the most global and popular sport, plays in public discourses around national identity and immigration in contemporary Europe. Football has become a highly contested terrain of change and resistance, where the tension between globalisation and the national-state is played out (Hase 2002; Levermore 2004; Sawyer and Gooding 2013). Contrasting visions are at play, which go beyond the field of sport. Ulrich Beck, for example, advocates a 'cosmopolitan vision' which would make the nation-state outdated:

> The national outlook, together with its associated grammar, it is becoming false. It fails to grasp that political, economic and cultural action and their (intended and unintended) consequences know no borders; indeed, it is completely blind to the fact that, even when nationalism is reignited by the collision with globality, this can only be conceptualized from the cosmopolitan perspective.
>
> (2006: 19)

At the same time, across Europe, nationalism is on the rise, as are forms of racism against minorities and immigrants (ENAR 2015). Appadurai argues that 'nation-states are struggling to retain control over their population in the face of a host of subnational and transnational movements and organizations' (Appadurai 1996: 170). And again, 'the 'task of producing locality (as a structure of feeling, a property of social life, and an ideology of situated community) is increasingly a struggle' (Appadurai 1996: 170). An example of the 'struggle' of 'producing locality' within the context of the Republic of Ireland, may be the attention given by media and public bodies to the decline of Gaelic Games in rural areas due to emigration and urbanisation.[12] Broadly speaking, national sport representatives are a viable tool for the state to affirm on a global stage what it is or aspires to be. The conditions that, during the nineteenth and twentieth centuries, made the founders of many European states believe in 'the myth of the nation-state' (Walby 2003: 1) have changed considerably, if not entirely. As evidenced by numerous examples in post-colonial countries, football and other popular sports have often played a role in the construction of national identities, and they continue doing so at many levels (Bairner 2001; Darby 2016; Naha 2018). However, some conditions are not the same anymore, and the spontaneous conversation among boys of immigrant background at the Ongar training pitch is an example of what I have been arguing.

Asked about their sense of national belonging, some of the players in Insaka admitted that being of mixed backgrounds and living as immigrants in a third country, they did not have a straight answer to give. This decision would depend on various factors, including the country of origin of their father ('You know, you go with your dad', said Jonathan, son of Congolese father and an Angolan mother). Other such factors were the country in which they felt more at home, or the country where they were made to feel at home. Some of the African boys, such as Sam and Yano, were born in other European countries but were taken to Ireland at an early age. Others moved several times during their childhood, having to work at creating bonds and then leaving and having to create new ones. At a training session I was once introduced to a cousin of Yano who spoke Italian with a strong 'Milanese' accent. He was born in Congo but had moved to Italy with his family at the age of three and had lived there until he was 16, when he moved to Ireland. He was now 19. He spoke various languages fluently, but what about his 'sense of national belonging'? He told me it was not very important to him the nation he belonged to, as long he could live in peace. What is implicit in the lived experiences of migration of many young people such as those I met during my time with Mountview and Insaka, and somehow lacking in both Beck's and Appadurai's conceptualisation of globalisation, is a question that has been analysed by Agamben (1995, 1998, 2005). For according to Agamben, one of the prevalent traits of contemporary sovereign state politics is the deepening of the shift from the 'rights of man' to the 'rights of the citizen', something that was already *in nuce* in the French *Declaration of the Rights of Man and the Citizen*.[13] Consequentially, 'non-citizens' – working immigrants, unaccompanied minors, refugees, asylum seekers, *sans papier*, *clandestini* and the many terminological declinations invented by the West to define the 'Other' living in its sovereign territory – are entitled to partial rights or no rights at all. Their destinies are in the hands of sovereign states that more often than not deal with them according to a juridical 'state of exception' (Agamben 2005). In contrast, 'citizens', especially citizen of Western countries, can fully enjoy the benefits of their hierarchical position. Their decision about 'national identity' can arguably be more predictable.

But yet there is also another element that must be taken into consideration in this discussion: the racialised identities of immigrants (Balibar and Wallerstein 1991). In Ireland, as in other European countries, some immigrants are stigmatised more than others – their trajectory of 'inclusion' is made more complicated by cultural and political factors. When the African boys say 'I want to play for Congo. Ireland they won't put you on' and 'No, if you are good enough they would', there is a perceived *problem* with someone being originally from Congo *and* representing Ireland. Towards the end of the 1980s, in his examination of the politics of race and nation in Britain, Paul Gilroy (1987) commented that 'There ain't no black in the Union Jack'. What about Ireland in 2018? Can 'black' people (of immigrant background) be considered 100% Irish or, using the ironic suggestion presented in Roddy Doyle's (2008) fiction story

'57% Irish', be allowed only partial 'Irishness'? Lentin and McVeigh (2006: 166) hold a pessimistic view of the possibility that 'the new communities of colour' are fully included in Irish society. They write:

> Globalisation has created the context in which we come to terms with racism – in Ireland and around the world. Increasingly, both multi-culturalism and interculturalism are abandoned as 'integration' becomes the watchword for managing racism in the 21st century. The problem of racism is both displaced and denied – now the real problem is located within the qualities of those minorities that need to be 'integrated'. It is not the racism of the 'host society' but the cultural and political incompatibility of the new communities of colour – immigrants, migrant workers, refugees and asylum seekers – that is asserted as the cause of the problems.
>
> (Lentin and McVeigh 2006: 166)

The story of Noe Baba

Sometime after the discussion surrounding national belonging and football that took place at the Ongar pitch, I came across the news regarding Noe Baba, a 15-year-old boy of Cameroonian background who was named captain of the Under-15 Republic of Ireland team.[14] His story fitted perfectly in the discussion I had elicited at the Insaka training pitch, because it could be considered proof that 'if you are good enough' Ireland would not have a problem in selecting you for its national team, even though you are 'black' or a member of an immigrant community.[15] However, reality has different faces and there is something that would impede all Insaka players from being selected for an Ireland side: none of them, at the time of my fieldwork, possessed Irish citizenship.

In the Irish context, however, there is a peculiar manifestation of this problem. Over the last 10 years, immigrant youth had been selected to represent the Republic of Ireland in football even if they did not bear an Irish passport. For this reason, they were only allowed to play home-games. This is the case, for example, of Emeka Omwubiko, originally from Nigeria, who was capped 11 times for the Republic of Ireland Under-17 team before being granted a passport and being allowed to travel abroad with the national team.[16] Noe Babas' story appears to be a more positive one, for he only arrived in Ireland in 2007 but by 2011 he was already playing regularly for the Irish national youth team – although even his football experience in Ireland has not been free from racial abuse.[17] On the internet, I found an article from a local newspaper about him, so I printed it out and brought to the next Insaka game, a friendly match organised in Belfast as part of the collaboration between Insaka and Glentoran FC. I waited to take the sheet out of my bag until all the players were on the bus, on the way back to Dublin.

I handed the photocopy of the article to some of the players, asking if they knew the story and what they would think about it. None of them had heard of it before. There was some incredulity among them, even though not everybody showed interest in it. 'He is a man', shouted a voice from the back after looking at the picture of the young Irish captain. 'He seems much older than 15', added another one. 'He looks like he is 30!' said a third voice eliciting laughter. Fredy seemed particularly attracted to the story and asked me for the sheet. 'Did you write it?' he asked. 'No, it is not something that I have written, I just thought the story was interesting', I answered. 'So, what do you think?' I bluntly and naively asked him before waiting for him to finish reading it. 'It's good', was his emphatic answer, before getting back to the reading. Then the sheet passed on to other boys, who were curious to read it. Even though I did not get very expressive feedback I could see that the story was doing its 'job', that of eliciting reflection and, maybe, inspiring new ideas about belonging. As a matter of fact, this resonates with Noe Baba's answer to the question of what it means for him to play for the Republic of Ireland national team: 'It makes me feel I am part of this place now'.[18]

Gilroy (1987) argues that sport discourses, in particular those around football, can shape national identities and our racialised identities. As it happened in other countries, the presence of players of immigrant background in the Republic of Ireland national football team does not only challenge the perception of homogeneous and fixed 'national' characteristics (to some degree these were already challenged by the presence of black players of Irish descent in the past, such as Paul McGrath), but further enhances the sense of inclusion of youth of immigrant background. The news surrounding Noe Baba's captaincy of a Republic of Ireland youth team resonates with the conversations about 'national teams' that I often observed and sometimes elicited during my time with Mountview and Insaka.

Arguably, James, Zuby and Ken could also see things differently now. As a matter of fact, the main aspiration James had for Insaka was precisely that of 'making one of them in a better place', meaning to help a boy (of African background) to become a professional footballer. Ken's aspiration was that of seeing young players of immigrant background being capped by the Irish national team. He believed that this could be a way to counter the spread of racism in Irish society and create role models for immigrant youth. As I learned during my fieldwork with Insaka, 'racism' was an explanation for many of the problems the team encountered. The recurring discourse on discipline appeared in the end to be just a wishful strategy to resist racial abuse and discrimination. At the same time, the team was playing and winning to keep alive the memory of their friend and teammate Toyosi. Will Noe Baba's example and other similar ones be able to determine changes in the acceptance of immigrant cultures into the 'national outlook' (Beck 2006: 19; Amelina and Faist 2012)? It is one of the questions that will be addressed in the final chapter of the book, where I will revisit the sites and main themes of my ethnographic study.

Notes

1 Here, my experience was similar to Gallagher's (2000), in that a white informant used racist talk with me assuming a shared kinship.
2 The bizarre story of this holiday centre turned into a refugee centre has been told in the documentary film *Seaview* (Gogan and Rowley 2008). As of April 2018, the Mosney Accommodation Centre hosted 793 refugees of 39 different nationalities. Reception and Integration Agency (RIA) *Inspection Report*, 3 April 2018, www.ria-inspections.gov.ie/en/RIAIR/2018%20Mosney%20Inspection%20Report%203%20April.pdf/Files/2018%20Mosney%20Inspection%20Report%203%20April.pdf [accessed 1 July 2018].
3 'A nation of welcomes? New figures challenge the Republic of Ireland's record on asylum and immigration', *The Detail*, 12 February 2018, www.thedetail.tv/articles/a-nation-of-welcomes-assessing-the-republic-of-ireland-s-record-on-asylum-and-immigration [accessed 20 September 2018].
4 The ban to work was lifted in June 2018 for those who have been in Ireland for nine months or more and have not had a first decision made on their refugee status. 'About 3,000 asylum seekers to have right to work', *The Irish Times*, 28 June 2018. Until June 2017, the weekly allowance was €19.10.
5 Unfortunately, such statistics, if at all in existence, have not been made available by the FAI for the purpose of this book.
6 In the early 1970s there were about 15,000 'hidden children' (from the title of Frigerio and Buergherr's 1992 book) or 'undocumented children' in Switzerland, mostly sons and daughters of Italian, Spanish and Portuguese seasonal immigrants.
7 One of the Eastern European boys, who was reluctant to pay his 'subs' (€2.5 per game), admitted to me that he was a regular at an inner city gym, where he could also practise martial arts. It cost him €40 per month.
8 'Respect' is a social responsibility programme launched in 2008 by the Union of European Football Associations (UEFA) with the slogan: Respect the Diversity, Respect the Opponent, Respect the Game.
9 He probably meant the Democratic Republic of the Congo, since this was the country is family was originally from.
10 In May 2011, Blanc and his colleagues were cleared of breaking anti-discrimination laws, but the inquiry stressed the following:

> It emerges very clearly that ways to limit the numbers of so-called dual-national players, including putting in place quotas were, in fact, debated … The general impression that emerges is really very unpleasant, with innuendoes that very often were borderline tending toward racist.
> (http://espn.go.com/sports/soccer/news/_/id/6519252/france-coach-laurent-blanc-cleared-discrimination [accessed 23 August 2011])

11 'Salvini su Balotelli: Capitano della Nazionale? Serve umiltà' (Salvini on Balotelli: Captain of the national team? You need humility), *Gazzetta dello Sport*, 4 June 2018.
12 'GAA officials in crisis talks as emigration threatens clubs' survival', *Irish Independent*, 18 January 2013.
13 In *Homo sacer*, Agamben (1998: 75) writes: 'In the phrase *La declaration des droits de l'homme et du citoyen*, it is not clear whether the two terms homme and citoyen name two autonomous beings or instead form a unitary system in which the first is always already included in the second. And if the latter is the case, the kind of relation that exists between homme and citoyen still remains unclear'.
14 'From Cameroon to Castlebar', *Mayo News*, 28 February 2012.
15 To date, a number of black players with Irish heritage have represented the Republic of Ireland on the football pitch, for example Paul McGrath and Chris Hughton. As

of August 2018, a player of immigrant background has yet to break into the Irish
men's senior national team.
16 See FAI (2007: 18).
17 'Rising star tackles racial abuse', *Irish Examiner*, 1 March 2012.
18 'Rising star tackles racial abuse', *Irish Examiner*, 1 March 2012.

References

Agamben, G. (1995). 'We refugees'. *Symposium*, 49(2), 114–119.

Agamben, G. (1998). *Homo sacer. Sovereign power and bare life*. Stanford, CA: Stanford
University Press.

Agamben, G. (2005). *State of exception*. Chicago: University of Chicago Press.

Amelina, A. and Faist, T. (2012). 'De-naturalizing the national in research methodologies: Key concepts of transnational studies in migration'. *Ethnic and Racial Studies*,
35(10), 1707–1724.

Appadurai, A. (1996). *Modernity at large: Cultural dimensions of globalization*. Minneapolis: University of Minnesota Press.

Archetti, E. (1999). *Masculinities, football, polo, and the tango in Argentina*. Oxford: Berg.

Armstrong, G. and Mitchell, J. (2008). *Global and local football*. London: Routledge.

Back, L. (1993). 'Gendered participation: Masculinity and fieldwork in a South London
adolescent community'. In D. Bell, P. Caplan and K. Wazir Jahan (eds), *Gendered
fields. Women, men and ethnography*. London: Routledge, 215–233.

Back, L. (1996). *New ethnicities and urban culture: Racisms and multiculture in young lives*.
London: UCL Press.

Back, L., Sinha, S. with Bryan, C. (2012). 'New hierarchies of belonging'. *European
Journal of Cultural Studies*, 15(2), 139–154.

Bairner, A. (2001). *Sport, nationalism and globalization*. New York: State University of
New York Press.

Balibar, E. and Wallerstein, I. (1991). *Race, nation, class: Ambiguous identities*. London: Verso.

Beck, U. (2006). *The cosmopolitan vision*. Cambridge: Polity Press.

Bell, V. (ed.) (1999). *Performativity and belonging*. London: Sage.

Bhabha, H. (1996). 'Culture's in-between'. In S. Hall and P. du Gay (eds), *Questions of
cultural identity*. London: Sage, 53–60.

Boden, S. (2006). 'Dedicated followers of fashion? The influence of popular culture on
children's social identities'. *Media, Culture & Society*, 28(2), 289–298.

Burdsey, D. (2011). 'They think it's all over … it isn't yet!'. In D. Burdsey (ed.), *Race,
ethnicity and football: Persisting debates and emergent issues*. London: Routledge, 3–20.

Carrington, B. (2010). *Race, sport and politics: The sporting black diaspora*. London: Sage.

Darby, P. (2016). 'Football and identity politics in Ghana'. In A. Bairner, G. Kelly and J.
Woo Lee (eds), *Routledge handbook of sport and politics*. London: Routledge, 137–149.

Deacon, R. (2006). 'Michel Foucault on education: A preliminary theoretical Overview'.
South African Journal of Education, 26(2), 177–187.

Denzin, N. (1997). *Interpretive ethnography*. Thousand Oaks, CA: Sage.

Denzin, N. (2007). 'Book review: Loïc Wacquant body & soul: Notebooks of an appren-
tice boxer'. *Cultural Sociology*, 1(3), 29–30.

Denzin, N. K. and Lincoln, Y. S. (2011). 'Introduction: The discipline and practice of
qualitative research'. *The Sage handbook of qualitative research*, fourth edition. London:
Sage, 1–20.

Dine, P. and Crosson, S. (eds) (2010). *Sport, representation and evolving identities in Europe*. Bern: Berg.

Dolby, N. and Rizvi, F. (eds) (2008). *Youth moves. Identities and education in global perspective*. New York: Routledge.

Doyle, R. (2008). *The deportees*. London: Vintage.

Du Bois, W. E. B. (2008 [1903]). *The souls of black folk*. London: Penguin.

Duneier, M. (1999). *Sidewalk*. New York: Farrar, Straus and Giroux.

Dyck, N. (2008). 'Anthropological perspectives on discipline'. In N. Dyck (ed.), *Exploring regimes of discipline*. London: Berghahn Books, 1–22.

ENAR – European Network Against Racism (2015). *Invisible visible minority*. Brussels: ENAR.

FAI – Football Association of Ireland (2007). 'FAI intercultural football plan'. Dublin: FAI.

Fanning, B., Killoran, B., Ni Bhroin, S. and McEvoy, G. (2011). *Taking racism seriously*. Dublin: Trinity Immigration Initiative & Immigrant Council of Ireland.

Fanon, F. (1987 [1952]). *Black skin, white masks*. London: Pluto Press.

Fletcher, T. and Hylton, K. (2016). '"Race", whiteness and sport'. In D. K. Wiggins and J. Nauright (eds), *Routledge handbook of sport, race and ethnicity*. London: Routledge, 87–106.

Foucault, M. (1979 [1975]). *Discipline and punish*. Harmondsworth: Penguin Books.

Frigerio, M. and Buergherr, S. (1992). *Versteckte Kinder (Hidden children)*. Luzern: Rex-Verlag.

Frigerio, M and Merhar, S. (2004). *Und Es Kamen Menschen. Die Schweiz Der Italiener (...And came men. The Switzerland of the Italians)*. Zurich: Rotpunktverlag.

Gallagher. C. (2000). 'White like me? Methods, meaning, and manipulation in the field of white studies'. In F. W. Twine and J. W. Warren (eds), *Racing research, researching race: Methodological dilemmas in critical race studies*. New York: NYU Press, 67–92.

Gallagher, M. (2010). 'Are schools panoptic?'. *Surveillance & Society*, 7(3/4), 262–272.

Gallagher, M. (2013). 'Using Foucault in school research: Looking beyond the Panopticon'. *Social Theory Applied*, webblog, 4 April. Available from: http://socialtheoryapplied.com/2013/04/04/using-foucault-in-school-research-thinking-beyond-the-panopticon/ [accessed 10 July 2013].

Garner, S. (2013). 'Reflections on race in contemporary Ireland'. In J. V. Ulin, H. Edwards and S. O'Brien (eds), *Race and immigration in the New Ireland*. Notre Dame, IN: University of Notre Dame Press, 175–204.

Gilroy, P. (1987). *There ain't no black in the Union*. London: Routledge.

Gogan, K. and Rowley, P. (2008). *Seaview*. Film, Ireland, 81 minutes.

Goldberg, D. T. (2002). *The racial state*. Hoboken, USA: Wiley-Blackwell.

Goldberg, D. T. (2015). *Are we all postracial yet?* Cambridge, UK: Polity Books.

Hall, S. (1997). *Representation. Cultural representation and signifying practices*. London: Sage.

Hase, M. (2002). 'Race in soccer as a global sport'. In J. Bloom and M. D. Willard (eds), *Sports matters: Race, recreation and culture*. New York: New York University Press, 299–319.

Hassan, D. and McCue K. (2013). 'The "silent" Irish – Football, migrants and the pursuit of integration'. In D. Hassan (ed.), *Ethnicity and race in association football: Case study analyses in Europe, Africa and the USA*. London: Routledge, 126–138.

Hoerder, D., Hebert, Y. and Schmitt, I. (eds) (2005). *Negotiating transcultural lives: Belongings and social capital among youth in comparative perspective*. Toronto: University of Toronto Press.

Hopkins, P. (2010). *Young people, place and identity*. London: Routledge.

Huizinga, J. (1980 [1938]). *Homo ludens: A study of the play-element in culture*. London: Routledge.

Hylton, K. (2009). *'Race' and sport. Critical race theory*. London: Routledge.

Ignatiev, N. (1995). *How the Irish became white*. London: Routledge.

King, C. (2004). 'Race and cultural identity: Playing the race game within football'. *Leisure/Loisir*, 23, 19–30.

Lentin, R. and McVeigh, R. (2006). *After Optimism? Ireland, racism and globalisation*. Dublin: Metro Eireann Publications.

Lentin, R. (2007). 'Ireland: Racial state and crisis racism'. *Ethnic and Racial Studies*, 30(4), 610–627.

Lentin, R. (2016). 'Asylum seekers, Ireland, and the return of the repressed'. *Irish Studies Review*, 24(1), 21–34.

Levermore, R. (2004). 'Sport's role in constructing the "interstate" worldview'. In R. Levermore and A. Budd (eds), *Sports and international relations: An emerging relationship*. London: Routledge, 16–30.

Loyal, S. (2011). *Understanding Irish immigration: Capital, state, and labour in a global age*. Manchester: Manchester University Press.

Loyal, S. and Quilley, S. (2018). *State power and asylum seekers in Ireland*. Basingstoke: Palgrave Macmillan.

Malcolm, D. (2008). *The Sage dictionary of sport studies*. London: Sage.

Mauro, M. (2005). *La mia casa è dove sono felice (My home is where I am happy)*. Udine: KappaVu.

Mauss, M. (1973). 'Techniques of the body'. *Economy and Society*, 2, 70–88.

McGee, D. and Bairner, A. (2011). 'Transcending the borders of Irish identity? Narratives of Northern nationalist footballers in Northern Ireland'. *International Review for the Sociology of Sport*, 46(4), 436–455.

McGinnity, F, O'Connell, P., Quinn, E. and Williams, J. (2006). *Migrant's experience of racism and discrimination in Ireland*. Dublin: The Economic and Social Research Institute Dublin.

Mezzadra, S. (2006). *Diritto di fuga. Migrazioni, cittadinanza, globalizzazione (The right to escape. Migration, citizenship, globalization)*. Verona: Ombre Corte.

Mezzadra, S. and Neilson, B. (2013). *Border as method, or the multiplication of labor*. Durham: Duke University Press.

Naha, S. (2018). 'A state without a nation? Historicising India's "conspiracy" against Bengal and its cricketers'. In D. Hassan and C. Acton (eds), *Sport and contested identities*. London: Routledge, 132–152.

Ni Chonaill, B. (2009). 'Perceptions of migrants and their impact in the Blanchardstown area: Local views'. Report, Dublin: Irish Research Council in Humanities and Social Science.

Ni Laoire, C., Carpena-Mendez, F., Tyrrel, N. and White, A. (2011). *Childhood and migration in Europe*. London: Ashgate.

NYCI – National Youth Council of Ireland (2017). *Make minority a priority. Insights from minority ethnic people and recommendations for the youth work sector*, Report. Dublin: NYCI.

Poli, R. (2007). 'The denationalization of sport: De-ethnicization of the nation and identity deterritorialization'. *Sport in Society*, 10(4), 646–661.

Rinehart, R. (2008). 'Exploiting a new generation. Corporate branding and the co-optation of action-sport'. In M. Giardina and M. Donnelly (eds), *Youth culture and sport*. New York: Routledge, 71–90.

Roediger, D. R. (2002). *Colored white: Transcending the racial past*. Berkeley, CA: University of California Press.

Rowe, D. (2018). 'Competing allegiances, divided loyalties'. In D. Hassan and C. Acton (eds), *Sport and contested identities*. London: Routledge, 155–174.

Sawyer, M. Q. and Gooding, C. C. (2013). 'Racism, body politics and football'. In D. L. Andrews and B. Carrington (eds), *A companion to sport*. Chichester: Wiley-Blackwell, 164–178.

Seiberth, K., Thiel, A. and Spaaij, R. (2017). 'Ethnic identity and the choice to play for a national team: A study of junior elite football players with a migrant background'. *Journal of Ethnic and Migration Studies*, published online 29 November 2017. DOI: 10.1080/1369183X.2017.1408460.

Walby, S. (2003). 'The myth of the nation-state: Theorizing society and polities in a global era'. *Sociology*, 37(3), 529–546.

Ware, V. and Back, L. (2002). *Out of whiteness: Color, politics and culture*. Chicago: University of Chicago Press.

Chapter 6

Follow up

The story that was not there

It's a Tuesday morning at the end of July 2018. I have embarked on a cycling exploration of the locations of my ethnographic study of sport practices of young people living in north-west Dublin. The bicycle allows me to move peacefully, and silently, through the maze-like design of these recent suburbs. It also helps in creating a counterpoint effect to the complicated emotional bequest of doing immersive qualitative research. Between January 2009 and June 2011, I spent most of my weekends attending football matches in this area and in formal and improvised pitches across Dublin and beyond. I regularly attended training sessions and became familiar with the people and the places. The people I was spending time with also became, to some extent, familiar with my presence. Since the completion of my PhD, in the spring of 2013, I have returned at least once a year to Dublin. I have kept in touch with some of the participants, following from afar their life trajectories, and paid attention to the developments in Irish sport and society (Mauro 2014, 2016a). However, I was not entirely prepared for some of the material changes in the urban landscape brought about by the post-recession recovery that some have defined as a 'new boom'.[1] When I finished my PhD and went back to Italy, Dublin was slowly recovering from the recession that started in 2008; the traces of something gone dramatically wrong were visible and intrinsically part of my fieldwork. The uncompleted all-weather pitch that Insaka used as their training ground, for example. The fields on the other side of the road, where horses were left to wander amid worn-out signs that announced the *imminent* construction of new houses. Those images were no longer there, their content irreparably altered.

This chapter will start from here, from the material changes in the setting of my study. It will then return to the questions introduced in Chapter 1, and explored throughout the book, with the aim of placing some of the themes into a longitudinal perspective. The aim is to critically situate my discussion of sport, belonging, and migration in Ireland in a constantly evolving reality. The chapter will also foreground a reflection from some young research participants on the contribution that sport, namely football, has played in the development of their subjective and collective identities. Before doing so, however, I feel the need to address some theoretical and epistemological problems that have accompanied the writing of this book.

Denzin provides a definition of ethnography that is fascinating and challenging at the same time, and one I wish to subscribe to. He writes:

> Ethnography is not an innocent practice. Our research practices are performative, pedagogical, and political. Through our writing and our talk, we enact the words we study. These performances are messy and pedagogical. They instruct our readers about this world and how we see it. The pedagogical is always moral and political; by enacting a way of seeing and being, it challenges, contests, or endorses the official, hegemonic ways of seeing and representing the other.
>
> (Denzin 2006: 422)

Among the critical tasks in conducting qualitative research in the way that I have done in West Dublin over a number of years, are that of combining critique with dialogue (Back 2002), and that of producing 'a text to read not with the eyes, but with the ears in order to hear "the voices of the pages"' (Tyler 1986: 136). On the one hand, one has to create a dialogue which enables the participants to share ethnographic authority of what emerges from the interaction with the researcher. This is a moral commitment that puts the research endeavour into perspective, as it requires an awareness of 'the need to redress inequalities by giving precedence … to the voices of the least advantaged groups in society' (Mertens *et al.* 2009: 89). It is not simply about producing knowledge, but about fostering positive change in the lives of the participants and their communities, and of society at large. In the words of Giardina and Denzin (2011: 320): 'it is not enough to simply understand any given reality. There is a need to transform it. Educators, as transformative intellectuals, must actively participate in this project'. The urgency for this approach to scholarly inquiry is made more pressing by growing patterns of inequality across Western societies, combined with scapegoating practices against immigrants and 'people of colour', which are becoming popular in political discourse, and openly accepted by large sections of societies, in many European countries (FRA 2018). All this can be a challenging task when the participants' express uncomfortable views or behaviours, for example in the way certain immigrants are racialised in popular discourse. To some extent, such tensions and emotional strains are part and parcel of the ethnographer's experience and need be critically and reflexively analysed.

On the other hand, the researcher is the one that instigated the dialogue and the one who will arguably be responsible for the final text which represents its most ambitious material outcome (the book). Sinha and Back (2013) advocate the adoption of 'sociable methods', which are participatory and dialogic in nature. In their work with young adult migrants in London, they invited some participants to collaborate in the writing and illustration of their own stories. They claim that they 'reimagined empirical enquiry in a way that blurred the relationship between observer and observed, data and analysis and participants and authors' (Sinha and Back 2013: 3). Their approach echoes the 'community authorship' advocated by Richardson (1992). Denzin (2014) invites us to be cautious about the possibility of 'giving voice', and to pay attention to dynamics of power (who gives voice?) and intentionality (how are agents being constructed?). Nevertheless, voice is, alongside agency and participation, a central component of childhood and youth research, as it emanates from article 13 of the United Nations Convention on the Rights of the Child (UNCRC 1989). During my research I have practised different forms of collaboration with participants, such as for example the video production with Adrian and Ciprian, and tried to elicit more. However, there are ethical and practical limitations to research collaboration with young, underage, participants, which only to some extent can be anticipated in the design of a study (Bucknall 2014).

After resistance

During the last months of my fieldwork with Insaka, the fence around the pitch that the team used for their training sessions was partly replaced and the holes covered. However, this did not stop local youth entering the pitch from a different point and the Insaka weekly trainings continuing as before. To access the pitch, people now had to climb a lower section of the fence and jump over it. No one among my key informants seemed to know for how long this situation would be tolerated by the Fingal County Council, which owned the pitch, and if the pitch would, at some point, be completed and opened to the public. The access to the pitch was eventually blocked at the end of the Summer 2012. The immediate effect was that Insaka was left without a training ground, and they had to meet in public parks across Blanchardstown. Pressed by this and other hurdles, the team soon disbanded. However, as we will see, it 'resurrected' some time later in a new, unexpected form. What remained of the three seasons played by the most unusual of teams in the Dublin Schoolboys Leagues? What did the young players bring with them from that experience?

By 2017, at the time of my cycling exploration, the 'ghost estates' and the horses had disappeared from Ongar, and new houses, roads and infrastructure had been built, including a rail station (Hansfield station, opened in June 2013), and two schools (a Primary School and a Secondary School under the patronage of Educate Together, both opened in August 2014).[2] The all-weather pitch where Insaka used to train and local youth used to meet, was inaugurated in June 2014 by the Minister for Transport, Tourism and Sport, Leo Varadkar. It is now managed by the Ongar Community Centre, and used by the pupils of the nearby St. Benedicts National School. It is these pupils, around a hundred of them, that I see playing freely during their lunch break on the former Insaka training pitch; some of them are even kicking a ball. I stop by the side of the road, and while sitting on the bike I spend a few minutes absorbing new impressions on a place I used to know. 'The true picture of the past flits by', writes Benjamin (1999: 247), 'The past can be seized only as an image which flashes up at the instant when it can be recognized and is never seen again'. I feel that the changes in the social and material landscape around the Ongar pitch tell me something significant about the peculiar trajectory of Insaka.

I can now see more clearly that the place I used to know, the pitch squatted by local youth and temporarily adopted by Insaka, was like the 'holey place' described by Deleuze and Guattari in A *thousand plateaus*. 'It is in their specificity, it is by virtue of their inventing a holey space, that they necessarily communicate with the sedentaries *and* with the nomads (and others beside, with the transhuman forest dwellers)' (Deleuze and Guattari 1988 [1980]: 415, emphasis in original). Deleuze and Guattari use the image of the 'holey space' to talk about nomadic lives, specifically those of the smiths, who are 'ambulant, itinerant' (Deleuze and Guattari 1988 [1980]: 413). They draw on an image from the film *Strike*, by Sergei Eisenstein, that 'presents a holey space where a disturbing group of people are rising, each emerging from his or her hole as if from a field mined in all directions' (Deleuze and Guattari 1988 [1980]: 413–414). At the time of my encounters with Insaka, the pitch was that holey space, a space where a 'disturbing group of people' (immigrants by virtue of colour or contingency, or both; nomadic lives in the eyes of the local majority) would emerge and play, *communicate with the sedentaries and with the nomads*, at the same time visible to everyone, because the pitch was placed at a crossroads, and invisible because they were not supposed to be there. This tension between visibility and invisibility (as in the novel by Ralph Ellison, 2001 [1952]) is only broken by the fool, the drunkard in this case, so drunk that he cannot control his racist feelings and he speaks out against the 'other'.[3] That holey space was not going to last, but its message does: as I will try to demonstrate, its temporality still speaks to us in different ways. As it happened, today the pitch is returned to 'public' use and it can be rented at different hourly rates: Voluntary (€50), Community (€80), Commercial (€105), Pay & Play (€88).[4] Which rate category would a team like Insaka, if it still existed, be assigned to? Among the new users of this space, as I learn from a notice hung on the fence ('New players welcome'), is the Garda Westmanstown Rugby Club, the rugby club of the local police force. Given the status of rugby in Irish society, it is evidently a rise on the social class ladder for this once marginal place.

My final meeting with James and Ken (Zuby is away that day, but I would reconnect with him later) takes place in a Nigerian restaurant. It is not the usual KKK, but a different one just a few steps away from it, in one of the basic buildings of the Coolmine Industrial Estate. The restaurant has only recently opened, and there is no sign at the door yet. As with other locations of my multi-sited ethnography, this one has also transformed over just a few years: new 'ethnic' shops and business have been added, while others have either closed or moved out. The 'Polish Small Business Centre' is still there, as is the 'Boshka Hair and Beauty Salon', but the Polish food store 'Mroz' has disappeared. Among the new entries there is the 'Sudanese Social Club' and 'Zouk', an Indian and Pakistani restaurant. Like the Ongar pitch, this rather hybrid place (industrial or commercial? Retail or production?) has been altered by migration and given a new, transient meaning. It is an example of what Sassen (2006: 181) would define as 'reconfiguration of economic spaces' brought about by globalisation and urban migration. The businesses hosted here are priced out of the Blanchardstown Shopping Centre, the true focal point of this large suburb, and have arguably given life to their own 'centre' in an anonymous industrial estate.

James and Ken invited me to talk about their new venture, the Insaka Sports Academy, based in the Abia state, Nigeria. But first we discuss the parable of the team they set up and ran for three years. There is no poster of Mohammed Ali to overlook our conversation, but simply a large TV screen that shows Formula One (the FIFA men's World Cup is over, and the Premier League has yet to start). Following the end of their third season, Insaka disbanded, despite having recruited new young players. As said, the costs to maintain a club were unbearable without support from private or public sponsors. At some point, James had tried to find sponsors for his project among the African immigrant communities. On one occasion, I attended a meeting organised at KKK with seven man who had different roles in the African diaspora community, from businessman to pastor. However, although some offered help, the outcome was not as satisfactory as desired by the organisers. The demands to set up a proper club were too high, particularly amid an environment that was not supportive of an 'ethnic' youth team. Since then, James and Zuby, who had won the league title and the league cup with a team built from scratch, have not found other coaching roles with Irish teams. Zuby, who holds a UEFA B coaching licence, contributed to some national and international projects promoted by SARI, such as the Soccernites and the Streetfootball World Cup, but he is now working full time in the care sector. 'I am a family man', he told me. 'You know, football is my passion, but there is nothing else I can do'. James is self-employed and spends part of the year in Nigeria to coordinate the Insaka Sport Academy, which is partly a collaborative project with Northern Irish club Glentoran FC. The reading of the trajectory of Insaka by my main adult informants reveals different layers of interpretation.

KEN: When James started holding trials in the park, these young players arrived in numbers. Most of them they would say they had been abused while playing with different teams. By getting them together the plan was to build confidence in them, self-esteem and particularly resilience. To let them be able to tackle the issues that affected them, such as racism and discrimination. Having done this, they would go to other teams; that was the whole idea. And some of them in fact moved on to play with other teams, even in England.

ZUBY: To win the league and the cup was an amazing achievement, we are obviously proud and happy with what we achieved, but it was labour for nothing. You have to look at the environment. In terms of society, to say that we benefited from it, no, they don't care, no one cares. They wanted to stop that team, they branded us the African team, you know the rest of the story.

JAMES: The idea with Insaka was to offer a chance to the kids, to bring them together. We wanted to show to them that they can struggle, they can make something out of themselves. We did it, but that's the end of the story. Black coaches don't get recognition. Now we are moving the same concept, the same vision, to Africa. We try to accommodate all the kids, our project is a charity, is not like other academies who are doing it mostly for profit.

At least two points worthy of attention emerge from these accounts. One is the function that a team like an Insaka allegedly served within the immigrant communities in West Dublin, and especially those from Africa. The second is the lack of opportunities for ethnic minority coaches in football, which is something that has been highlighted in more mature contexts of immigration such as the UK, and especially England (Cashmore and Cleland 2011; FARE 2014; Bradbury 2018). Across Europe, there is a significant body of research on 'ethnic' or 'mono-ethnic' sports clubs created within immigrant communities to cater for young people and adults who share the same ethnic or national backgrounds (Blecking 2008; Andersson 2009; Poli et al. 2012; Theeboom et al. 2012). Their function is, on the one hand, to foster a sense of belonging to the community of origin and, on the other hand, to create an environment where people, at least on the sporting pitch, are not to made to feel outsiders in the hosting society. Studies conducted in the UK (Burdsey 2006, 2007; Bradbury 2011) show that ethnic minorities may find in ethnic clubs more protective environments, a sort of safe haven against different forms of discrimination experienced in sport and beyond.

These types of clubs are often seen negatively across continental Europe (Agergaard 2018), as they are perceived as forms of self-segregation. At the political level there is the assumption that migrants would benefit more from entering local 'ethnically mixed' sports clubs instead. By entering local clubs, migrants would have the opportunity of directly interacting with 'natives', and to acquire 'bridging social capital' (Jarvie 2017: 169). However, Agergaard provides an alternative interpretation of such teams. She contends that 'ethnic minority sports clubs may develop migrants and descendants' feelings of social belonging and possibly even trust in the receiving society in becoming members of civil society organisations' (Agergaard 2018: 240). In setting up a club they will have to 'gain knowledge of laws and administration of civil organisation in their host society' (Agergaard 2018: 240).

The case of Insaka is particular, because, as shown from the accounts of the adult protagonists and from my participant-observation, it provided a safe space for migrant teenagers to play and develop their football. As we will see, this function assumed a special value in the aftermath of the death of Toyosi Shittabey, a friend and former teammate. On the other hand, it was unique as a football team in a country of recent immigration, because, despite the initial motto they had adopted ('All Africa'), it was a truly multi-ethnic and multi-national team – an experiment where everyone was welcome regardless of their origins and background. By competing in an official league, the team had also to deal with the institutional laws and the rules involved in running a club. As a matter of fact, they were fully participating in this particular civil society organisation. However, Insaka operated in a sort of institutional and symbolic middle ground: in a limbo. It had been allowed to enter the league despite not having an official playing ground, a proper office, not even a training ground. This arguably happened because there are few clubs across the country operating Under-18 teams, and the league was eager to recruit new ones. More importantly, club registration regulations were, at that stage, more relaxed than today. Following reforms introduced by the FAI and the Schoolboys Football Association of Ireland (SFAI) in 2014, the registration procedures of a club have become more complex and demanding. For example, according to the requirements for the two-year 'Club Licence', the club needs to run 'a minimum of two 11-a-side teams and two Development Teams'.[5]

The peculiar, temporal trajectory of Insaka in the Irish football system can be read from a different perspective, which takes into account the vitality of immigration for any social body (Goldin *et al.* 2012). In unanticipated ways, Insaka successfully displayed a different style of football, at least at this level. The team also gave visibility to issues, such as underlying discrimination and racism, which are part of the everyday experience of black people in Ireland, but little talked about by the majority of the population. In this regard, despite *or* because of its precarious status and its troublesome existence, Insaka produced something that was made to last, like a small-scale 'configuration pregnant with tensions' (Benjamin 1999: 254). To make this point clear, I will draw on the concepts of *rhizome* and *intermezzo* by Deleuze and Guattari. They explain that 'a rhizome has no beginning or end; it is always in the middle, between things, interbeing, *intermezzo*' (Deleuze and Guattari 1988: 26). And further:

> The middle is by no means an average: on the contrary, it is where things pick up speed. *Between* things does not designate a localizable relation going from one thing to another and back again, but a perpendicular direction, a transversal movement that sweeps one *and* the other way, a stream without beginning or end that undermines its banks and picks up speed in the middle.
>
> (Deleuze and Guattari 1988: 27, emphasis in original)

The rhizome/intermezzo is what escapes the strictures of the state apparatus and, by doing so, it creates new spaces, free multiplicities. At the same time, we may wonder if the function served by Insaka at this particular historical conjuncture (*to create an intermezzo where things pick up speed*), probably with the indifference of the majority, would have been undermined had the team been allowed to operate in more stable circumstances. This could have happened if Insaka were included among the many beneficiaries of the €2 million grants allocated by the

Irish government for sporting projects in Dublin 15 and Dublin 7 between 2011 and 2012. Among the actions funded within that governmental scheme, are, for example, €25,000 for the 'Changing Rooms' of Hartstown/Huntstown FC, €7682 to Mountview Boys and Girls FC as 'Equipment Grant', and €181,303 to St Mochta's FC to build an 'All-weather pitch and floodlighting'.[6] A small funding to the most recent of youth clubs would have certainly made a difference to the rickety nitty gritty of their weekly routine. It might even have ended up normalising their 'diversity effect' – their being perceived as an element of disturbance and unacceptable dissonance. However, the dominant political discourse on interculturalism, and the racialisation of African immigrants in sport and beyond, made all this unlikely to happen, and in the end practically impossible. I will return to this point and expand upon it in the final part of the chapter.

Growing up, growing out

As noted in the previous chapters, both teams at the centre of my investigation were characterised by a level of mobility of the young players totally unexpected to me. Some boys, both immigrants and Irish, would change club at end of every season, for different reasons. This told me something important about how they interpreted their sporting experience, but also about how they built relationships with places and people (Hopkins 2010). This study is focused on young people who migrated to Ireland at some point in their childhood; none of the participants with an immigrant background was born in the country. Some had only joined their families or a parent quite recently, at the age of 11 or 12, after having lived with relatives, usually the grandparents. They represent the most sensitive link of the migration network, because their agency in the migration process had arguably been very limited (Ensor and Goździak 2010). The challenges they had to face and still face are different from those, like their younger siblings, who are born in Ireland. They also differ from those of their parents, who will with more confidence identify as 'home' the place they left behind (Berger and Mohr 2010 [1975]: 62–63).

When I started working on the follow up to my ethnography I realised the complexity of the task ahead. Once they reached adulthood, and, more importantly, once they had obtained an Irish passport, many had moved abroad. Around 10 of my research participants had moved to England, mainly to London. Others had moved, or moved back, to France, Canada, Belgium. A few, still in their early 20s, had become fathers and set up families. Some remained untraceable. In the end, however, I was able to reconnect with some of them, and I carried out eight interviews.

The remarkable changes in their lives implied another step to overcome, which was purely methodological. While my original study had been essentially ethnographic in nature, combining observation and conversations and informal interactions with the participants, this time I had to rely mainly on semi-structured interviews, combined in some cases with phone conversations, emails and WhatsApp messages. At the same time, my participants were now young adults who could hopefully manage with a certain degree of confidence a more formal research dialogue. But where should the interviews be carried out? The place where researchers meet their participants will impinge on the quality of the account that participants give of themselves (Adler and Adler 2002). In the end, the choice for our interviews' setting fell on the Shopping Centre. This was not surprising to me, as I was aware that most of the social life of young people residing in Blanchardstown revolves around the mall. Usually shopping malls fall in the category of 'non-places', as coined by Augé (1995). For him, a non-place is 'a space which cannot be defined as relational, or historical, or concerned with identity' (Augé 1995: 78). However, as I also learned from my work with migrant youth in Italy, shopping malls may be adopted by youth living in urban environments as a safe, productive space for socialisation (Mauro 2016b). Finally, the Blanchardstown Shopping Centre was not a completely new research setting for me, as Insaka would use the parking lot as their meeting point for Sunday's away games.

The main topic of our new conversations was the role played by sport, and especially football, in growing up in Ireland. I asked them to try to evaluate their experiences of playing football throughout their childhood and adolescence. With their help I wished to highlight what forms of belonging they believed they had been able to develop. I could then try to compare their views of today with what I had observed and documented before. Spaaij (2015: 305) contends that 'the experience of belonging is best understood as a process (i.e. becoming) rather than a state (i.e. being). Belonging is dynamic and situational: it can shift and change over time, be contested and plural'. This is particularly pertinent for young people whose lives are caught in between cultures, and whose imaginary is arguably occupied by multiple (ethnic, national, racial, gendered) affiliations. Obviously, youth sporting clubs do not operate in a vacuum, they express particular social and cultural histories, such as those, for example, of an Irish working class suburban community in the case of Mountview. Moreover, their intervention is situated within wider discourses on immigration politics, which in the Republic of Ireland focuses mainly on integration and interculturalism (Lentin 2010). They may also, to some extent, be influenced by discourses on the use of sport as a vehicle of social inclusion of ethnic minorities, refugees and immigrants. For all these reasons, youth sports clubs provide a dynamic space where different layers of belonging can be negotiated. Spaaij argues that the sports club 'is a site where the everyday experience of belonging and the politics of belonging intersect' (Spaaij 2015: 305). In the next section I will try to explore this duality through the accounts of some participants.

Sense of togetherness

I met Benni in one of the few quiet corners of the 'centre', the Café of the Draíocht Arts Centre, just across the road from the main entrance of the shopping mall. This became my favourite setting for the interviews. I was aware of the fact that Benni had become a football referee, an interesting topic in itself to discuss, but I decided to start our conversation from his passion for cricket as a black child growing up in South Africa, and moving to Ireland at the age of 11. I reminded him that the first time that we met, at the Ongar pitch, he told me that cricket was his first passion.

> Yeah, cricket is still in the back of my heart, but I do not watch it or play it anymore. I am doing athletics now, and obviously I am football referee, I have been one for a few years now.

Similarly to many young males that I met, Benni had played for various teams during his childhood and adolescence (four in total). As with other former players, he underlines that Insaka was a whole different thing.

> Insaka was different than the other teams. I joined it because all my friends were there, some were also in my school, that was the good thing about that. But we were good. The team sent a message that together we could do almost the unbelievable, we were strong and after we stopped doing all the fighting and started playing no one in the league could beat us. After Insaka went bust, I was thinking to join another team, because after the success we had people were looking at us, they would come and say 'hey come play with us'. But it was not the same anymore. I was kind of lost in the field of sports, to be honest. In my last year at school I tried every single sport, I asked myself what am I good at? Athletics was some-thing I did well, I have always been fast, so I tried and I enjoyed the com-petitive edge, that feeling.

Benni's words resonate with those of Yano, son of a Congolese father and an Angolan mother. Yano still plays football with a senior team based in the area where he lives, an ethnically diverse neighbourhood of Blanchardstown.

> I used to love training with Insaka, meeting and playing with people you get along with, and that you understand each other. That brought us together. But looking back I also think that that team made me com-municate better. Some people were very shy before joining the team. The fact that we were all Africans gave me confidence in myself, something that I did not have. It helped me stay out of trouble. And the coaches were very disciplined. They had that kind of discipline for having played at profes-sional level, which was great.

Fredy now lives in London, he works in Finance; 'in the City', he underlines. 'London is a busy, dynamic place where to make money and move forward', he says. 'I see myself like I want to build my own career here and when I decide my time is up I go back and settle'. Home for him is Dublin, Ireland, where he moved at the age of six, from Angola. When I ask him what stays with him of the time spent with Insaka he instinctively points to 'football knowledge'.

> Playing with that team made me see things a lot different in respect to football, the type of coaching got me more inside of the game. When I watch football now I see it differently. Obviously, that team was something else from the teams I played before, it was more multicultural. I mean, we were all from different backgrounds but the bond was good, it was really family oriented, we were like a family.

Fredy was one of the three Insaka players that had a trial with Glentoran FC, an outcome of the collaboration that still continues these days with the academy set up by James in Nigeria. The trial did not go well for any of them, but Fredy cultivated for a while the dream of a career in football.

> After I left Insaka I had the chance to enter a football programme for Under-19 elite players, in Dublin, run by Ken's brother Harry, who works for the FAI. It was like a school, you had training every day. But after it finished I lost passion, you see others getting trials and you are left behind. I looked at my situation, time was moving on, so I left football. Now I don't have time for playing it, but I watch it a lot, watching football is my main passion.

I approached my meetings with them cognisant of the limits of 'interviewing' as a means to understand and investigate social life, particularly with young people who, through social media and digital forms of communication, are 'increasingly observers of their own lives' (Back 2012: 18). At the same time, I trusted the 'life story approach' (Thomson et al. 2002) could help my participants and myself to connect key moments of change in their personal life with wider social processes. By inviting them to tell a story, as a way of storying their lives (Anderson and Thomson 2014), I could entice them to identify certain biographical passages as 'critical moments'. Thomson et al. (2002: 339) argue that young people sometimes live 'through experiences that they may subsequently come to understand as critical moments'. For Benni, Yano and Fredy, playing for Insaka was that critical moment that fortified a sense of togetherness among youth with an African background. It also sent a message to Irish society, a message that 'together we could do almost the unbelievable'. For Yano, that experience helped him to gain self-confidence and 'to communicate better'. All this counters the understanding of 'ethnic' clubs essentially as forms of self-segregation, which would not help ethnic minorities and immigrants to better 'integrate' in the hosting society. Rather, it may provide young people with valuable resources to use later in their lives, when they will, for example, go on to play with other local teams or practise different sports.

Differently from other clubs, Insaka did not represent a specific history or a 'community', where newcomers have to learn how to fit in. It was truly an 'intermezzo where things pick up speed' (Deleuze and Guattari 1988 [1980]: 25), or a little vessel where everyone is welcome as long as they are passionate about the game, and they can control and pass the ball. According to Benni, Yano and Fredy the sense of togetherness was one of the strengths of the team, but what they may mean by this is that it was *essentially* about a group of African boys coming together under two African coaches. How did the 'white' boys fit into this picture? Being all of Eastern European backgrounds, the non-Africans in the team represented 'different shades of white' (Fletcher and Hylton 2016: 89) – different and symbolically subordinate to the 'white Irish'. What they all had in common was that they also were born in a country different from the one where they were living. Benni provides a reflection on the idea of Insaka being an 'African team':

> I think the white players saw themselves as minorities. If they went to an Irish team they would also suffer, they were seen as different. But it is different for the ones who grow up here. I see it when I referee youth matches. If you look at the Under-16, for example, you would not tell the difference between some Eastern European and the Irish: same accent, the way they talk, they dress, they cut their hair. They are more integrated now. But then, it was different for the guys in Insaka, they felt part of that of journey with us. We may just have come a different way, but we had the same way of thinking.

Yano adds a different layer of meaning to the relationship between the African boys and those of Eastern European background playing for Insaka.

> I never saw the colour, you know. They were some of us, we also lived in the same area, go to the same schools. It's been a few years, but we still see each other, we speak and we are friends on social media. For me football has always been a way to meet people and make friends. If it wasn't for football I would have not blend in, it was like that when I was in Tallagh and the same when I moved to Blanch with my family. This is what it is for me.

I would have liked to hear Ciprian's view on this, but he declined my invitation to talk about his past. He simply expressed his interest in *not* looking back to his younger self. Back at the time when he was playing with Insaka, he had opened up to me about his passion for football and hip hop, and his views on identity, Romania, and life opportunities in Ireland. His refusal made me question my motivation for doing this. Was my interest intrusive? After leaving Ireland, I had been irregularly in contact with him and a few others, but before contacting him this time I had noticed that the video clips he and Adrian had produced as a hip hop duo were no longer available on YouTube. Any reference to his hip hop past had also been removed from his social media accounts.[7] Something had certainly changed in his relationship with Adrian, but more importantly he seemed not at ease in looking back at a time in his life that I thought was 'interesting'. On the phone he told me that his life was all about his work (as a housepainter), his family (he is the oldest of four siblings in a single parent household), and the church on Sunday. There was no place for football. I sensed our dialogue was not necessary at this time, or justified to him. In the study of childhood and adolescence, it is not uncommon that participants in qualitative longitudinal projects may, at some point, refuse to revisit their past (Anderson and Thomson 2014). Although I did not originally set out to conduct a longitudinal study, my interest in revisiting some critical moments in young participant's lives demanded an interest from their part to collaborate. This also made me reflect on the expectations of youth researchers, and on the fact that transition from childhood into adulthood (a central theme in the sociology of youth), particularly when implicated in patterns of migration and relocation, can be a non-linear, fractured project, and something not everyone would feel at ease in revisiting for the purpose of 'research'.

My meeting with Adrian happened in rather different circumstances. His reply to my approach was warm and friendly. He invited me to meet him at the fastfood restaurant that his mother runs with his help and that of his younger brother. We sat at the back of the restaurant, located on a busy Blanchardstown road, and were joined by another young man of Romanian descent, with whom Adrian shares his greatest passion: motor racing. His social media accounts are full of pictures of cars. He took out non-alcoholic drinks and we sat down for a chat. My first impression was that he is still the 'old' Adrian. He likes to boast about the things he likes and does not like, and he wants to show that he is a young man with 'attitude'. He wears a hat with 'I want to F***k Rhyanna' embroidered on the front. 'I bought it in Romania', he tells me. He still plans to go back to Romania, at some point. 'I don't want to get old in this country, man', he tells me. We talk for about two hours, covering many sides of his life. Obviously, it is his view on his time with Insaka that I am most interested to hear about. Adrian left the team when he decided to go back to Romania to stay with his father. He later returned to Ireland, but by that time the team had disbanded.

> Insaka was good, but even there, you know, it was a struggle, with the pitch and all. It was not easy, but the coaches were very good, you could learn a lot from them. I always felt fine in the team. I am still friends with some of the boys. We happen to meet from time to time, it is not a big place here. Some of them are good, have kids, they have become fathers. After I finished with Insaka I played for a while with a Romanian team in a Sunday senior league. It was good, we won the league, but it costs money to play, you have to pay even if you get a yellow card. It is not serious, football is not serious in this country.

The fact that Adrian joined a 'Romanian' team after leaving Insaka, and that he hangs out essentially with young people who share his biographical trajectory (his girlfriend is also from Eastern Europe and raised in Ireland) may superficially be a sign that he is not comfortable with 'diversity'. However, his time with Insaka, playing football and being somehow successful at it, appears to have created a safe space where racial diversity can be experienced and valued. This is confirmed by an 'incident' that occurred during our meeting. His friend Paul was taking active part in the conversation, although he admitted he was not very interested in football. At some point he explained that Ongar, the neighbourhood, 'was fine when I moved there in 2011, but now it's hard, they can rob you, stop you to take your phone, things like that'. At then, out of the blue, Paul used the 'N' word to define youth of African background. I instinctively held my breath and felt Adrian's eyes looking at me and then at his friend. He was visibly embarrassed. Paul quickly apologised: 'I mean blacks, sorry'. Then Adrian articulated on this:

> There are no people who are racist, I tell you. They say that Romanias are all gypsies, they say it, you know. I tell you 70/80 per cent of the people are fine, then there are 20 per cent of fuckers, they think foreigners take their jobs and things like that, but they are people who don't work. Some people don't like blacks, but those people are everywhere.

In somewhat confusing terms, Adrian felt the urgency to express his feelings on this issue, and he then underlined, again, that while playing for Insaka he felt 'one of the boys', because he had also suffered racism.

Premier parents

Nothing has apparently changed in the other major setting of my ethnography, the playing pitch of Mountview FC. I visit it on the day of the Summer Champions Mini-League. It is a small scale festival, where children under 12 play 5-a-side games in mixed-sex teams, and also alongside players who may normally play for a different club. There is a food stall and an inflatable castle for the little ones. It is a sunny day, the field is divided in two pitches, which are surrounded by parents and siblings of the young players. I look for some faces known to me, but there are few. Kids grow fast and their parents rarely remain involved with the club after their children have outgrown youth sport. Mick is taking pictures, he is the official photographer of the day, and Willie arrives a little late with his baby son. I watch a few games being played and I notice that there are fewer 'black' children compared with similar events I had attended a few years back. It is superficial evidence, just a visual impression that hints at a potential change in the demographic profile of the club and the local community.

When I meet Mick the following day at the nearby Community Centre, though, he confirms my impression. The club has gone through some remarkable changes. Until 2013, the club was running 13 teams, at some stage even 18, while the club has only seven now, and an Academy for 4–7 year olds. 'We just found it difficult to manage. You need more volunteers and sport is more heavily regulated now, you have more police checks, more training, child protection. Costs have also gone up', he says. One particular aspect strikes my informant about the present state of youth football: parents' expectations.

> I have noticed that football has changed. There are expectations from certain parents, they expect coaches to be a certain standard, to do certain things, but they are just volunteers, come on. If parents don't like the training they may even bring their children somewhere else, to another club. Some parents these days expect their kids to be on trial, to play in the Premier and things like that. We call them 'Premier Parents' for that.[8]

I ask him about young players with non-Irish background, as Mountview had a reputation for being quite an inclusive and diverse club. This should be put into perspective, as generally all youth clubs in the Blanchardstown area host significant numbers of children with an immigrant background, compared with clubs located in other parts of the city and the country. This is due to the social and demographic characteristics of the area, historically one of the most ethnically diverse in the country (CSO 2017).

> We have seen numbers of the immigrant kids drop off a bit, particularly with those of African background, and I don't know what are the reasons. Some families may have moved over to the UK or have gone back home, this is what I heard, but this is just my personal opinion. It has become too expensive for them to live here. I don't know if it has to do with the housing crisis, the rent, I don't know. The fact is that we don't have as many as we used to have. We have still some children from Eastern European backgrounds, from Poland, Moldova, Romania.

At the time of my ethnographic fieldwork, young players of Eastern European background were rare at Mountview FC, and it was something that caught my attention, as I was aware of the presence of a large Polish community across different areas of Blanchardstown. At the same time, young players of African descent, from countries such as Nigeria, DR Congo, Ivory Coast, were in good numbers. Another evident change relates to the financial contribution of the families, the fees. There are no more 'subs', subscription money paid before each game by the young players into the hands of the coach. Today the young players' families are asked to pay an annual fee of €200, which can be paid in two instalments during the year. This is becoming common practice among youth clubs, as the same approach has been adopted by other local teams, such as Verona FC and St. Mochas FC, with fees roughly of the same amount. A slightly different path is followed by the largest youth club in the area, Corduff FC, which runs 27 youth teams across all age groups. At Corduff FC, the fees are €5 per week for Under-8s to Under-12s, and from Under-13s upward there is an annual fee of €185.

Willie is no longer involved with the club or active in coaching. For a while he coached a senior team, which included some of the players who used to be in his successful Under-14 team. However, now he is busy with work and a young family to support. He claims to be still passionate about the game, and plans to be back into coaching in the future. 'I will be back here, where else should I go? This is my home. I would like to coach kids, that is what I can do. I like it better than coaching at senior level', he says. While we watch an Under-10 match, I ask him what he thinks may be the reason for fewer African boys playing for the club these days. 'That may even be the fees, I don't know. It is more expensive to register a kid to play these days, and if you have more than one, the costs may be too much for certain families'.

As shown earlier, as teenagers reach the age of 15–16 they lose interest in playing competitive sport. Consequently, clubs struggle to set up teams in the Under-16 divisions and over. To address this issue, in November 2017, the DDSL announced the introduction of a Youth league that replaces the Under-17s and 18s leagues. Willie's team disbanded when the team members were turning 16, but after a while some of them re-joined their coach in a team playing in a senior amateur league. 'They asked me to coach a senior team and I took the chance. Some of the boys that were with me at Mountview joined me there and so we kept the team going for a couple of seasons'. This lasting bond created with the coach is testimony to the role that youth coaches may play as mentors and educators, beyond the sporting field. It is something that it is underlined in documents and reports produced by European institutions (for example, Amara *et al.* 2005; ENGSO 2012).

As noted, many of the participants in this study claimed to have often changed teams. During his childhood, Patrick, originally from DC Congo, played in four teams and Mountview was his last. He now regrets moving so often.

> I was 11 when I moved to Ireland, I did not have any English, so football definitely helped me. It's all about what you like, I liked school but I liked football more. Football brought me closer to Irish society, I made new friendships, learned English – you know the manager wants you to understand his instructions and he will help you. That was football for me. What I regret is having changed so many teams. I was moving every year. That limited my development as a player. They said I was very talented, but actually changing clubs did not help. When I was at Stella Maris a guy came to me claiming he had connections with big English teams and persuaded me to change club. Then I had to leave because my family moved to another area. Every time you move to a new team you need to know the system, to build a bond, a relationship with your teammates, it's like making new friendships, basically. But I was young, I did not know.

Today Patrick does not play or follow much football. After finishing college, he spent two years in England and then he returned to Dublin, where he runs his family barber salon. More importantly, he tells me, he is an evangelist preacher. 'God called me to work for him, we are born with a purpose and growing up I understood mine'. Congo, his native country that he taught about to his team-mates when he was playing for Mountview, is a distant place now. 'My home is Dublin, Ireland. I was born in Congo but if you bring me back there now I do not know where I am'.

Like Patrick, Philippe also played with different teams during his childhood.

> I stayed longer at Mountview because I felt more at ease. Playing in a mixed team made definitely a difference to me as there were other kids like me in the team, coming from Africa. But I left when I was I think 15–16, I think, I had lost interest. After that, I went back to football and played a few times at senior, with Willie's team, but then I gave up. I always liked the game side, but I was not keen on training. Now I just go to the gym, that's all the sport that I do.

When I ask Philippe to elaborate on the reasons for quitting football as a teen-ager he recollects an incident that I witnessed, and documented in Chapter 3.

> I left the team about the same time Eric left, we were close at that time, he has moved back to France now. I was not playing much at that time. But Eric left after the racist incident, just after that. Some opponent called it a racist name. I think he left for that. When it happened he just walked out, he was annoyed, he could not take it. That is what he told me, I was not there that day.

These accounts highlight the importance of the role of sport institutions, in primis sport governing bodies, in acknowledging the crucial role that sport can play to favour social inclusion or integration of migrant youth and ethnic minorities (Marivoet 2014; Agergaard 2018). Unfortunately, among many in the field of sport, it is the prevalent belief that football, so to say, will take care of itself. In other words, that the game is naturally inclusive and that there is no need to intervene with particular policies. However, as these accounts suggest, attention should be paid to the promotion of a culture that is respectful and welcoming of diversity, and that actively tackles racism and discrimination. This was the main goal of the FAI Intercultural Plan, which will be discussed at the end of the next section. Before doing that, I will look at the structural changes introduced to youth football in Ireland.

The state of youth football

There is certainly no lack of opportunities for young people to play football, and other sports, in Blanchardstown. There are about 10 schoolboys' football clubs, with many teams for all ages. However, the structural changes introduced over the last few years by the main sporting bodies have created more demands to clubs and families. Further, the costs clubs have to sustain have often increased, for example for renting training or playing pitches, insurance, referees fees and others, and this has arguably made football in general less inclusive for those placed lower on the social class ladder. This has implications for immigrant families, but also for the 'New Irish', who may have acquired citizenship rights without seeing an improvement in their social and occupational mobility (Kelly et al. 2016: 20–21). As in other Western countries of immigration, the labour market in Ireland is segmented across ethnic lines, with certain nationalities occupying predominantly specific sectors. For example, more than half of male Polish are occupied in the construction industry, while Nigerians are concentrated in the health services (care) and business services (for example as security guards and sales assistants) (Loyal 2011; Kingston et al. 2015). Loyal (2011: 159) contends that 'there is an overlooked social class dimension to immigration in Ireland'. And further, 'class analysis in Ireland has to be rethought, recalibrated, and expanded within this new context in which migrants almost constitute a sub-proletariat with low wages, unskilled jobs and insecure employment' (Loyal 2011: 160). Despite the recent renewed growth of the Irish economy, some sections of society have benefited less than others from the wealth created in the country, and inequality has widened during the recession (Savage et el. 2015). To add more details to the picture, one has to consider the dramatic increase in the cost of housing, which in 2018 has reached the highs of the original Celtic Tiger economic boom. Since 2013, rents have risen incrementally each year, and in 2018 they were nationally on average 52 per cent up from the lowest point touched in 2010. However, in Dublin the increase has been of 81 per cent.[9] All this may arguably play a role in the distribution of children with an immigrant background across youth football clubs (Darmondy et al. 2016). It is something that has not gone unnoticed by some youth clubs; for example, Corduff FC proudly claim to be 'the most progressive club in the greater Blanchardstown area', and that their fees are lower compared with other youth clubs.[10] As it happens, they appear to have today a larger presence of children with an immigrant background in their teams.

In this context, some critical attention should be paid to the overhaul of the youth football system undertaken by the FAI since 2014. The focus of these interventions is openly on performance and results, something that may negatively impinge on the inclusiveness of the game for children and young people from poorer backgrounds. The recent creation of national youth leagues for Under-17, Under-15 and soon Under-13 has caused feelings of uncertainty amongst grassroots youth clubs. In 2017, the FAI announced an Under-15 national league, the Under-15 Airtricity league, which will join the existing Under-17 and Under-19 divisions. In 2019, an Under-13 national league will also be launched. The Airtricity League gathers the 20 clubs participating in the top league of Irish football (Premier Division) and in the second league (First Division). According to the FAI, the aim of these changes is to enhance the level of competition and quality of the game from youth level upwards (FAI 2016).

Announcing the introduction of the Airtricity Under-15 League, Rudd Dokter, the FAI High Performance Director, underlined that 'the very best Under-15 players throughout the country will now play against the highest quality opposition, thus enhancing their development as they progress to top level senior football'.[11] In parallel to this, the introduction of national youth academies has been announced. It is an approach inspired by the system in place in countries such as the Netherlands and France, and reflects the general trend in leading football countries to bring more competition and 'productivity' throughout the system. It also reflects the professionalisation of youth football that has occurred over the last 30 years (Tallec Marston 2012), and an emphasis on early specialisation and athletes' selection characterising youth sport in the Western World (Côté et al. 2012). However, some prominent Dublin school-boys' clubs have challenged the decision to include St. Kevin's in the new Under-15 League, a club that is not linked to any of the 20 clubs of the Airtric-ity League. Historically, the best schoolboys' clubs in the country are inde-pendent from the top senior Irish clubs. Youth clubs such as Home Farm, Cherry Orchard, Belvedere, St. Kevin's, and others, have nurtured dozens of future professional players, and Ireland Internationals, who at some point moved to an English or Scottish club, with important financial rewards for the Irish clubs. They now fear the new national youth league will make their work impractica-ble, with the best 12/13-year-olds moving to the Airtricity clubs. The whole situation has been defined a 'mess' by some critics, who believe that grassroots football, which historically has received limited support from the FAI, will be further marginalised after these changes take full effect.[12] As it happens, there is no lack of funding for the FAI's project. In 2018, the total funding of youth development for Airtricity League clubs was brought to €1.15 million.[13]

Against the backdrop of major changes in the youth football system, with implications for the participation levels of children and young people of immig-rant background, it is interesting to pay some attention to the Intercultural Pro-gramme of the FAI. It was first introduced in 2007 as 'Intercultural Plan' and it ran until 2010 with four overarching objectives: (1) combat 'racism' in football; (2) promote participation among minority ethnic and multicultural com-munities; (3) develop a culture of football that is dynamic and globally com-petitive; (4) contribute to the wider process of integration (FAI 2007). The Plan followed in the steps of UEFA's 10-point plan to tackle racism and dis-crimination in football (Kassimeris 2008), and to support its implementation the FAI received a grant of 50,000 Swiss Francs from UEFA. SARI, who had lobbied for the grant at the first UEFA-FARE Unite Against Racism Confer-ence, was a major contributor to the design of the Intercultural Plan, alongside other organisations such as Show Racism the Red Card and the National Con-sultative Committee on Racism and Interculturalism (NCCRI), a government advisory body. However, over time, SARI's role became less visible, and the organisation claim it has been overtly marginalised by the FAI.[14] This claim is in some way supported by the publication of the 'Handbook on volunteering of migrants in sport clubs and organisations' (SPIN 2016), curated by the FAI on behalf of the European Sport Inclusion Network (SPIN), and funded by the European Union. The Handbook provides an overview of projects in several European countries, including Ireland, but there is no mention of SARI, which for more than 20 years has been working in this field with the direct contribution of volunteers of migrant background.

Despite this problematic relationship with key actors, the FAI has received large sums from the government. Between 2008 and 2015, the Department of Justice and Equality paid almost €900,000 to the football governing body towards the implementation of its intercultural projects.[15] Amongst the actions prioritised in the original Intercultural Plan were training modules for referees, stewards and players. However, over the years a series of racist incidents happening both at the top level of Irish football and at grassroots and youth level has made observers question the efficacy of the plan, and the commitment of the FAI to its implementation.[16] Hassan and McCue (2011: 63), comment that 'it is unfortunate that this plan, which promised so much, has come unstuck due to a weakness in its implementation'. An example of the impasse highlighted by Hassan and McCue is the fact that no statistical data are made available by the FAI about racist and discriminatory incidents happening through the Irish football system.[17] This contradicts one of the actions included in the original Plan: 'Establish a system to record and analyse all racist and sectarian incidents in football; figures to be published in FAI annual report' (FAI 2007: 6).

As of 2018, the 'Intercultural Programme', has become simply one of the seven programmes coordinated by the FAI Grassroots Department, and its objectives seem less ambitious than they were originally: 'The Intercultural Football Programme seeks to increase participation in football among people from minority ethnic and cultural backgrounds, whilst also challenging and preventing the spread of racism within the game' (FAI 2016: 18). No figure is released of the financial resources allocated for the Intercultural Programme today, but some information is available on the initiatives being promoted. For example, at grassroots level, the Intercultural Programme is implemented through events to promote participation among migrants and ethnic minorities. According to the FAI, in 2015 'the programme had over 700 participants with 45 per cent of participants having family origins from overseas' (FAI 2016: 18). Another field of intervention is the organisation of workshops for grassroots leagues. However, these are reactive rather than proactive interventions; they are intended as 'anti-discriminatory training', which is part of the procedure that a club has to undergo when sanctioned for racist or discriminatory behaviour.[18] No details are available on the number of such interventions being undertaken throughout the year.

The New Irish, sport and society

After having paid attention to the material changes in the setting of the study, to the personal accounts of some of the protagonists, and finally to institutional reforms in the field of football, this final section will shift the focus towards dominant discourses on sport and migration in Irish society. Such discourses (Foucault 1980) provide the framework, the symbolical and cultural context, within which young people with an immigrant background practise football and other sports, and articulate their racialised position in Irish society. As noted by Palidda (2017: 15):

> more than any other, the emigrant-immigrant is at the mercy of the dominant practices in the country of origin as well as in the territory of arrival, and they are also vulnerable to the dominant discourse, because they try to adapt to what – perhaps – the dominant is willing to accept as a migrant.

A growing body of literature contends that the sporting field has become one of the main venues – arguably the most mediatised one – for the public articulation of national identity (Bairner 2001; Levermore 2004; Garrat 2010; Marjoribanks and Farquharson 2012). So far, despite immigration being a defining trait of Irish society for 20 years, limited attention has been paid, both by researchers and the mass media, to the influx of immigration in Irish sports. What I mean by this, is the impact that first generation migrants and their descendants may have on national and international competitions. In 2010, 15-year-old Cameroon-born Noe Baba made moderate headlines when he captained an underage Ireland men's football team. In the following years, other players with an immigrant background have represented Ireland at youth level. In November 2018, Michael Obafemi, an 18-year-old of Nigerian background born in Dublin and raised in England, became the first second-generation migrant to play for the Republic of Ireland men's senior team. Interestingly, this fact was overlooked by most commentators, who rather focused on the young age of the player, being the first born in the 2000s to play for the country.

In November 2017, the selection of New Zealand-born Bundee Aki for the rugby Ireland men's team caused some controversy. Writing in *The Irish Times*, columnist Una Mullally summarised the issue as following: 'There has been a certain amount of discussion surrounding the inclusion of Aki in the Irish team – a discussion about "nationhood", identity, and who gets to wear the green jersey'.[19] She emphatically argued that 'questioning Bundee Aki's right to play for Ireland says more about us than him'. Non-Irish nationals have also represented the country in golf and cricket, but without stirring a public debate around national identity (Storey 2013). Given the visibility and the global popularity of football, one is tempted to wonder how the potentially increasing inclusion of second-generation migrant players will be received. Black players have represented Ireland in football, for example Paul McGrath and Chris

Hughton, but the fact that at least one of their parents was Irish-born enabled them to be perceived, in popular discourse, as 'Irish'. Success on the football pitch arguably helped this process. As noted by Free (2010: 46), 'McGrath's popularity in Ireland undoubtedly owed something to his success at a time when the national team was becoming a symbol of postcolonial renaissance in Ireland. He was reassuringly 'Irish' despite his mother's migration and his inter-"racial" mix'.[20] The children of immigrant parents cannot claim Irish ancestry or 'blood' and their position, as evidenced by some recent cases, is more easily contested when it comes to definitions of Irishness.

In July 2017, 18-year-old Gina Akpe-Moses won the gold medal in the 100 m European Under-20 Championship. The first Irish woman to win a European sprint title, Akpe-Moses was born in Nigeria and raised in Ireland since the age of three. Her success was hailed with delight and surprise by the national mass media, given the historical poor record in sprinting by Irish athletes, but it also stirred controversial comments on social media. Some have noted that the rise of young athletes of African descent (the 2018 Junior national titles in the women's 100 m and 200 m have also been won by two black teenagers of African descent) may boost Ireland competitiveness in disciplines where traditionally results have been scarce. Others simply acknowledge that this is a natural evolution in Irish history, in a country that only in the recent past has started to attract migrants after having been for a long time a country of emigration. However, in the case of Akpe-Moses, as for Mario Balotelli in Italy, skin colour is a particular sensitive factor for the hard-core defenders of 'ethnic purity'. The example in Figure 6.1 is taken from a long Twitter thread started by Irish

Figure 6.1 Twitter thread on the Republic of Ireland 4 × 100 m women team, July 2018.

Athletics (the national governing body for Athletics) to celebrate the Irish women 4 × 100 m team that qualified for the final at IAAF World U20 Championships, in July 2018.[21] The Irish team that day was formed of a white Irish (Molly Scott) and three black Irish (Gina Akpe-Moses, Rhasidat Adeleke and Patience Jumbo-Gula).

Racist comments like the one in Figure 6.1 are promptly countered and contested by other Twitter users, who hold more positive views on Ireland's multicultural society. However, the fact that such a debate takes place, and draws numerous (often anonymous) participants, is evidence of the complex relationship between sport and the nation-state, between perceptions and projections of 'national identity' and international sport events. It is certainly not an issue unique to Ireland, but a current that traverses many Western countries, and that is made more acute by the political crisis of the nation-state (Agamben 1998). Looking at Europe's multicultural societies, Gilroy (2000: 249) argues that 'the frontiers of cultural difference can no longer be made congruent with national borders'. Garner pays specific attention to issues of race and immigration in contemporary Ireland and contends that

> only certain categories of immigrants are seen as problematic (often but not exclusively from outside Europe). Not recognising this phenomenon would be an illustration of epistemological ignorance. Moreover, the discursive focus on 'problematic' immigrants has reracialised the Irish population. On Amnesty International's Survey[22] of racial abuse, the 'Black Irish' group reports the highest levels of racist experiences.
>
> (2013: 186)

Drawing on these points, and on the immersive exploration of personal stories (football related) and public issues (football and non-football related) undertaken in the previous chapters, the conclusion will try to address the following question: can we think of a non-racialised sport in a racialised society?

Notes

1 'Is there a boom? Is it getting boomier?', *The Irish Times*, 15 April 2017.
2 Educate Together is an independent NGO founded in 1978 that runs schools 'that guarantee equality of access and esteem to children irrespective of their social, cultural or religious background', www.educatetogether.ie/about/what-is-educate-together [accessed 2 July 2018].
3 In the introduction to his novel, Ellison recounts a similar incident, which happened in his New York neighbourhood: 'A wino lady let me know exactly how I rated on her checklist of sundry types and characters' (Ellison 2001 [1952]: xxvii).
4 www.ongarcc.ie/All-Weather-Pitches-9465.html#.W12MDNhKiRs [accessed 20 July 2018].
5 www.ndsl.ie/files/resources/NDSL_Club_Licence.pdf [accessed 9 January 2018]. In April 2014, the FAI also introduced the Child Welfare Policy, www.fai.ie/sites/default/files/atoms/files/FAI_Child_Welfare_Policy_-_2014.pdf [accessed 7 June 2018].

6 Leo Varadkar, present Taoiseach (Prime Minister) and Minister for Sport between 2011 and 2014, is originally from Blanchardstown and was elected in the Dublin 15 area. In the Summer of 2014, he claimed: 'I have been able to allocate almost €2 million for 29 sporting projects in Dublin 15 and Dublin 7' http://leovaradkar. ie/2014/07/varadkar-announces-e733000-boost-for-sport-in-dublin-west/ [accessed 8 May 2018].

7 His Facebook profile was public, as was those of most of the young players. I had access to Facebook through my wife's account (with her permission).

8 Within the Irish schoolboys' league system, there are different divisions in the same age group, with the top one being the 'Premier'. For example, in the Dublin & District Schoolboys Leagues (DDSL), the Under-12 league is organised into nine divisions: C1/C/B1/B/A1/A/Major1/Major/Premier, www.ddsl.ie/competitionstabs.aspx?oid= 1015 [accessed 10 August 2018].

9 'Dublin rents to rise to €2,500 before they start to slow', The Irish Times, 13 February 2018.

10 'Duff makes DDSL move', The Dublin Gazette, 29 September 2017, https://dublin gazette.com/sport/duff-make-ddsl-move/ [accessed 5 August 2018].

11 'Where are the players: Rebuilding the supply of talent in Irish football', The Irish Examiner, 19 December 2017.

12 'Explaining the mess that has become of the FAI's new Under-15', Balls.ie, 4 July 2017, League. www.balls.ie/football/under-15-league-368373 [accessed 3 June 2018]. According to their official accounts, in 2013 the FAI had an income of €36.7 million, of which only €1.1 million went into development and grants to grassroots football. In the same year, €9.55 million was spent on staff. 'The FAI millions: where they come from and how they're spent', The Irish Times, 27 June 2015.

13 'League of Ireland youth funding increased to €1.15 million', RTE, 13 February 2018, www.rte.ie/sport/soccer/2018/0213/940459-league-of-ireland-youth-funding-increased-1–15million/ [accessed 3 August 2018].

14 Perry Ogden, Executive Chair of SARI, personal communication, 4 August 2018.

15 The payment was done in six instalments: €235,000 (2008); €232,000 (2009); €232,000 (2010); €168,899 (2011); €100,000 (2012); €20.000 (2015). Office for the Promotion of Migrant Integration, Department of Justice and Equality, personal communication, 27 September 2018.

16 See for example, 'Referee told Sikh boy to remove turban', Guardian, 14 December 2008; 'Schoolboy soccer club fined for taking players off pitch in stand against racism', Irish Examiner, 1 July 2014; 'U12 football match abandoned over "racist" comments from adult supporters', Irish Independent, 22 February 2017.

17 Between 2007 and 2008, the FAI registered five 'racist incidents' in men's organised amateur football. This figure was included in the European report on Racism, ethnic discrimination and exclusion of migrants and minorities in sport (FRA 2010).

18 Des Tomlinson, FAI Intercultural Officer, personal communication, 2 August 2018. In April 2010, in the aftermath of Toyosi Shitta-bey's death and a few incidents involving Insaka, the NDSL sent an invitation to its 81 clubs members to attend an 'Anti-Racism Workshop' held by FAI officials along with a representative of Show Racism the Red Card. Only nine clubs, including Insaka, sent representatives to the event.

19 'Questioning Bundee Aki's right to play for Ireland says more about us than him', The Irish Times, 10 November 2017.

20 The importance of success with the national team for black players, in order to be fully accepted as 'Irish', appears to be indirectly confirmed by the racist abuse suffered by Cyrus Christie during the last FIFA World Cup qualifying campaign. 'Republic of Ireland defender Cyrus Christie the target of racist abuse after World Cup play-off loss', The Independent, 21 November 2017.

21 The tweet is dated 13 July 2018. As of 9 August 2018, it received 121 comments, 740 retweets and 2400 likes.
22 *The views on black and ethnic minorities*, Amnesty International, Dublin, 2001.

References

Adler, P. A. and Adler, P. (2002). 'Teen scenes: Ethnographies of adolescent cultures'. *Journal of Contemporary Ethnography*, 31(5), 652–660.

Agamben, G. (1998). *Homo sacer. Sovereign power and bare life.* Stanford, CA: Stanford University Press.

Agergaard, S. (2018). *Rethinking sports and integration: developing a transnational perspective on migrants and descendants in sports.* London: Routledge.

Amara, M., Aquilina, D. and Henry, I. (2005). *Sport and multiculturalism.* European Commission DG Education and Culture. Available from: www.isca-web.org/files/Sport%20 and%20Multiculturalism%20EU%202004.pdf [accessed 1 August 2011].

Anderson, S. and Thomson, R. (2014). 'Inventing adulthoods'. In A. Clark *et al.* (eds), *Understanding research with children and young people.* London: Sage/The Open University.

Andersson, T. (2009). 'Immigrant teams in Sweden and the case of Assyriska FF'. *Soccer & Society* 10(3–4), 398–417.

Augé, M. (1995). *Non-places. Introduction to super-modernity.* London: Verso.

Back, L. (2002). 'Guess who's coming to dinner? The political morality of investigating whiteness in the Gray Zone'. In V. Ware and L. Back (eds), *Out of whiteness. Color, politics and culture.* Chicago, IL: University of Chicago Press, 33–59.

Back, L. (2012). 'Live sociology: Social research and its futures'. In L. Back and N. Puwar (eds), *Live methods.* Oxford: Wiley-Blackwell/The Sociological Review, 18–39.

Bairner, A. (2001). *Sport, nationalism and globalization.* New York: State University of New York Press.

Benjamin, W. (1999). *Illuminations.* London: Pimlico.

Berger, J. and Mohr, J. (2010 [1975]). *A seventh man.* London: Verso.

Blecking, D. (2008). 'Sport and immigration in Germany'. *The International Journal of the History of Sport*, 25(8), 955–973.

Bradbury, S. (2011). 'Racism, resistance and new youth inclusions'. In D. Burdsey (ed.), *Race, ethnicity and football: Persisting debates and emergent issues.* London: Routledge, 67–83.

Bradbury, S. (2018). 'The under-representation and racialised experiences of minority coaches in high level coach education in professional football in England'. In D. Hassan and C. Acton (eds), *Sport and contested identities.* Routledge: London, 11–29.

Bucknall, S. (2014). 'Doing qualitative research with children and young people'. In A. Clark, R. Flewitt, M. Hammersley and M. Robb (eds), *Understanding research with children and young people.* London: Sage/The Open University, 69–84.

Burdsey, D. (2006). 'If I ever play football, dad, can I play for England or India?' *Sociology*, 40(1): 11–28.

Burdsey, D. (2007). *British Asians and football: Culture, identity, exclusion.* London: Routledge.

Cashmore, E. and Cleland, J. (2011). 'Why aren't there more black football managers?' *Ethnic and Racial Studies*, 34(9), 1594–1607.

Côté, J., Coackley, C. and Brune, M. (2012). 'Children's talent development in sport: Effectiveness or efficiency?' In S. Dagkar and C. Armour (eds), *Inclusion and exclusion through sport.* London: Routledge, 172–185.

CSO – Central Statistics Office (2017). *Census 2016. Population and migration estimates.* Dublin: Government of Ireland.

Darmondy, M., Ginnity, F. and Kingston, G. (2016). 'The experiences of migrant children in Ireland'. In J. Williams, E. Nixon, E. Smyth and D. Watson (eds), *Cherishing all the children equally?* Dublin: Oaktree Press.

Deleuze, G. and Guattari, F. (1988 [1980]). *A thousand plateaus. Capitalism and Schizophrenia.* London: Athlone Press.

Denzin, N. (2006). 'Analytic autoethnography, or déjà vu all over again'. *Journal of Contemporary Ethnography,* 35(4), 419–428.

Denzin, N. (2014). 'Critical and post-structural inquiries'. Conference Paper, Tenth International Congress of Qualitative, University of Illinois at Urbana-Champaign, USA. Available from: www.youtube.com/watch?v=NppBzyIAo9Q&t=138s [accessed 1 July 2018].

Ellison, R. (2001 [1952]). *Invisible man.* London: Penguin.

ENGSO – European Non-Governmental Sports Organisation (2012). 'Manifesto for a truly inclusive sport'. Available from: www.engso.com/admin/upload/Manifesto_social_inclusion_final.pdf [accessed 2 May 2012].

Ensor, M. O. and Goździak, E. (eds) (2010). *Children and migration: At the crossroads of resiliency and vulnerability.* London: Palgrave Macmillan.

FAI – Football Association of Ireland (2007). *Intercultural football plan. Many voices, one goal.* Dublin: FAI.

FAI – Football Association of Ireland (2014). *Intercultural standards report.* Dublin: FAI.

FAI – Football Association of Ireland (2016). *Strategic plan 2016–2020.* Dublin: FAI.

FARE – Football Against Racism Europe (2014). *Ethnic minorities and coaching in elite level football in England: A call to action.* FARE/Sports' People Think Thank.

Fletcher, T. and Hylton, K. (2016). '"Race", whiteness and sport'. In D. K. Wiggins and J. Nauright (eds), *Routledge handbook of sport, race and ethnicity.* London: Routledge, 87–106.

Foucault, M. (1980). *Power/knowledge: Selected interviews & other writings 1972–1977,* C. Gordon (ed.). New York: Pantheon Books.

FRA – European Union Agency for Fundamental Rights (2018). *Fundamental rights report.* Vienna: European Union Agency for Fundamental Rights.

Free, M. (2010). 'Migration, masculinity and the fugitive state of mind in the Irish emigrant footballer autobiography: The case of Paul McGrath'. *Estudios Irlandeses,* 5, 45–57.

Garner, S. (2013). 'Reflections on race in contemporary Ireland'. In J. V. Ulin, H. Edwards and S. O'Brien (eds), *Race and immigration in the New Ireland.* Notre Dame, IN: University of Notre Dame Press, 175–204.

Garrat, D. (2010). '"Sporting citizenship": The rebirth of religion?' *Pedagogy, Culture & Society,* 18(2), 123–143.

Giardina, M. and Denzin, N. (2011). 'Acts of activism ☞ politics of possibility. Towards a new performative cultural politics'. *Cultural Studies Critical Methodologies,* 11(4), 319–327.

Gilroy, P. (2000). *Between camps.* London: Allen Lane/The Penguin Press.

Goldin, I., Cameron, G. and Balarajan, M. (2012). *Exceptional people. How migration shaped our world and will define our future.* Princeton, NJ: Princeton University Press.

Hassan, D. and McCue K. (2011). 'Football, racism and the Irish'. In D. Burdsey (ed.), *Race, ethnicity and football: Persisting debates and emergent issues.* London: Routledge, 50–66.

Hopkins, P. (2010). *Young people, place and identity*. London: Routledge.

Hylton, K. (2009). *'Race' and sport. Critical race theory*. London: Routledge.

Kassimeris, C. (2008). *European football in black and white*. Plymouth: Lexington Books.

Kelly, E. *et al.* (2016). 'How did immigrants fare in the Irish labour market over the Great Recession?' *OECD Economics Department Working Papers*, No. 1284, OECD Publishing, Paris. Available from: http://dx.doi.org/10.1787/5jm0v4f4r8kh-en [accessed 24 April 2018].

Kingston, G., McGinnity, F. and O'Connell, P. (2015). 'Discrimination in the labour market: Nationality, ethnicity and the recession'. *Work, Employment and Society*, 29(2), 213–232.

Jarvie, G. (2017). *Sport, culture and society. An introduction*, third edition. Abingdon: Routledge.

Levermore, R. (2004). 'Sport's role in constructing the "interstate" worldview'. In R. Levermore and A. Budd (eds), *Sports and international relations: An emerging relationship*. London: Routledge, 16–30.

Lentin, R. (2010). '"All I have to do is dream?" Re-greening Irish integrationism'. *Translocations*, 6(2). Available from: www.translocations.ie/docs/v06i02/Vol%206%20Issue%202%20-%20Revisit%20-%20Lentin,%20edited.pdf [accessed 15 February 2012].

Loyal, S. (2011). *Understanding Irish immigration: Capital, state, and labour in a global age*. Manchester: Manchester University Press.

Marivoet, S. (2014). 'Challenge of sport towards social inclusion and awareness-raising against discrimination'. *Physical Culture and Sport. Studies and Research*, LXIII, 3–11.

Marjoribanks, T. and Farquharson, K. (2012). *Sport and society in the global age*. Basingstoke: Palgrave Macmillan.

Mauro, M. (2014). 'A team like no "other". The racialized position of Insaka in Irish schoolboys' football'. In J. O'Gorman (ed.), *Junior and youth grassroots football. The forgotten game*. London: Routledge, 54–73.

Mauro, M. (2016a). 'Transcultural football. Trajectories of belonging among immigrant youth'. *Soccer and Society*, 17(6), 90–105.

Mauro, M. (2016b). *The Balotelli generation. Issues of inclusion and belonging in Italian football and society*. Bern: Peter Lang.

Mertens, D. M., Holmes, H. M. and Harris, R. L. (2009). 'Transformative research and ethics'. In D. M. Mertens and P. E. Ginsberg (eds), *The handbook of social research ethics*. Thousand Oaks, CA: Sage, 85–101.

Palidda, S. (2017). 'Migrations as a total political fact in the neo-liberal frame'. In E. Di Giovanni (ed.), *Mobilities between old and new boundaries*. Palermo: Palermo University Press.

Poli, R., Berthoud, J., Busset, T. and Kaya, B. (2012). *Football et integration (Football and integration)*. Berne: Peter Lang.

Richardson, L. (1992). 'Trash on the corner: Ethics and technography'. *Journal of Contemporary Ethnography*, 21(1), 103–119.

Sassen, S. (2006). *Cities in a world economy*, third edition. Thousand Oaks, CA: Pine Forge Press.

Savage, M., Callan, T., Nolan, B. and Colgan, B. (2015). 'The Great Recession, austerity and inequality: Evidence from Ireland'. ESRI Working Paper, No. 499, Dublin: The Economic and Social Research Institute (ESRI).

Sinha, A. and Back, L. (2013). 'Making methods sociable: Dialogue, ethics and authorship in qualitative research'. *Qualitative Research*, 12(4), 473–487.

Spaaij, R. (2015). 'Refugee youth, belonging and community sport'. *Leisure Studies*, 34(3), 303–318.

SPIN – European Sport Inclusion Network (2016). *Handbook on volunteering of migrants in sport clubs and organisations*. Report, Vienna: SPIN.

Storey, D. (2013). 'Sport, culture and identity'. In C. Rees (ed.), *Changes in contemporary Ireland: Texts and contexts*. Newcastle upon Tyne: Cambridge Scholars Publishing, 80–95.

Tallec Marston, K. (2012). 'A lost legacy of fraternity? The case of European youth football'. In R. Holt and D. Ruta (eds), *Routledge handbook of sport and legacy*. London: Routledge, 176–188.

Theeboom, M., Schaillée, H. and Nols, Z. (2012). 'Social capital development among ethnic minorities in mixed and separate sport clubs'. *International Journal of Sport Policy and Politics*, 4(1), 1–21.

Thomson, R., Bell, R., Holland, J., Henderson, S., McGrellis, S. and Sharpe, S. (2002). 'Critical moments: Choice, chance and opportunity in young people's narratives of transition'. *Sociology*, 36(2), 335–354.

Tyler, S. E. (1986). 'Post-modern ethnography: From document of the occult to occult document'. In J. Clifford and G. M. Marcus (eds), *Writing culture. The poetics and politics of ethnography*. Berkeley, CA: University of California Press, 122–140.

UNCRC – United Nations Convention on the Rights of the Child (1989). Geneva: United Nations.

Conclusion

As I set out to write the final pages of this book, I realise that 10 years have passed since the start of my study of youth sporting practices in Ireland. During this time, many things have happened in my life, including parenthood and three relocations, and I have taken long breaks from the research to follow other projects and life commitments. As with the lives of my participants, mine has also moved on from the events that I observed, experienced and documented during my early fieldwork in Blanchardstown. Nevertheless, the idea of taking this work to completion in the form of a book has continued to linger in the back of my mind. In a way, I never mentally stopped to labour around the possibility of giving a comprehensive, coherent representation to an experience (the ethnography and its long aftermath) which has been intense, fluid and often contradictory. At times, during the writing of the book, I found myself at a loss, like the protagonist of *Correction*, the novel by Thomas Bernhard (2003 [1975]), who re-writes the same text three times and every time the previous version is reduced and 'destroyed'. In the end, the different versions appear having each a distinctive character and, after the death of the protagonist, a friend takes on the work of 'correcting' them until a puzzling finale: 'The end is no process. Clearing' (Bernhard 2003 [1975]: 249).

Understandably, mine is no work of 'fiction': it deals with real life and with social dynamics experienced by real people. For this reason, 'the end' can arguably be interpreted as a process, as something that is always in the making and it will never be completed. The ethnographic text, as with any research work, will be read, hopefully discussed and dissected by others, who will use it to complement their understanding of certain issues, and as a starting point for further investigations. They will also, possibly, offer more pertinent answers to some of the questions that I address. Writing in *Slate*, Douglas Hunter laments that 'most academic books aren't written to be read – they're written to be "broken"'.[1] Every academic in the humanities and social sciences would, to some extent, be familiar with an approach to reading specialist texts without having to actually read them 'cover to cover'. They will skip certain parts and go straight to others, scroll through the index and the bibliography for elements of interest; for something that they expect to find, because they are not prepared to be surprised. They, consequently, will themselves write books that reflect this attitude (book breaking). The point, Hunter claims, is that 'academic writing is often hostile to storytelling as a way of conveying important truths'.

I do not mind if this book will be 'broken'; ideally, it would work like a rhizome, which 'may be broken, shattered at a given spot, but it will start up again on one of its old lines, or on new lines' (Deleuze and Guattari 1988 [1980]: 8). Having said that, from the start I made clear that I wished this book to be read as a text that tells meaningful stories. I wanted the protagonists of my study to emerge as complex, fractured and contradictory characters as they may be – as we all may be, particularly as young persons. I obviously focused my attention on certain issues that I wished to learn more about, and possibly comprehend beyond their individual, localised dimensions. In doing so, I kept in mind the teaching of Wright Mills:

> Know that many personal troubles cannot be solved merely as troubles, but must be understood in terms of public issues – and in terms of the problems of history-making. Know that the human meaning of public issues must be revealed by relating them to personal troubles – and to the problems of the individual life.
>
> (2000 [1959]: 225)

In my writing, I also wanted the reader to follow me when I felt confused, and lost for explanations. This book is born out of curiosity for human life, and as an act of love for the unpredictable forms of social interaction enabled by sport and leisure practised by young people. It is also an act of commitment for the less privileged, for those living and struggling at the margins of dominant media narratives about 'immigration', 'multiculturalism' and 'sport as a tool for integration'. In a way, both settings of my study, at the particular conjuncture of the ethnographic fieldwork, provided a pristine environment to explore issues of sport, belonging and social inclusion in contemporary Ireland. Sport and state institutions had little contact with, and apparently minimal influence on, the activities of the social groups I spent months and years interacting with. Most of the times I was the only travelling spectator to away games, or at trainings, of both teams I worked with.

As I showed in Chapter 6, over the years things have evolved in terms of the organisation and institutional structure of youth football. The Irish sport governing bodies have started a process of rationalisation and specialisation whose aim is to improve the competitiveness of the game. The social and economic scenario has also, to some extent, changed, as Ireland has resumed economic growth after some years of recession, further enhancing the role of the country as a central hub of economic globalisation. At the same time, patterns of inequality have deepened, affecting both Irish natives and immigrants, and particularly certain categories of immigrants (non-EU, refugees, asylum seekers). The two processes, changes in youth sport and socioeconomic developments, are interlinked, the 'productivity' of the youth football system is functional in the growth of the global industry of football, and enhances the international prestige of the country in international competitions. The role of the state in this dynamic, albeit not immediately evident, deserves specific attention. Reflecting the political hegemony of neoliberalism, the Republic of Ireland, similar to many European nation-states, is receding from its role of 'pastoral state' (Bauman 1995) that historically provided social security and welfare to the whole of the population. The free market ideology implies that the state has to make sure that the private sector is left free to operate and proliferate (Mezzadra and Neilson 2013). That is its main role in the eyes of powerful financial corporations and transnational organisations such as the World Bank and the International Monetary Fund (IMF), whose influence on national policies has increased over the last 30 years. However, a more sensitive task is left to the nation-state: that of continually (re)producing a cohesive dimension, a sense of 'identity' based on common history (and historiography), language, religion, and finally culture, a pervasive and ambiguous concept. Against the backdrop of human mobility justified by the needs of neoliberal economy, the 'racial state' (Goldberg 2002) operates by delimiting the access to rights and resources of migrants. Like other nation-states, the Republic of Ireland has been described as a fitting example of a racial state (Lentin and McVeigh 2006; Loyal 2011; Garner 2013) and even as a 'racist state' (Lentin 2007). While claiming respect for their 'cultures' according to the principle of equality, a pillar of modern democracy since the 1789 French Revolution, the state curtails migrants' roles in society. However, it is on the terrain of culture that the division between 'us' and 'them', functional to the racial state and to social cohesion according to the same paradigm, becomes more evident and persistent. Focusing on the Irish case, Loyal contends that

> Discussions of culture are simultaneously discussions of power. Culture is a place where political power can weave itself into people's everyday lives. And it is precisely because state power has to dissolve itself into and be expressed through a nationally defined culture that states see multicultural societies as problematic.
>
> (2011: 249)

Sport played by young people at grassroots level pertains essentially to the domain of culture. To what extent is it entangled in, and framed by, the processes that I have described? I think I have provided sufficient examples of how sport, and particularly a global, popular sport as football, functions as a site where social and cultural belonging is negotiated and actively constructed by young people. One of the most significant impressions emerging from this study is how young people can move across cultural and ethnic differentiations in their exploration of culture, as creative students of culture (MacDougall 2006). Sport provides them with one of the very few settings where they can engage with adults and peers on a voluntary basis, expressing a level of agency that is generally denied to them at school and at home. Furthermore, by playing in a team they can arguably acquire a valuable role in the eyes of the adult society and in that of their peers. But, contradictorily, the significance, and the intensity, of their interactions increases as they move away from the eyes of the adults. This, importantly, also relates to ethnic and racial identifications, and processes of racialisation that dominate society at large.

The interactions that were taking place at the all-weather pitch in Ongar and at Mountview Park before and after training sessions and matches represented fruitful effects of transcultural dialogue. These interactions could be fortified by a winning record of the team, strengthening the sense of togetherness among its players. In this context, the context of youth team sport, a sense of belonging can take different forms, and be articulated on different layers: to the team, to a group of friends of similar background, the club, the community where it operates, and to the majority society. These forms of belonging can overlap or they can exclude each other. What determines their 'durability' is up to different factors, some unpredictable and others that could be influenced by policy interventions. The unpredictable ones depend, for example, on the winning record, as winning is at the heart of all competitive sport. Winning creates shared, collective memories. The more predictable, and substantial, factors pertain, on the one hand, to the role of adults in charge of the team and the club, and on the other hand, to the institutions governing the game and defining the boundaries of the sporting practice, writing the rules, and providing resources for the training of game officials, coaches, and club administrators. At a higher level operates the state itself, which, for example, can grant or deny citizenship rights (which, though, may not guarantee full acceptance in the 'national outlook').

From what I have described, the sporting practice of these adolescents, both those of immigrant background and Irish natives, appears to be defined by a dichotomic dynamic. The football team provides them with an opportunity to challenge racialisation processes that dominate society at large, and even to reinvent their 'assigned' roles in creative ways ('We are Congolese, man. We are the best'). On the other hand, the same context, left to operate without an awareness among the adult mentors of the fertile contribution that diversity can bring beyond sport performance, will damage and even destroy the transcultural dialogue created by young people. Ethnic minority players are valued simply for their qualities as players, and as long as they are able to conform to certain unwritten codes of demeanour. Their 'diversity' is not accepted per se. Obviously, there is the possibility that (native) coaches and club administrators appreciate their 'nonconformity', accepting the fact that a two-way process of socialisation is taking place, but that is more the exception than the rule. This leads to a crucial question: is a non-racialised sport possible in a racialised society?

Over the last two decades the international governing bodies of football, FIFA and UEFA, have intensified their efforts to make the game truly inclusive, designing and implementing anti-discriminatory programmes and soliciting the national governing bodies to do the same (Kassimeris 2008). Their efforts resonate with policy interventions promoted by European institutions such as the European Union, the Council of Europe and others. A number of sport organisations across Europe have started specific initiatives targeting immigrant communities and ethnic minorities. These initiatives send out messages of inclusion, respect of diversity, and anti-discrimination that may or may not attune with broader attitudes towards social diversity and immigration present in certain societies (Mauro 2016). As such, they may represent a sort of counter narrative: sport is more inclusive than society at large. This would reflect the idea of sport being a level playing field, a social configuration where everyone is accepted and valued simply on the basis of their sporting prowess and talent, and where social, ethnic or national backgrounds do not matter. As commendable as they may be, are such interventions capable of creating an alternative version of society – more inclusive, less divisive, non-racist – for young people? Green contends that 'Youth sport, and developments therein, are almost inevitably dependent upon the impact of such social divisions as class, gender, ethnicity and disability, as well as the intersections between them' (Green 2016: 259). It is difficult to question this statement, and it is precisely for this reason that non-discriminatory policies are valuable, as they can at least reduce the impact of such divisions in the sporting practice of young people. Given the amount of financial resources at their disposable, and in the face of increasing professionalisation and adultification of youth sport, football governing bodies should be made accountable for their efforts in tackling discrimination and in spreading an inclusive, open and truly universalistic sporting culture.

Note

1 D. Hunter, 'Book breaking and book mending', *Slate*, 25 July 2018. Available from: https://slate.com/human-interest/2018/07/academic-publishing-and-book-breaking-why-scholars-write-books-that-arent-meant-to-be-read.html [accessed 10 September 2018].

References

Bernhard, T. (2003 [1975]). *Correction*. London: Vintage.
Bauman, Z. (1995). *Life in fragments: Essays in post-modern morality*. Oxford, UK: Blackwell.
Deleuze, G. and Guattari, F. (1988 [1980]). *A thousand plateaus. Capitalism and Schizophrenia*. London: Athlone Press.
Garner, S. (2013). 'Reflections on race in contemporary Ireland'. In J. V. Ulin, H. Edwards and S. O'Brien (eds), *Race and immigration in the New Ireland*. Notre Dame, IN: University of Notre Dame Press, 175–204.
Green, K. (2016). 'Social divisions and youth sport. Introduction'. In K. Green and A. Smith (eds), *Routledge handbook of youth sport*. London: Routledge, 259–264.

Goldberg, D. T. (2002). *The racial state*. Hoboken, USA: Wiley-Blackwell.

Kassimeris, C. (2008). *European football in black and white*. Plymouth: Lexington Books.

Lentin, R. (2007). 'Ireland: Racial state and crisis racism'. *Ethnic and Racial Studies*, 30(4), 610–627.

Lentin, R. and McVeigh, R. (2006). *After Optimism? Ireland, racism and globalisation*. Dublin: Metro Eireann Publications.

Loyal, S. (2011). *Understanding Irish immigration: Capital, state, and labour in a global age*. Manchester: Manchester University Press.

MacDougall, D. (2006). *The corporeal image. Film, ethnography and the senses*. Princeton: Princeton University Press.

Mauro, M. (2016). *The Balotelli generation. Issues of inclusion and belonging in Italian football and society*. Bern: Peter Lang.

Mezzadra, S. and Neilson, B. (2013). *Border as method, or the multiplication of labor*. Durham: Duke University Press.

Wright Mills, C. (2000 [1959]). *The sociological imagination*. Oxford: Oxford University Press.

Index

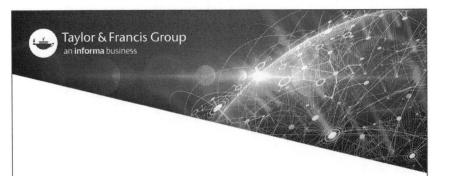